FEEDING FRENZY

D1638999

PAUL MCMAHON has authored reports on sustainable food systems as an advisor to The Prince of Wales's International Sustainability Unit and to the UN's Food and Agriculture Organization. He co-founded and now helps run SLM Partners, a business that invests in sustainable agriculture in Australia and across the world. Born in Ireland, he holds a PhD from Cambridge University.

FEEDING FRENZY

The New Politics of Food

PAUL MCMAHON

P

PROFILE BOOKS

First published in Great Britain in 2013 by
PROFILE BOOKS LTD
3A Exmouth House
Pine Street
London EC1R OJH
www.profilebooks.com

1 3 5 7 9 10 8 6 4 2

Typeset in Bembo by MacGuru Ltd
info@macguru.org.uk

Printed and bound in Great Britain by
Clays, Bungay, Suffolk

A CIP catalogue record for this book is available from the
British Library.

ISBN 978 1 78125 034 1
eISBN 978 1 84765 879 1

The paper this book is printed on is certified by the © 1996 Forest
Stewardship Council A.C. (FSC). It is ancient-forest friendly. The
printer holds FSC chain of custody SGS-COC-2061

FSC
www.fsc.org
MIX
Paper from
responsible sources
FSC® C018072

CONTENTS

INTRODUCTION

A gleaming steel fence is going up in a remote part of Africa. An alien construction, it dissects a landscape of open fields, mud huts and dirt tracks, where straight lines are elusive. On one side, diesel-powered tractors chew up the soil, containers packed with seed and fertiliser wait to be opened, and foreign managers look forward to a bumper harvest. On the other side, a local farmer in a tattered shirt scratches at the soil with a simple hoe, fearing that he may not be able to grow enough food for his family. Villagers cluster around the gate to the property, looking for work but muttering that the land rightly belongs to them. There are rumours that the young men are arming themselves so they can resist what they regard as a foreign 'land grab'.

This story is playing out on the western fringes of Ethiopia, in a steamy region close to the border with South Sudan. The land has been acquired by a billionaire sheikh as part of an initiative launched by the Saudi government, which wants to grow more of its food abroad. Ethiopia, like most of Africa, may be better known for food scarcity and famine, rather than food abundance and exports, but this is one of dozens of similar projects to be launched across the continent since 2008.

1

The appearance of steel fences and satellite-guided tractors in one of the poorest parts of the world is a direct result of the turmoil that has gripped global food markets over the past five years. Food prices more than doubled between 2007 and 2008. Grain stocks fell to a dangerous level, and there were fears that supplies would not be available at any price. After a brief dip, prices rebounded in 2010 and jumped again in 2012. Food is a lot more expensive than a decade ago and does not look like getting any cheaper. We seem to be stuck in a never-ending food crisis.

Everyone can see the effect in their supermarket and restaurant bills. Higher food prices squeeze our incomes, meaning there is less to spend on everything else. But for the poor of the world the impacts are more dramatic. About one in eight people now go hungry each year. Millions of people have been forced deeper into poverty. High prices have sparked food riots and demonstrations in more than thirty countries. In January 2011 an iconic photograph emerged of a protester in Tunisia facing down riot police armed with nothing more than a baguette – a symbol of how anger over food helped spark the 'Arab Spring'.

Ferment in food markets has been seized upon by professional doom-mongers who believe the human race is living beyond its means. 'The Coming Famine', 'World on the Edge', 'Climate Change Peril', 'Peak Food', 'Peak Oil', even 'Peak Dirt' – these are some of the ideas and book titles that have circulated in recent years, all warning of an impending food collapse. Malthus, the nineteenth-century prophet of population catastrophe, is back in fashion. And another controversial idea is re-emerging after a long period of stigmatisation – population control. Rich people in rich countries are once more telling poor people in poor countries to have fewer children.

There is no doubt that we are entering a challenging time. The human population will grow from 7 to 9 billion over the next forty years. Every year there are an extra 80 million mouths to feed. As the global middle class swells in size, people are demanding more expensive diets, which adds to the pressure on the planet's resources. There is a question mark over the sustainability of modern agriculture because of its dependence on fossil fuels, the damage it inflicts on the environment and its vulnerability to a changing climate. Even the UK government's chief scientist, Professor Sir John Beddington, has warned that 'the food system is failing'.

Can we feed a world of 9 billion by 2050? Is the current market turmoil an early sign that the global food system will not cope?

This book tries to answer these questions. It describes how the global food system works today, highlighting the huge inequalities and imbalances that pervade it. It reveals the real reasons behind the recent increase in food prices, exploring issues such as the role of biofuels, climate change, financial speculation and the rise of the Asian consumer. It looks at how demand for food is likely to develop over the next forty years and investigates whether food supplies will be able to keep up.

At the most basic level, this means assessing the biophysical potential of our planet – the amount of land, water, energy and other natural resources that is available. It is a matter of hard science. But just because we can produce enough food does not mean that everyone will eat. Food security is determined not only by how much food is available but by whether people can access it and afford it. Therefore, the real answer will depend on the social, economic and political dimensions of the global food system. In particular the fate of millions of people will be determined by whether nations choose to compete or collaborate in a time of relative scarcity.

Judging by the response to the recent crisis, we are in for a period of intense competition. This book lifts the lid on the extraordinary scramble for food that is now taking place around the world. It reveals how countries are manipulating trade and hoarding agricultural surpluses, even if this starves their neighbours; how financial investors are distorting markets through their willingness to bet on anything; how private corporations are rushing to secure supply chains before their competitors can get there; and how a bizarre array of fortune-hunters and policymakers are scrambling to acquire farmland in some of the poorest countries of the world, in ways that echo the colonialism of the past. Many people no longer trust markets to provide. Food has become a geopolitical issue of the highest importance.

If these trends continue, they could lead to a nightmare scenario of exploitation, hunger and conflict. But this book also maps out an alternative vision that could deliver better outcomes. It is a way forward that addresses the heated debates that often flare up in connection with the future of food and farming. It overcomes simple dichotomies such as organics versus genetic engineering, family farms versus large commercial estates, free trade versus government subsidies. It builds on the work of innovators all around the world who have found ways to produce more food with fewer resources while generating wealth for farmers and consumers. Which path will the world choose? The answer will matter to politicians and generals, to farmers and investors, to consumers and citizens — and, not least, to the African farmers watching the steel fences go up around their land.

The sense of crisis that pervades the world's food system is surprising because it came after a long period when food and agriculture were taken for granted. When I grew up in Ireland in the 1980s, the newspapers were full of stories of butter mountains and wine lakes forming across the European

Community. For the next twenty years, the main issue was what to do about food prices that were too *low*. Politicians fretted about what to do with food surpluses; farmers clamoured for more government subsidies; development experts lamented the poverty being inflicted on peasants in poor countries. Yet, beneath a veneer of equilibrium, the world's food system was marked by injustice, inequality and a basketful of economic perversities. Maybe it was inevitable that it could not be sustained. The next two chapters of the book explain how this situation came about.

THE UNEVEN PACE OF AGRICULTURAL INNOVATION

Cereal yields per hectare, in tonnes

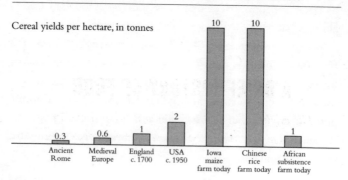

multiplied by...

Area worked per farmer, in hectares

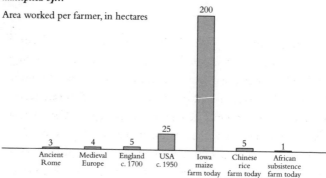

...which equals

Cereal production per farmer, in tonnes

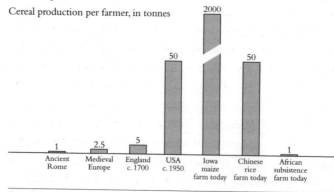

Source: M. Mazoyer & L. Roudart, *A history of world agriculture from the neolithic age to the current crisis*, Earthscan, 2006

A BRIEF HISTORY OF FOOD

*The origins of agriculture, how it developed and the
huge gaps that exist between farmers today*

Shennong, Emperor of the Five Grains, the Divine Farmer,
is venerated as the father of Chinese agriculture. According
to legend, he was born with the head of an ox and the body
of a man. He spoke after three days, walked within one week,
and was able to plough a field at the tender age of three – not
only that, but he is said to have invented the plough in the first
place. Legend goes that before he appeared his people were
starved and sickly, barely surviving by eating grass. Shennong
taught them how to farm and introduced plants that could
serve as food, herbs and medicines. A walking laboratory, he
had the unusual benefit of a transparent stomach and was able
to test hundreds of plants by seeing the effect they had inside
his body. One story tells how he became the first person to
taste tea, after some charred leaves were blown into a pot of
boiling water. But his most important discoveries were the
five grains that underpin Chinese civilisation – wheat, rice,
millet, soybean and sorghum. Thanks to these grains, his people
enjoyed hundreds of years of peace and abundance.

The story of Shennong reveals the building blocks of agriculture, which societies have tried to improve and perfect ever

since. It starts with the selection and cultivation of plants that can turn solar energy into the carbohydrates, proteins, fats and micronutrients we need to survive. The world has roughly 250,000 plant species, of which about 50,000 are edible, and of which we regularly eat no more than 250. They include a range of cereals, roots, tubers, fruits, vegetables, herbs, nuts, spices and oils. In addition, we have domesticated animals, which convert less palatable plants into more nutritious forms. Today, meat and dairy products provide about one quarter of human protein intake (and fish another 5–6 per cent). Nevertheless, the legend of Shennong shows how our farming systems have been designed around a small number of crops that provide energy in bulk. Today, 15 crops supply 90 per cent of our calories, and 3 crops – wheat, rice and maize – provide 60 per cent of our calories. The latter are grass plants, which have particular advantages because their grains are energy-rich, contain valuable proteins, store well and can be processed into many kinds of food.

The other building blocks of agriculture serve to maximise the production of these useful plants. All living things need water to grow. Shennong taught his people how to build wells and how to plant seeds at the right time to benefit from seasonal rains. Plants require nutrients such as nitrogen, phosphate and potassium, which are taken from the land when each crop is harvested. Shennong renewed fertility by resting fields and recycling dung and urine from farm animals. Another challenge is minimising the impact of weeds and pests. Shennong invented the plough and the rake, which helped farmers to break up weeds. All these interventions require work, which brings us to the last component of agriculture – applying power. Mechanical power is needed to pull ploughs, harvest crops, herd animals, process food and transport loads to and from the fields. Being half ox, Shennong had little trouble pulling heavy implements through the fields. For mere humans, it was more of a struggle.

These five processes – selecting plants and animals, managing water, renewing fertility, protecting from pests and applying power – constitute the basics of a farming system. They appeared in different parts of the world, starting about 10,000 years ago, bubbling up like springs from the underlying reserves of human ingenuity. These streams of agricultural development then proceeded at various paces, sometimes accelerating, at other times stagnating, sometimes joining together to follow a common path, at other times breaking off in unique directions. The pace of change accelerated in the twentieth century, propelling some societies forward but leaving others high and dry. This history can help us understand the contours of the global food system today.

Early origins
Archaeologists believe that farming developed independently in China, Central America, Papua New Guinea, tropical Africa and, probably earliest of all, in the Fertile Crescent, an arc stretching from present-day Iran, through southern Turkey and down to the Levantine coast of the eastern Mediterranean. This region was unusually rich in wild varieties of grass plants, for example wheat and barley, which could be adapted for human cultivation. It also contained wild animals, such as sheep and goats, whose herding instincts made them amenable to domestication.

Farming communities first developed in the fertile river valleys. The annual floods not only provided water but also deposited a fresh supply of nutrients on the land after each harvest, renewing fertility. The soils on the flat, open flood plains were easy to work. To kill weeds, farmers scratched the soil with an ard, a basic v-shaped wooden implement that functioned more like a hoe than a plough. In most cases, they hauled the ard themselves – people were the beasts of burden.

This farming system underpinned the 'hydraulic civilisations' that emerged on the Tigris, Euphrates, Nile and Indus rivers from about 3500 BCE (Before Common Era). Flood waters were controlled by a network of canals and dykes, and building and maintaining this infrastructure required a high degree of social organisation. A ruling class emerged to organise the people, together with the earliest forms of writing, mathematics and government administration. This system generated a reliable food surplus – each farming household produced more than was needed to sustain itself. This freed others to become soldiers and priests, shoemakers and metal-workers, scribes and bureaucrats, kings and pharaohs. The idle time between one season's harvest and the next planting also meant that large numbers of people could be put to work erecting grand monuments in honour of their gods and rulers. There would have been no pyramids without full granaries.

As populations grew, and farmers stepped out of the river valleys, they faced new challenges. Perhaps the most daunting was how to replace soil nutrients without the benefits of annual floods. It might be possible to get a good crop for one or two years, but yields would then inevitably fall as the soil was exhausted. In response farmers turned to shifting cultivation, also known as swidden agriculture or 'slash and burn'. Farmers cut the native vegetation, set it on fire, and, after allowing the ash to fertilise the soil, planted a crop. Rather than trying to maintain the fertility of the land, they simply moved on once yields dropped. They would then return many years later, after the natural vegetation had regrown, to start the cycle again. With a low population density, this system could be practised within an area indefinitely, so long as enough time was given for the land to recover. But population pressure, together with the lure of fertile virgin land, meant that people continually pushed into new areas. As a result, farmers spread out from the earliest centres of innovation, clearing vast forests along the way.

The Bantu people carried the torch of farming through much of Africa. Originally from West Africa they began to migrate east and south more than 3,000 years ago, bringing agriculture with them. By 200 BCE the Bantu around the Great Lakes in East Africa used slash and burn methods to cultivate sorghum, millet and yams. They cleared vegetation with axes and fire, buried seeds with digging sticks and aggressively weeded the plots by hand. They used iron tools as early as anyone else. As their numbers grew, they gradually expanded throughout East and Southern Africa, displacing or assimilating tribes of hunter-foragers. By 300 CE (Common Era) peoples of Bantu heritage occupied nearly all the lands suitable for growing sorghum and millet. However, it would be another thousand years before they developed cities or states, perhaps because they had a vast continent into which to expand and could continue to practise shifting cultivation even when their population increased.

Mediterranean and European farmers did not have that luxury, as they eventually bumped up against the sea and against each other. This forced a shift from slash and burn agriculture to sedentary systems that made the most of the land available. By the time of ancient Greece and Rome, farmers had solved the puzzle of how to restore fertility. The answer was integrating crops and livestock. Cereals, especially wheat, were cultivated on the most fertile land, which was left fallow every second year. Animals were grazed on peripheral pastures, then penned overnight on the fallow land, where their dung and urine acted as fertiliser. In this way, animals were used to concentrate fertility from extensive pastures on to small areas of cultivated land. Oxen were also used to pull iron-tipped ards – the first major replacement of human power by animal muscle. The Greeks and Romans utilised the less fertile hillsides to grow vines and olives.

This farming system was not much more productive than slash and burn, which explains why food insecurity was so prevalent throughout antiquity. As the populations of Athens and Rome grew, this system was also pushed beyond its ecological limits. Hills were stripped of trees for wood and fuel, shrubs and grasses were over-grazed, the land was over-ploughed. Intense winter rains led to massive soil erosion, leaving hillsides bare and turning valleys into marshes. The loss of self-sufficiency in food production compelled both Athens and Rome to use military force to colonise and exploit other lands. Egypt, with its reliable Nile waters, became a bread-basket for each city in turn. Under Julius Caesar, Roman rule spread to almost all parts of Europe where wheat could be grown – in many ways the Roman Empire was an empire of wheat. Slavery was another consequence. A slave did not have a family; therefore, any agricultural surplus he or she produced was available to the slave-owner.

For a thousand years after the collapse of the Roman Empire, feudal Europe followed the same basic system of cereal cultivation combined with livestock husbandry. There were some innovations. The ard was replaced by the more effective mouldboard plough, which cut deeper and turned the sod – this aerated the soil, broke weeds, aided mineral-isation and was better suited to wetter, heavier soils. More animals could be kept over winter, especially in colder climates, because of the use of hay and stabling. Consequently, Northern Europe became more densely populated than the Mediter-ranean region for the first time. Twice the amount of cereals per hectare could be produced compared to antiquity, which allowed for a doubling of the European population. The greater surplus allowed medieval cities such as Paris to flourish and fed the artisans who built the Gothic cathedrals of the High Middle Ages. Yet, as the number of people grew, agriculture again began to hit its ecological limits. This contributed to a series of famines, plagues and wars in the fourteenth century that slashed the size of the population by one-third. It would be another 200 years before the European population started to grow again.

As in so many aspects of civilisation, China outpaced Europe at this time. Agriculture first began around 7500 BCE on the plains of the Yellow River in the dry north. The main crop was not rice but millet, a hardy small-seeded grass that could cope with droughts. Pigs and chickens were first domesticated here. By 400 BCE, the same time as the Athenian Golden Age, the Chinese operated sophisticated irrigation schemes, used cast-iron tools and employed oxen to pull ploughs. The Yellow River brought water (sometimes too much) but it was poor in nutrients, especially nitrogen, because it flowed from barren regions that lacked vegetation. To restore fertility on the land, Chinese farmers applied animal manure and human sewage (known as night soil). Thanks to Emperor Shennong, they also discovered the unique properties of the soybean. As well as providing food – the beans could be eaten directly (as in Japanese *edamame*) or made into tofu – this plant was a legume, which meant that bacteria in nodules on its roots fixed nitrogen directly from the atmosphere. After harvest, the plants could be ploughed into the soil as green manure. This allowed crop rotations without any fallowing.

When this farming system, along with Han Chinese culture, spread to the more humid south and east of present-day China, it incorporated the rice-growing culture of the Yangtze Delta, which was almost as ancient. This turbo-charged productivity, as wet rice grown in paddy fields could be harvested twice or even three times a year. From there, the system spread north to Korea and Japan. Chinese practices also filtered through to Southeast Asia – the modern states of Vietnam, Cambodia, Thailand, Laos, Myanmar and Indonesia – where they mingled with Indian influences. Rice had been grown in the Ganges Valley of India for almost as long. The 'rice economies' that emerged were built on a farming system that delivered high yields per hectare, but required a lot of labour, which explains why population density in much of Asia was (and still is) considerably higher than in Europe.

For a thousand years, the Islamic world acted as a conduit between the farming systems of Asia and Europe. The Prophet Muhammad's successors in the eighth and ninth centuries carved out an empire that stretched from Spain and North Africa, across the Middle East to the Indus Valley and Central Asia. They inherited the agriculture of antiquity and improved it. Farmers built sophisticated irrigation networks, using new technologies such as waterwheels and the shadoof (a pail hung from a horizontal pole that pivoted on a post). They developed complex crop rotations, produced harvests all year round and did not have to fallow because of their incorporation of legumes and manure. Crops from all over the empire were brought together and jumbled up in new combinations. Sugar cane, sorghum, Asian rice, lemons, bananas, coconut, aubergine, artichoke, spinach, watermelon – all were brought to the Mediterranean from Asia and Africa at this time. This system supported several of the world's largest cities: Baghdad had more than 1 million inhabitants by the tenth century. Ironically, many of these regions are now the biggest food importers in the world.

Modern revolutions

Europe, the laggard, finally began to catch up in the seventeenth century. The key innovation was the elimination of fallowing. Instead of resting fields, farmers planted turnips, clover or other legumes after a cereal harvest. These fodder crops helped to restore fertility while producing more feed for animals. This meant that twice as many animals could be kept, which generated more manure, which – together with the nitrogen-fixing action of the legumes – delivered higher cereal yields. In addition, more working animals meant extra muscle on the farm.

This new system first emerged in Flanders and then flourished in England from about 1700. It allowed twice as much food to be produced with the same amount of labour. For the first time ever, the farming population could support a non-farming population bigger than itself: by 1830 only a quarter of British people were directly involved in producing food. This set in motion a virtuous cycle of development: cities provided a market for food surpluses, and farmers provided a ready market for manufactured goods such as farm implements; this led to further increases in food production, allowing more rural labour to be released for jobs in factories or mines. The humble turnip may have been as important as the steam engine in fuelling the Industrial Revolution.

Europeans were soon carrying their turnips and tools around the world. If the Muslim Empire had been a catalyst for the earlier transmission of crops across Eurasia, European empires connected all the continents of the world together, facilitating the greatest exchange of plants and animals in human history. Agriculture had developed independently in the Americas, and to a high level of sophistication, based on a different set of indigenous plants and animals. Under the 'Columbian Exchange', the Spanish and Portuguese carried maize, potatoes, tomatoes, squashes, peanuts, chillies, chocolate, beans, cotton and rubber back from the Americas. They took wheat, rice, cattle, horses, pigs and sheep in the other direction. They also brought disease, military violence and a system of forced labour in silver and gold mines that devastated the productive agricultural systems of native American societies. It also led to a massive collapse in the local population, so Europeans initiated a more sinister exchange. They brought sugar cane and coffee, the tropical plants of the Muslim world, to the Americas. They then shipped African slaves across the Atlantic to grow these foods within brutal plantation economies.

The Europeans, in particular the British, also brought their basket of agricultural technologies to the temperate zones of North America, South Africa, Australia, New Zealand and Argentina, where they established settler colonies of farmers. The landscape and climate looked similar to home, the same European farming systems tended to work. But there was one major difference. Whereas the challenge in Europe was little land and lots of people, the opposite was the case in these colonies. Here, once the natives had been killed or pushed back, there was almost limitless land, but there was a shortage of labour to farm it. This created an incentive to develop labour-saving devices. The USA would be at the forefront of the next advance in agriculture: mechanisation.

From the nineteenth century, new mechanical equipment began to replace human labour on the farm. There were machines for preparing the soil – metallic ploughs, brabant ploughs, harrows, rollers, sowers, ridgers. There were reapers and binders for hay-making and harvesting. Giant, steam-powered threshers began to trundle across the landscape. It was possible to halve the labour force necessary in agriculture and, therefore, to double the amount of food produced per worker.

One thing holding back mechanisation was the lack of a suitable source of power. Animals had limitations, steam engines were heavy, and sparks from steam boilers could ignite a field of ripe crops, with disastrous consequences. The internal combustion engine solved this problem. A 100-horse-power engine was just that – a machine that could replace 100 horses on the farm. It provided tremendous pulling power and allowed fewer men to work much more land more quickly. The first oil-powered tractor was built in the USA in 1889. Commercial sales began in 1902. By 1950 there were 3.5 million tractors in the USA – virtually every farm had one. The wave of mechanisation gradually spread from the New World back to the Old, as more European labour was lured to the cities and rural wages rose.

Mechanisation went hand in hand with another nineteenth-century revolution – in transport. Steam railways and riverboats penetrated the interior of continents, bringing settlers and tools in, and food and commodities out. As a result, the agricultural frontier expanded like a shock wave. Between 1850 and 1910 the amount of arable land in the USA, Canada and Australia more than tripled, growing from 51 million to 166 million hectares. This was the equivalent of putting all of France, Germany, Italy and the UK under crops. But there was no point growing all this food if there was no one to buy it – international transport was just as important in linking settler colonies to world markets. Steamships carried the huge surpluses from the productive farms of North America and Australia. Between 1870 and 1900 the price of transporting American wheat to Europe was reduced by a factor of three. Now, food could be grown in Kansas, sent by railway to Chicago, moved via canal and river to New York and then shipped across the Atlantic to Europe. By 1937 agricultural goods accounted for half of all world trade.

The globalisation of food can be seen in the meal of a typical labourer in the London of Sherlock Holmes. At the turn of the twentieth century, a London worker ate bread made from North American wheat, washed down by a pint of beer brewed from Canadian barley. The butter on his bread came from Ireland, the marmalade from Spain. On Sunday, he might tuck into roast beef, shipped from Argentina or Australia. He drank tea imported from India, sweetened with sugar grown on the former slave plantations of the Caribbean. He sat at the apex of a food system that sucked in produce from all around the world.

The new mechanised agriculture of North America and Australia produced a lot more food per farmer, but not much more per hectare. Crop yields in the USA in 1950 were not so different from those achieved in Britain a hundred years before. Increased food production had mainly come about through the expansion of cultivated land. But by the end of the Second World War, virtually all suitable land in the temperate colonies was under the plough. The American frontier had reached the Pacific Ocean; white settlers had spread to every part of Australia. If food production was to continue to increase, farmers would have to get more out of existing farmland. How could this be done?

The first step was the development of new fertilisers. For thousands of years, farms had been largely self-supplying, requiring few inputs and instead using animals, legumes and fallowing to restore fertility on cultivated fields – perhaps with a little help from the Chinese chamber pot. In the mid-nineteenth century this began to change. Researchers at Rothamsted in England identified the crucial role of nitrogen, phosphate and potassium in plant growth and began to look for readily available sources that could be added to fields. This led to islands off Peru, where the droppings of millions of birds had built up into layers of nutrient-rich guano. Importation of guano to Britain began in 1820 and reached a peak of 300,000 tonnes per year in 1858. At this time, it was the biggest source of income for the Peruvian government. But deposits that had taken thousands of years to accumulate were gone in fifty. Afterwards, efforts turned to mining saltpetre deposits in the Atacama Desert – which sparked a war between Chile and Peru – and to an array of eclectic sources, including sal ammoniac distilled from Egyptian camel dung. None was satisfactory: by the turn of the twentieth century artificial fertilisers were only used on a quarter of farmland in Europe.

The breakthrough came in Germany with the invention of the Haber-Bosch process. This used heat, high pressure and an iron catalyst to convert hydrogen and atmospheric nitrogen into ammonia, which could then be made into nitrogen fertiliser. This was straightforward chemistry, but complex engineering. Both Fritz Haber and Carl Bosch won Nobel Prizes in Chemistry for their work. In 1913 production started at a factory owned by the German chemical giant BASF. The flow of ammonia was temporarily diverted to the production of explosives during the First World War but fertiliser production resumed and increased rapidly once the war ended. Britain learnt its secrets after occupying defeated Germany and purchasing confidential plans from two BASF engineers in the 1920s. Factories proliferated around the world thereafter.

For the first time, farmers were not limited by the need to recycle nutrients within their boundaries – they could simply buy them from outside. But there was no point in having all these nutrients if plants were not able to absorb them. This spurred the breeding of higher yielding crop varieties. Progress came through hybridisation, which involves the controlled mating of inbred parents to derive plants with larger grains and shorter stalks. Hybrids had to be bought from specialist seed companies each year, which was a big change, as before farmers had simply kept some seeds back from a harvest for the next season. From the 1930s hybrid seeds became widespread in the USA. There were similar advances in animal breeding, as animals were selected to respond better to more nutritious feed. A dairy cow in 1900 could produce 2,000 litres of milk a day; now, with enough feed, she can yield up to 10,000 litres.

Breeding to maximise the useful parts of plants (such as seeds or fruits) sacrificed other aspects of plant performance, such as resistance to pathogens or general hardiness. The new varieties were high performance but fragile – the race horses of the plant kingdom. This led to the development of a wide range of herbicides, insecticides and fungicides to kill weeds, pests and diseases. Farmers became even more dependent on chemistry, spending $40 billion on crop protection worldwide by 2008.

The new plant varieties were also thirsty, which contributed to a massive expansion of irrigation. Across the world, the total area of irrigated land grew from about 80 million hectares in the 1930s to 275 million hectares in 2000, an area ten times the size of the UK. A new form of irrigation was invented, the centre pivot system, in which long lines of sprinklers rotated around a central water source. You will see them if you fly across the USA or Australia: perfect green discs, in otherwise dry landscapes, that look like they have floated down from outer space.

The modern agricultural revolution charged forward in North America, Europe and other developed regions. In Asia, Japan just about kept up. It built fertiliser factories, irrigation networks and advanced seed breeding facilities. Indeed, dwarf varieties of wheat developed by the Japanese were later used by scientists all over the world to improve yields.

But the agricultural productivity of the other ancient Asian civilisations stagnated. Millions died in famines in China and India during the twentieth century. By the 1960s, as populations grew rapidly, there were real fears about whether these countries could continue to feed themselves.

Disaster was averted by the transfer of key innovations from West to East. A doughty plant scientist from Iowa called Norman Borlaug played a key role – and won a Nobel Peace Prize for his efforts. From his research centre in Mexico, he developed high-yielding dwarf varieties of wheat suited to hot climates and introduced them to India in the late 1960s, helping the country to double its wheat production in just six years. At the International Rice Research Institute in the Philippines, another American, Henry Beachell, developed a high-yielding dwarf variety of rice that was adopted throughout Asia. In what became known as the 'Green Revolution', governments rolled out a package of hybrid seeds, artificial fertilisers and irrigation during the 1960s and 1970s. Within twenty years cereal production in Asia had doubled. It has been estimated that 2 billion people would not be around today without this Green Revolution.

Unfinished business

The pace of agricultural change quickened during the twentieth century – more has changed in the last seventy years than in the previous 700. We have developed increasingly sophisticated ways of breeding plants and animals, managing water resources, replenishing soil fertility, removing weeds and pests, and delivering on-farm power. As a result, people are better fed than ever before. Globally, between 1950 and 2000 the human population increased by two and a half times but the amount of food produced more than tripled. The Emperor of the Five Grains would be impressed.

21

Yet, the modern agricultural revolution has come at a price. It has been built on cheap and abundant energy, mostly in the form of fossil fuel. Hydrocarbons not only power the tractors on the farm, and the ships and trucks that carry food around the world, but they are a major input for the production of fertilisers and agro-chemicals. Furthermore, modern farming can destroy the natural resources on which it depends. Aquifers are pumped dry; land is poisoned by chemicals; over-ploughed soil washes away; the inappropriate use of pesticides and antibiotics breeds resistant pests and diseases. Farming can create pollution that harms the rest of society, and it is a major source of greenhouse gas emissions, which is likely to cause the climate to change in dangerous ways. There is a question mark over whether the modern agricultural revolution can be sustained.

Equally, there are large parts of the world that have been barely touched by this revolution. A chasm opened up between the most productive and least productive farmers. In 1900, an efficient farmer in the USA produced about 10,000 kilos of cereals per year, whereas a poor farmer in Africa produced 1,000 kilos. One system was ten times more productive than the other. Today, the African farmer still produces 1,000 kilos a year whereas a modern American farmer can produce 2,000,000 kilos. The most efficient system is now 2,000 times more productive.

These farmers might as well be living on different planets, or at least in different millennia. The American farmer drives a 300-horsepower tractor, plants genetically modified seeds, uses global positioning satellites to apply fertilisers and manages a farm measured in hundreds of hectares. In contrast, four-fifths of all farmers in sub-Saharan Africa only use hand tools, including a type of ard, because they cannot afford oxen, let alone tractors. They plant low-yielding seeds, make little use of industrial fertilisers and commonly use slash and burn to restore soil fertility. The average farm is about two hectares in size, about as big as three football pitches. The typical African farming system would not look out of place in Europe during the Middle Ages or among the Bantu people 2,000 years ago.

The agricultural revolutions carried some societies a long way but they barely touched others. The result, by the start of this century, was a patchwork global food system clunkily held together by international trade. Countries played different and sometimes surprising roles, determined as much by political and economic choices as by geography. The next chapter provides a snapshot of this system and reveals the imbalances, injustices and perversities that lay just beneath the surface, threatening a fragile equilibrium.

FOOD EXPORTERS AND IMPORTERS ON THE EVE OF THE CRISIS
Net trade in food, measured in calories, 2005–2007

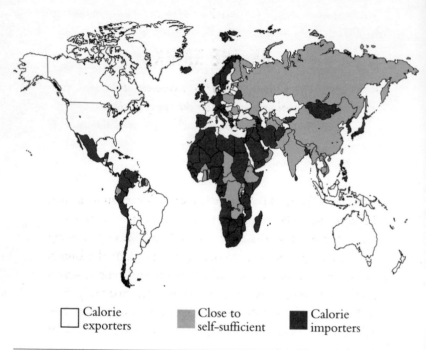

☐ Calorie
exporters

■ Close to
self-sufficient

■ Calorie
importers

Note: 'Exporters' export >10% of calorie consumption; 'Importers' import >15% of calorie consumption; 'close to self-sufficient' are in between
Source: FAO Statistics Division, 2010

2

ON THE BRINK

Who feeds the world? A taxonomy of the global food system on the eve of crisis

Who feeds the world? This is not a simple question to answer. In 2009 the UK government commissioned a two-year research project on the future of food and farming, drawing on the brainpower of more than 400 experts. At the launch of the final report, in a packed Whitehall conference room, a leader of the project explained how one of the first things they had tried to do was to 'map the global food system'. But they did not get very far. 'We gave up,' Professor Lawrence Haddad admitted. 'It was too complicated.'

Part of the problem is that trade statistics that focus on the monetary value of food can be misleading. For example, the Netherlands had a food trade surplus worth $14 billion in 2006, but this is because it exported small quantities of expensive processed food while buying in shiploads of cheap raw commodities. It depends on imports to sustain its dense population. Conversely, Russia had a food trade deficit of almost $15 billion in the same year, but this was because it imported high value products such as meat while exporting large quantities of grain. If it was cut off from the rest of the world, Russia would probably still be able to feed its people, although on a tedious diet. Similarly, trade figures that deal in tonnages of food are hard to interpret. You are not only comparing apples with oranges, but wheat with wine, pork with potatoes, sugar with spice, all of which have different dietary qualities.

The best solution is to follow the calories. All foods can be converted into calorific values based on the amount of dietary energy they deliver to the eater. This cuts out differences in price that are driven by taste, scarcity or luxury value. Of course, man cannot live on calories alone: we need a range of proteins, fats and micronutrients to stay healthy. But calories are the baseload for our diets and a handy common denominator. By looking at which countries have calorie surpluses and which have calorie deficits, we can get a much clearer idea of where the staple foods are coming from.

The United Nations' Food and Agriculture Organization (FAO) calculated the net trade in calories for 176 countries between 2005 and 2007. If we overlay this data with levels of economic development, five main country 'types' begin to emerge. It is a crude typology, and not all countries fit neatly into a single category, but it can help to identify groups of countries that have similar roles in the global food system. The way in which these groups of countries interacted – or didn't interact, as the case may be – tells us a lot about how the system functioned on the eve of the recent crisis. And, as following chapters will explore, the way these blocs interact will help shape the geopolitics of the future.

Established food powers

The FAO database shows that only forty-one countries were net exporters of calories in the 2005–2007 period. Of these, some fourteen were advanced, industrialised economies. They include the USA, Canada, Australia, New Zealand and a few European Union countries such as France. For decades, these countries have been the powerhouses of the global food system, both as exporters and as designers of international trade policy. This is where we should turn first to understand how the system evolved.

One of the reasons why these countries generate agricultural surpluses is that they have been blessed by nature. The USA, with its long growing season, reliable precipitation and good soils, has greater potential for farm production than any other country in the world. The mild climate and long summer days of Western Europe make it ideal for growing wheat. Canada and Australia enjoy abundant land – there are almost two hectares of arable land for each person, eight times the global average. New Zealand has plenty of lush pastures, earning it the slightly ridiculous sobriquet 'The Saudi Arabia of Milk'.

These countries are also the inheritors of the modern agricultural revolution described in the last chapter. Farms are large, mechanised, heavily capitalised and high-tech. Farmers make use of hybrid seeds, nitrogen fertilisers, pesticides and the latest satellite guidance technology. The virtuous cycles of agricultural and industrial development have gone hand in hand with reliable infrastructure, functioning markets, and, by and large, benign systems of government. Those employed in agriculture now make up a tiny proportion of the workforce, generally less than 3 per cent. In the USA there are more prisoners and fast food chefs than farmers. But these farmers are incredibly productive.

Indeed, one of the major challenges in these countries has been how to deal with *over*-production. The result has been a complex system of subsidies and tariffs. This problem emerged in the USA in the 1930s, when economic depression and rising European protectionism caused prices to crash and drove millions of farmers into poverty. The first US farm bill was passed in 1933 as part of President Roosevelt's 'New

Deal'. New bills, each more bloated than the last, have been passed about every five years since. European countries such as France and Germany have a long tradition of protecting their farmers, and since 1962 this principle has been enshrined in the generous Common Agricultural Policy of the European Union. By 2007 government support accounted for 25 per cent of farmer income in the European Union, 19 per cent in Canada and 10 per cent in the USA. (Farmers in Australia and New Zealand used to benefit from subsidies too, although they have been mostly dismantled over the past thirty years.)

These policies achieved the goal of raising the incomes of farmers to the level of the rest of society, but they tended to stimulate over-production of staple crops. Prices fell. The challenge of what to do with agricultural surpluses remained.

One solution was to feed them to animals. This not only absorbed large quantities of surplus grain – a cow, pig or chicken needs to eat many kilos of feed to put on one kilo of meat, so there was a powerful multiplier effect. It also satisfied consumers: in almost every part of the world people tend to eat more meat as they get richer. By 2000 almost 70 per cent of the grain produced in the USA was used as animal feed. Nearly half of all revenues in agriculture came from livestock. Increasingly, animals were reared in confinement, fed a diet of grains or soybean meal, bred to grow as quickly as possible, and doused with antibiotics and hormones to stay alive. For centuries, domesticated animals, as providers of fertiliser and power, had been reared to assist with cereal cultivation. The shift to synthetic fertilisers and tractors broke this link, and industrial livestock production then turned the relationship full circle. Now, the purpose of cereal cultivation was increasingly to provide feed for animals.

Animal production was not the only way to turn low priced grains into higher value products. Businesses became ever more inventive in reconstituting the basic building blocks of maize, soybean and wheat into processed, branded foods that could be sold at greater profit. The development of high fructose maize syrup (or corn syrup) is a classic example. Scientists worked out that enzymes could be used to turn maize starch into an artificial sweetener that was cheaper to produce than refined sugar cane. It is now commonly used in soft drinks, breakfast cereals, yoghurts, soups and condiments. By the early 2000s one-tenth of the US maize crop was used to make this syrup. Indeed, maize is now used in everything from textiles to carpets to detergents. It is also used to produce fuel, a new phenomenon whose implications are only beginning to be felt.

Yet, as farm productivity increased decade by decade, still the grain surpluses persisted. This made export markets of crucial importance, especially to the USA. Public Law 480, later renamed as 'Food for Peace', was first passed by President Eisenhower in 1954 with the aim of distributing America's food surplus to the world. Food was either given away for free (food aid) or sold to countries on concessional terms. This was partly motivated by economics and partly by Cold War foreign policy: the USA offered cheap food to developing countries to lure them away from the Soviet bloc. Senator Hubert Humphrey, a future American Vice President, was explicit about this in a speech in 1957. 'Before people can do anything they have got to eat,' he told American Senators. 'If you are looking for a way to get people to lean on you and to be dependent on you, in terms of their cooperation with you, it seems to me that food dependence would be terrific.' The cheap food tap was turned on and off depending on whether regimes stayed friendly – Vietnam, Iran and Chile all experienced this on/off treatment. Later, Washington used export subsidies to artificially lower the price of American grain on world markets, ensuring that this dependency continued.

In his history of the grain trade, Dan Morgan describes how 'grain became one of the foundations of the post-war American Empire'. This was a break with history. Previous empires had tended to suck food in from their peripheries. The USA sent food out. Even now, it is the world's sole 'food superpower'. The USA typically ships as much grain abroad as the next four biggest exporters put together. Because of its dominant share in so many markets, what happens in the USA has a huge influence on global prices. If American farmers sneeze, the world takes notice.

Emerging food exporters

Nonetheless, over the past thirty years American dominance of food trade has come under challenge from a number of 'middle income' countries with competitive agricultural sectors capable of generating their own surpluses. These emerging food exporters include Latin American countries such as Brazil, Argentina, Uruguay, Paraguay and Bolivia. In Asia, Thailand, Vietnam and Myanmar are all net exporters of calories, mostly in the form of rice. In recent years, large grain surpluses mean that some of the former countries of the Soviet Union – Russia, Ukraine and Kazakhstan – can also be placed in this group.

These countries are blessed with favourable natural conditions for food production. They possess a large amount of arable land per person, as a group almost twice the global average and, in the case of Russia and Argentina, much more than this. The loess soils of Argentina, Uruguay, Russia and Ukraine – deep, nutrient-rich and easily worked – are ideal for grain cultivation. The fertile river deltas of Southeast Asia, with ample rainfall and year-round growing conditions, can produce three harvests of rice each year. These countries have adopted many of the innovations of the Western agricultural revolutions, such as synthetic fertilisers, hybrid seeds, agro-chemicals and modern machinery, adapting them to local conditions.

Brazil has come from nowhere to provide the stiffest challenge to American farmers. Up until the 1970s the country hardly counted in global food trade. In fact, it was a net food importer. But a spike in commodity prices at this time, together with a temporary US prohibition on soybean exports, opened up a space for Brazil. Farmers began moving from the crowded south to the massive central plains, the Cerrado. For centuries, this vast area of grassland and scrub was considered an infertile wasteland – its name means 'closed land' in Portuguese. The reason was its poisonous soil, which was highly acidic and contained a large amount of aluminium. Then, in the 1960s scientists working for the state-owned agricultural research institute, Embrapa, discovered that the soil could be improved by adding lime and phosphorus. They also developed tropical versions of the soybean, a plant that originated in temperate China. Millions of hectares were transformed into large, mechanised farms, growing soybeans, maize, beans and rice. Today, in what *The Economist* magazine calls the 'miracle of the Cerrado', the region accounts for 70 per cent of Brazil's crops.

Grain production in Brazil more than doubled between 1990 and 2007, as did yields per hectare. Ranchers pushed further north, clearing forest to establish new pastures and expanding their cattle herds. At the same time, the government encouraged the development of a biofuels industry based on fast-growing sugar cane. Brazil is now the world's largest exporter of beef, poultry and sugar. It vies with the USA as the top exporter of soybeans and is number three in maize. There used to be a popular joke about Brazil that it was 'the country of the future, but always would be'. Now, the future has finally arrived, at least for the large-scale commercial farmers that dominate the industry.

Other new global players have emerged from the ashes of the Soviet Union. Russia, Ukraine and Kazakhstan contain thousands of miles of rolling plains blanketed in a thick, fertile soil known as Black Earth. A natural breadbasket, coveted by Napoleon and Hitler, there is a long history of wheat export from this region via the Black Sea. Grain production plummeted in the 1990s after the Soviet Union collapsed, but since the turn of the century there has been a renaissance, as private investors took over old collective farms and governments improved infrastructure. Grain began flowing through the Black Sea ports once again. By 2009, these three countries accounted for almost one-fifth of all the grain on world markets. Russia was the third largest wheat exporter in the world.

These emerging agro-exporters have been the loudest opponents of rich world subsidies and tariffs, blaming these policies for lowering world prices and giving less efficient producers in Europe and North America an unfair advantage. Many of these countries are part of the 'Cairns Group', an alliance (also including Australia and New Zealand) that presses for freer trade in food. However, their commitment to free trade under all circumstances may be wavering. As we shall see, the events of the last few years have raised questions about whether they can be relied on as a steady source of supply for global markets.

The (barely) self-sufficient

In theory, our third country type should not be too worried about what happens on global markets. These are the self-sufficient developing countries whose agricultural systems have managed to keep pace with growing populations. Although they are dotted around the world – they include Côte d'Ivoire, Malawi, Guatemala and Turkey – by far the most important are the populous countries of Asia – China, India, Pakistan,

Bangladesh and Indonesia. These five Asian countries contain more than 3 billion people, so their agricultural productivity matters to us all. Rising demand for food in these countries, in particular China, is often blamed for destabilising world markets. But, at least until recently, these countries could feed themselves and were largely disconnected from world markets.

The farming systems of the self-sufficient Asian countries are a more labour-intensive and capital-light version of the modern agriculture of the Western world. Eager participants in the Green Revolution of the 1960s and 1970s, these countries have embraced synthetic fertilisers, hybrid seeds and pesticides. Indeed, Chinese farmers use more fertiliser per hectare than their American counterparts. The big difference is in the size of the farms and the number of people working on them. It is common for half the working population in these countries to be engaged in agriculture (although this is falling as industrial development accelerates and more people move to the cities). Farms tend to be small (often less than one hectare), plots are intensively worked, and there is less reliance on large machinery. The amount of food produced per unit of land is comparable with farms in North America or Europe, but productivity per farm worker is considerably lower.

Just like Britain in the eighteenth century, agricultural revolutions have underpinned the economic transformation of these Asian countries. China is a good example. It had to fix its agricultural problems before it could become the new workshop of the world. In the late 1950s and 1960s the 'Great Leap Forward' initiated by Mao Zedong – who collectivised all the land and organised farmers into communes – led to a disastrous famine in which 30 to 40 million people died. Starting in the late 1970s, the communes were dismantled, farmers were given back their land, and households were allowed to keep some of their profits. At the same time, the government invested in irrigation, roads, storage and the tools of the Green Revolution, while liberalising internal markets. A wave of agricultural entrepreneurship was unleashed, propelling more than 200 million rural Chinese out of poverty. It has been called the biggest and fastest wealth creation event in human history.

Grain yields in China doubled between 1977 and 2005. The number of people going hungry plummeted. By the turn of the century, China was the biggest producer of food in the world and largely self-sufficient. It had managed to feed 20 per cent of the world's population with only 8 per cent of the world's arable land. In many ways, Chinese agriculture is a great success story.

India underwent a similar, if less complete, transformation. In the 1950s India was dependent on foreign food, often in the form of American aid. The years 1965 and 1966 saw crop failures and near famine. As a result, Indian officials were open to new ideas when Norman Borlaug came calling with his Green Revolution toolkit. Following the adoption of new seeds, fertilisers and more irrigation, India was able to end its dependence on international food aid. India is now the second largest producer of food in the world. In dollar terms, it has run a small food trade surplus since the 1990s – rice is the biggest export, along with products such as cashew nuts, soybean meal, cotton and tea. Over the past fifty years, India's rural poverty rate has fallen considerably, although, because the population has continued to grow, malnutrition and grinding poverty still affect hundreds of millions of people.

The success of China, India and other populous Asian countries in achieving self-sufficiency was no accident and no triumph of free market forces. It was the result of deliberate government policy and wide-ranging state intervention. Aside from investing in infrastructure, governments used tariffs to protect farmers from foreign competition, established

minimum prices for crops, subsidised farm inputs such as fertilisers and seeds, and offered cheap credit. A recent report by the
Organisation for Economic Co-operation and Development
(OECD) concluded that Indian and Chinese subsidies are only
slightly below the rich world average and higher than in most
developing countries.

Rich food importers

The net food importers of the world, which depend on global
food markets for their survival, could be grateful that the most
populous Asian countries had achieved self-sufficiency as it
meant that more food was available for them. There is a simple
way to divide up the food importers – there are rich countries
and poor countries. The rich food importing countries either
have dense populations, small amounts of fertile land, limited
quantities of freshwater, or all three. Farmers are a small proportion of the population. But these countries possess some of the
highest income levels in the world and, therefore, can buy their
way out of trouble.

For some countries, this wealth comes from winning big in
nature's lottery. The pay-out is usually in the form of oil or gas.
For example, the members of the Gulf Cooperation Council
– Saudi Arabia, United Arab Emirates, Kuwait, Qatar, Bahrain
and Oman – are endowed with fossil fuel reserves valued at
some $35 trillion. Above these reserves is mostly desert, and
populations are growing fast, partly because of immigration,
so these countries import about three-quarters of their food.
For decades, they have followed a simple strategy: hydrocarbon
exports pay for carbohydrate imports.

Other food importers have grown rich through manufacturing while outgrowing their agricultural capacity. This is
the case for Japan, a country of 127 million people and the
world's biggest net importer of food. Historically, its highly

advanced farming systems helped to propel industrialisation and development. Yet, in the late twentieth century, as the population grew and developed more expensive tastes, the agricultural limitations of this small, mountainous country became apparent. The government used generous subsidies to bolster rice production, just about maintaining self-sufficiency in a food that has strong cultural resonance. But this came at the expense of almost everything else. Japan became a massive importer of wheat, maize, soybeans, dairy products and all types of meat. By 2006 Japan was importing more than 60 per cent of its calories and running an annual food trade deficit worth $28 billion. It requires an area of farmland three times the size of the country to grow all the food Japan consumes. It also requires a large area of ocean, as the country is a voracious consumer of seafood as well.

South Korea, with a population of 50 million, travelled a similar path. A major land reform in the late 1940s and early 1950s spread ownership of land to the rural peasantry and there was a drive for self-sufficiency in the 1960s. But less than one-fifth of South Korea's territory is arable land, partly because the country is so mountainous and partly because expanding cities have swallowed up much fertile land. Korean farmers have not been able to keep up with accelerating demand. By 2006 the country was the sixth largest net importer of food in the world, shipping in about 60 per cent of its calorie needs.

To an uncanny extent, countries like Japan and South Korea are following in the footsteps of the UK. As we have seen, Britain was at the forefront of the eighteenth-century revolution in European agriculture. Productivity was so high that between 1697 and 1792 it was a net exporter of grain. Yet, industrialisation and an exploding population meant that farmers could not keep up. The shift to imports was accelerated by the repeal of the Corn Laws in 1846, which reduced tariffs on foreign grains. The country became increasingly reliant on food from the USA, Canada, Australia and New Zealand. By 1938 Britain imported 88 per cent of its wheat, 96 per cent of its butter, 76 per cent of its cheese, 74 per cent of its fruit and about half of its eggs and meat. There were sporadic attempts to reverse this dependence, for example, when German U-boats threatened during the Second World War, and when farmers received a boost from European subsidies during the 1970s and 1980s. But by 2006 the UK was importing 40 per cent of its food and running a food trade deficit worth $23 billion – the third highest in the world. The difference is that most of this food now comes from fellow members of the European Union, not the British Empire.

And what of the European Union as a whole? As we have seen, some of its member states (like France) produce large food surpluses, while others (like the UK) are big importers. But it is more useful to look at the European Union as a single entity. Its food markets are protected by a single tariff wall and its farmers operate under the same Common Agricultural Policy.

Food self-sufficiency was one of the original goals of the architects of European integration. Western Europe had become heavily dependent on US food aid after the Second World War and remained a net importer of grains, oilseeds, sugar, beef and butter right through the 1970s. By the early 1980s, thanks to the Common Agricultural Policy, this import dependency had been reversed. The member states of what was then called the European Community were self-sufficient in grains, meat and dairy. Indeed, they were soon grappling with the familiar problem of excess production and began competing with the USA to sell food to poor countries at subsidised prices.

However, the EU grain surplus peaked in 1992 and thereafter began a long decline. This was partly due to changes in the nature of European subsidies. Instead of paying farmers based on production, Brussels started paying farmers based on the amount of the land they held, irrespective of how much they grew on it. Indeed, some were encouraged to set land aside. Agricultural production stagnated, even as demand continued to grow. In 2004, for the first time in twenty years, EU grain imports cancelled out grain exports – there was no surplus left.

Europe also became increasingly addicted to soybeans. The rise of the soybean is one of the most striking developments in world agriculture in the last twenty years. It is the one plant that challenges the primacy of cereal crops in the global food system. A nitrogen-fixing legume, this hardy plant can be grown in temperate and sub-tropical conditions. Soybeans can be consumed directly or processed into soymilk, tofu, soy sauce, flour, meat substitutes and a range of other food products. However, nine out of ten soybeans are crushed to produce oil and meal. The vegetable oil is used for cooking, salad dressings and in processed foods. The soybean meal is used as a high-protein feed for pigs, poultry and cattle. It is by far the most important feed for animals today. The volume of soybean trade has quadrupled since 1990 and is now equal to half the total trade in grains.

Many of these soybeans end up in the European Union. The trading bloc has imported soybeans and soybean meal to feed its animals since the 1960s but the volume of imports increased substantially during the 1990s. American pressure forced Brussels to reduce trade tariffs, and European farmers cut back on planting oilseeds because they were less profitable. At the same time, animal producers started buying more soybeans because the emergence of Mad Cow Disease led to bans on the feeding of meat and bone to animals. This was a major factor in the ballooning EU food trade deficit at the start of this century. By 2008 the EU trade deficit in agricultural products stood at 60 million tonnes. Soybeans and soybean derivatives accounted for around two-thirds of this amount. There were also large imports of sugar, maize, fruit and vegetables. The EU is still the second biggest exporter of wheat in the world, and exports smaller amounts of meat and dairy products, but in calorie terms it takes in a lot more than it sends out.

The EU's struggle to achieve self-sufficiency is like the story of a dieter who makes heroic efforts to shed pounds, and makes a lot of progress, only to relapse and pile everything back on. The dream of the original architects of the Common Agricultural Policy has been buried underneath a hill of beans. Western Europe has reverted to the position it held a hundred years ago – a wealthy, densely populated region that relies on the rest of the world to feed its expensive tastes.

Poor and food insecure

Other food importers are just as reliant on world markets but they are in a more precarious position because they are poor. Most developing countries have a food deficit, importing more calories than they export. These poor food importers are found across Central America, in West and Central Asia and amongst the nations of North Africa and the Middle East not blessed with oil. But the largest concentration and the most extreme examples are found in sub-Saharan Africa. This region is the big loser in the global food system, although it may hold the key to its future.

The agricultural revolutions that transformed so much of the world mostly skipped sub-Saharan Africa. The region has the lowest agricultural yields in the world: farmers produce about 1.2 tonnes of grain per hectare, compared to an average of 3 tonnes across the developing world and as much as 8 tonnes in North America and Europe. Local food production has not been able to keep up with a rapidly growing population. As a result, whereas sub-Saharan Africa was a net exporter of food in the 1970s, it is now a major importer. Between 2005 and 2007, only 4 of the 47 countries that make up sub-Saharan Africa were net exporters of calories; the rest relied on imports and food aid to varying degrees. The African continent had become hooked on cheap grain from more advanced agricultural regions.

In many countries, a two-tier food system has emerged. Cities on the coast or on navigable rivers buy food from abroad, because it is cheaper and more reliable. Isolated rural areas grow food for subsistence, with little connection to urban markets. Some farmers grow tropical commodities such as sugar, coffee, cocoa or fruit for export to the rich world. But the price of these commodities has fallen since the 1960s because of over-production and substitution – for example, sugar cane was replaced by high fructose maize syrup in the USA and by sugar beet in Europe. The terms of trade tilted against developing countries, widening their food trade deficits.

Rather than experiencing the virtuous cycle of agricultural and industrial growth, agriculture has thrust these countries into a vicious poverty trap. The majority of the working population is engaged in agriculture. Because of low productivity, limited agricultural surpluses and poor market access, they do not generate sufficient income to invest in more advanced farming techniques, and they struggle to compete against the cheap, subsidised imports flowing into the cities. Indeed, rather than feeding the cities or buying the industrial output from these cities, the rural poor are fleeing there en masse. The constant flow of rural migrants suppresses urban wages and produces a huge class of under-employed. The failure of agriculture weighs down the entire economy. It is one of the chief reasons for the extreme poverty of these countries. It also helps explain why Africa is the only continent where the number of malnourished people has actually increased over the last twenty years.

Although sub-Saharan Africa provides the most extreme examples of under-performing agriculture, more prosperous middle income countries have shown signs of slipping down the same slope. Egypt was self-sufficient in food in 1960, but its population has exploded from 28 million to 82 million since then, and Egyptian farmers have not been able to keep up. The country is now the largest wheat importer in the world. Thanks to Norman Borlaug and the Green Revolution, Mexico was mostly self-sufficient in food by the 1980s, but it became dependent on cheap maize from the USA after its markets were opened up by the North American Free Trade Agreement (NAFTA) in the 1990s. Another pioneer of the Green Revolution, the Philippines, has followed a similar trajectory, as successive governments failed to support the farming sector. The Philippines is now usually the world's largest importer of rice.

Overall, the least developed countries of the world, which ran an agricultural trade surplus as late as 1981, are importing an ever higher proportion of their food. They have been actively encouraged by the USA, and by the economists of the World Bank, the International Monetary Fund and the World Trade Organization (WTO), who spent the 1980s and 1990s forcing poor countries to dismantle import tariffs and farm subsidies as part of a drive towards freer trade. There was a strong whiff of hypocrisy about this, as American and European policymakers urged these governments to get out of agriculture while maintaining subsidies worth $300 billion per year for their own farmers and dumping food on markets at artificially low prices. 'Do as I say, not as I do', seemed to be the motto.

According to Akin Adesina, Vice President of a non-governmental initiative called the Alliance for a Green Revolution in Africa, this was an 'absolute disaster' for developing countries, especially in Africa. 'Today African farmers are almost the only ones in the world who receive absolutely no government support of any kind,' he said. African farmers 'are left on their own to sink or swim, and as we have seen they are simply sinking'.

A fragile equilibrium

Not all countries fit neatly into the five food types outlined above. But it is a useful typology. In 2006, about 500 million people lived in advanced economies with highly productive farming systems capable of generating large surpluses – chief among them was the USA. Just over 700 million people lived in middle income countries with developing farming sectors also capable of producing surpluses for export. These surpluses were eagerly snapped up by the 500 million consumers in wealthy countries that had outgrown their own agricultural capacities. Foreign food was also critical to the survival of a much larger number of people, approximately 1.4 billion, who lived in poor countries where farmers had been unable to keep pace with population growth. Sitting on the sidelines were the populous self-sufficient countries that had invested heavily in domestic food production and were (just about) able to feed themselves. Some 3.4 billion people could be found in these nations, with almost three-quarters in China and India alone.

At the start of the twenty-first century, the world's food system appeared stable, even boring. In real terms (after accounting for inflation), the price of food had been on a steady decline since 1950, apart from a brief spike in the 1970s. Policymakers filed food security away in the bottom drawer, confident that markets would always provide. Those activists and researchers who still worried about agriculture complained that prices were too *low* – they criticised European and American subsidies for dumping food on world markets and hurting poor farmers. But the challenge of feeding the world appeared to have been solved. This sentiment was captured by Giovanni Federico, a European academic who published an economic history of agriculture in 2005. 'The gist of this story is that agriculture has been an outstanding, and somewhat neglected, success story,' he wrote. 'In the past two centuries, it has succeeded in feeding a much greater population a greater variety of products at falling prices, while releasing a growing number of workers to the rest of the economy.'

Yet, if you scratch the surface you find that the world's food system had deep flaws. The long period of low prices starved agriculture of investment. In advanced economies, farmers were getting old and getting out. Farming was not seen as a dynamic sector for young people coming out of college, nor for private investors looking to deploy capital. Public funding of agricultural research and infrastructure shrank. Developing countries suffered even more: the proportion of foreign aid devoted to agriculture fell by two-thirds between the 1970s and 2007, while government budgets in poor countries were slashed. This globalised neglect of agriculture contributed to a worrying fall in productivity growth. Agricultural yields, on a per hectare basis, grew half as fast between 1990 and 2007 as they did during the previous twenty years. The agricultural revolutions of the twentieth century were running out of steam.

The global food system was also becoming more and more unbalanced. Over the past fifty years, trade in food has grown at a more rapid pace than global population. The number of people in the world doubled between 1965 and 2008 but the volume of trade in cereals and oilseeds increased by three and a half times. National calorie deficits and surpluses widened. What is striking, even counter-intuitive, is that rich countries were mostly selling food to poor countries. Of the 46 poorest countries in the world (those with a Gross Domestic Product of less than $2,000 per person) all but 3 countries imported more calories than they exported. On the other side of the equation, the 41 countries in the FAO database that were net exporters of calories were more than twice as wealthy as the world average. This led to some bizarre outcomes. The biggest food exporter was the USA, where less than 3 per cent of workers were engaged in agriculture; some of its best customers were poor countries where up to three-quarters of the workforce were farmers.

Worst of all, the food system was damaging the health of a large part of humanity. Among the wealthy, the problem was over-consumption, as people were seduced by cheap meat and unhealthy processed foods, while adopting more sedentary life-styles. This was a long-established problem in North America and Europe but it has recently taken root among the growing middle class in developing countries. In 2010 the International Obesity Taskforce estimated that 475 million people were obese and a further 1 billion overweight. This raises the risk for chronic diseases such as diabetes, heart disease and cancers, otherwise known as the 'diseases of the rich'.

Far more troubling was the number of people who ate too little. The FAO estimated that almost 900 million people were malnourished between 2004 and 2006, which was almost the same figure as thirty-five years before (even if it represented a smaller proportion of world population). An additional 1 billion people suffered from 'hidden hunger', lacking essential micronutrients such as vitamins and minerals in their diets. Some 9 million people died each year from lack of food – greater than the entire populations of London or New York and more than all deaths from AIDS, malaria and tuberculosis combined. It is estimated that somewhere in the world a child dies every twelve seconds from hunger-related causes.

How did this happen? There was plenty of food in the world to meet everyone's needs. But it was unevenly distrib-uted. In many developing countries, farming systems were not productive enough to generate reliable local surpluses. Moreover, people were too poor to buy food at prevailing prices. Three-quarters of the hungry were found in rural areas, part of the 1 billion rural poor who eked out an existence on less than $1.25 per day. The vast majority relied on farming for their livelihoods. Which brings us back to the failure of agriculture in large parts of the world: its failure to achieve greater productivity, its failure to generate decent incomes for farmers, its failure to kick-start virtuous cycles of rural and industrial growth. The French academics Marcel Mazoyer and Laurence Roudart, in an insightful history of agriculture published in 2006, called this a generalised 'crisis of the peasantry'.

The global food system of the early twenty-first century was both impoverishing *and* starving one-eighth of humanity, while leaving an even larger number overweight and at risk of disease. The equilibrium that had emerged was unjust, even perverse. But it was also unstable. It was vulnerable to environmental, economic and demographic pressures that had been building for many years. What if the established food powers found a better economic use for their agricultural surpluses, for example by converting food to fuel? Would the emerging food exporters be able to fill the gap? What if the mega-nations of Asia lost the battle for self-sufficiency and instead entered world food markets in a big way? Would the rich importers be able to buy their way out of trouble? If markets began to tighten, would there be any crumbs left for the poorest of the world, whose farming systems were already in crisis? And what about the environmental damage caused by modern farming methods – the excess water use, the soil degradation, the pollution and deforestation. Could we go on expecting yield increases year after year, especially if climate change began throwing uglier weather into the equation? The world was about to find out.

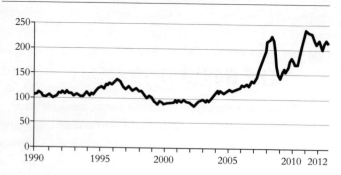

THE FOOD PRICE SPIKE
FAO food price index, 2002–04=100

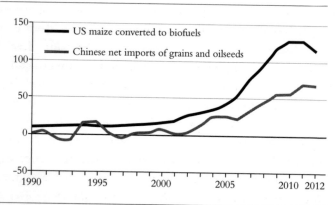

CHANGES IN DEMAND ON EACH SIDE OF THE PACIFIC OCEAN
Million tonnes

US maize converted to biofuels

Chinese net imports of grains and oilseeds

Source: FAO

3

THE WORLD FOOD CRISIS

*Richer diets, biofuels, wild weather and ecological
limits – the true causes of high food prices*

On 12 January 2010 a massive earthquake struck Haiti, killing
more than 300,000 people and leaving 1 million homeless.
When visiting the country a few months later, I saw the scale
of the destruction – it was like the capital city, Port-au-Prince,
had been smashed by a fist. But I also heard stories about how,
two years earlier, Haiti had been convulsed by a less visible
shock – a sudden rise in the price of food.

The cost of basic foods in Haiti rose by a half in the
early part of 2008. Residents of the slums of Port-au-Prince
complained that a plate of rice and vegetables that used to
cost $1.25 now cost almost $2. As most Haitians earn less than
two dollars a day, this had a huge impact on their nutrition.
Many people went hungry. To fill their stomachs, some turned
to eating a local speciality made from mud, salt and vegetable
oil – 'dirt cookies'. In April 2008 anger erupted on the streets
of the capital. Rioters looted shops, broke down the gates to
the National Palace, and turned on a UN peacekeeping force,
killing one soldier. In all, five people died in the rioting. The
violence also precipitated a political crisis, forcing the prime
minister from office.

The economic shock wave that swept over Haiti in 2008 had its epicentre in global food markets. From the beginning of 2007 to the middle of 2008 the international price of wheat, maize and soybeans roughly doubled. The price of rice, the world's most important food staple, tripled in just a few months. The media was full of stories about a 'World Food Crisis'.

Prices fell steeply towards the end of the year as the 'great recession' took the heat out of all markets and favourable weather allowed farmers to produce a record grain harvest. Some commentators thought the crisis was over. Yet, the global food system has been rocked by powerful aftershocks every couple of years since. Food prices spiked again during the summer of 2010, when the cost of wheat rose by two-thirds. Maize prices doubled over the following twelve months, and tropical commodities such as sugar, coffee, cocoa and cotton followed suit. There was another rally in the summer of 2012 after a heatwave decimated American crops. Maize and soybean prices reached their highest ever levels, and wheat was not far behind. Rice has not regained the giddy peaks of 2008, but, at the time of writing, it was still more than twice as expensive as in the years before the crisis began. We seem to be in a permanent food crisis with no end in sight.

In wealthy countries, where farmgate prices are only a small part of the final sale price of food, a doubling of the cost of wheat may only increase the price of bread by 10 per cent. This leaves less change in the pocket of consumers but it is not a matter of life and death. The impact is very different in poor countries. There, more people rely on unprocessed grains for their staples, so a doubling of commodity prices is transmitted directly to their wallets. Moreover, in these countries people are already spending up to three-quarters of their income on food, so they have little margin to spare. As a result, price rises drive more people into extreme poverty and hunger.

The UN Food and Agriculture Organization (FAO) initially estimated that the total number of malnourished people rose from 850 million to more than 1 billion in 2009, the highest figure on record. New data and methodology caused them to revise this figure downwards, to around 870 million, although they pointed out that this refers to chronic malnutrition and does not capture the damaging effects of temporary price spikes. Some of the poorest countries, such as Haiti, suffered greatly from sudden rises in food prices, forcing people to go hungry. Across Africa, the number of malnourished people increased by almost 30 million. Worldwide, the food crisis slowed the progress that was being made in reducing hunger. Children and women suffered the most.

Throughout history – whether in Ancient Rome, the France of Marie Antoinette, or Tsarist Russia – high food prices have been a recipe for revolution. This time was no exception. Haiti was one of more than thirty countries that experienced protests and violence as a result of higher food prices in 2008. When the government of Mozambique tried to raise food prices in 2010, clashes between demonstrators and security forces left seven dead.

Events in the Middle East showed that political leaders were right to be nervous. For decades, Arab autocrats had relied on cheap food to maintain stability. There was an implicit social contract: 'we give you cheap bread, you don't demand democracy'. When the price of grain skyrocketed, the system began to crack. In 2008, a wave of small bread riots began in Jordan, Morocco, Algeria, Lebanon, Syria and Yemen. In Tunisia protesters faced down riot police armed with nothing more than baguettes. In Egypt, bread prices rose by more than one-third, and more people became dependent on subsidised bread. By March 2008 about a dozen people had died in Egypt's bread lines, some in fights, some from exhaustion. President Mubarak ordered the army to take over the baking and distribution of subsidised bread to the public, effectively militarising bread production. But it was too late. When young Egyptians took to the streets in January 2011, anger over the price of food was one of their motivations. 'They are eating pigeon and chicken,' the crowd chanted, 'and we are eating beans all the time.'

What caused the sudden rise in food prices over the last five years? There is general agreement that it is not possible to identify a single cause: it has been described as a 'concatenation of trends', the product of 'cumulative effects'. Nevertheless, it is possible to separate proximate causes from ultimate causes. It is like peeling away the layers of an onion.

Near the surface, there were certain economic factors that magnified the volatility of food markets. One was the manipulation of food trade by governments. Another was speculation in commodity markets by financial investors. Both will be explored in later chapters. A third factor was the fall in the value of the US dollar, which depreciated by almost a third against other currencies in the years leading up to 2008. Most agricultural commodities are denominated in dollars, so falls in the dollar tend to lead to a countervailing rise in quoted prices. Finally, some blame money-printing by central banks since the 2008 financial crash for flooding the world with liquidity and inflating the prices of real assets such as commodities.

These factors certainly magnified volatility in food markets. Yet, alone, they could not have caused the crisis. It is better to see them as multipliers, which acted on deeper issues. Ultimately, food prices leapt because of a fundamental mismatch between supply and demand. Global production of the major food staples was lower than consumption in seven of the eight years from 2000 to 2008. In other words, for seven out of eight years the world was running a food deficit, living off its reserves. This led to a run-down in global food stocks. By 2008 there was little spare capacity in the system. No wonder prices jumped.

Therefore, it is to supply and demand that we must turn to understand the fundamental causes of the food crisis. This means looking at production and trade data from around the world. It means studying the interactions between the five 'food types' outlined in the previous chapter. The role of key nations was changing, in ways that upset the equilibrium that had prevailed for a quarter century.

The drumbeat of demand

On 31 October 2011, a day traditionally associated with honouring the dead, it is thought that a baby born somewhere became the 7 billionth person alive. This was the latest milestone in a population explosion of mind-boggling rapidity. It took a leisurely 122 years for humanity to grow from 1 billion to 2 billion, a figure reached in 1927. It took 33 years to reach 3 billion. From 1960 each extra billion has been added more quickly than the last, so that it took just 12 years to go from 6 to 7 billion. The *rate* of growth is actually slowing: it now stands at about 1.1 per cent each year compared to a peak of 2.2 per cent in the 1960s. But because this is a small percentage of a very big number the size of the increase is still staggering: each day, there are 219,000 more mouths to feed. This translates directly into demand for food, especially for basic carbohydrates such as rice, wheat and maize.

Population growth is the relentless drumbeat behind the march of food demand. Yet, there is an even more important factor at work. The beat is speeding up because diets are changing. As people become wealthier they increase their consumption of meat, dairy products and vegetable oils. We saw this happen in Britain during the nineteenth century, in North America in the twentieth century and in Japan and South Korea in recent decades. Now it is the turn of the fast developing countries of Asia, Latin America and the Middle East. Meat consumption in developing countries is growing ten times faster than in industrialised countries. The trend is especially obvious in China, where meat consumption increased from 20 kilos per person in 1985 to 53 kilos in 2007. This has a multiplier effect on other foods, as chicken, pigs and cattle are frequently raised on grain or soybeans.

So, can we blame new demand from China and other Asian countries for the spike in global food prices? Have they fallen off the self-sufficiency wagon? The media was full of stories to this effect in 2008. But a number of experts rejected this thesis. They pointed out that data on Chinese trade in grains (which includes rice, wheat, maize, barley and millet) does not show any significant increase in imports during this period. Indeed, between 1997 and 2007 China was a net exporter of grains, albeit on a small scale. How could Chinese demand be a cause of the food crisis if the country was such a small player in world markets?

However, a closer look at the figures reveals a different picture. Grain production in China fell behind consumption each year between the 2000/2001 season and 2005/06. Local farmers were not able to keep up with demand. The only way that China was able to increase its consumption, while still exporting small quantities of grain, was by drawing down stocks: Chinese reserves fell by two-thirds during this period, reaching a twenty-year low in 2006. Better harvests after this point meant that production was able to overtake consumption once again – Chinese state planners breathed a sigh of relief. But this did not lead to a resumption of exports on any scale. Instead, China withheld grains to rebuild its stocks.

Moreover, since 2008 China has become a net importer of grains, largely because it has started to import maize to use as animal feed. This took many people by surprise, including the US Department of Agriculture, which has consistently under-estimated Chinese demand. The numbers are still small in the context of China's massive agricultural sector, but the country has gone from regularly exporting about 7 million tonnes of grain ten years ago to importing 10 million tonnes during the 2011/12 harvest cycle. This swing of 17 million tonnes is more than Brazil's total grain exports. It is enough to have an effect on the market.

When we add trade in oilseeds to the analysis the picture is even clearer. Oilseeds include peanuts, rapeseed, sunflowers and cottonseeds, but the king is the soybean. Although China is the original home of the soybean – Emperor Shennong is credited with its discovery – the country has not been self-sufficient in the crop since 1995. Imports have grown exponentially since the government made a strategic decision to develop the domestic pig industry by using imported feed. China has overtaken the European Union as the world's biggest buyer of soybeans. By 2011 the country was importing 56 million tonnes per year. This is an extraordinary amount, enough to fill 840 Panamax ships, the giant cargo vessels that squeeze through the Panama Canal.

If we add oilseeds to China's grain trade, its growing calorie deficit becomes clear. Chinese farmers have not produced enough grains *and* oilseeds to satisfy domestic demand since 1998. The country's net import of these crops was just a few million tonnes until the 2003/04 harvest – less than 2 per cent of consumption – but in the following years this deficit widened considerably. By the middle of 2008 China was shipping in 34 million tonnes of grains and oilseeds per year; by 2012 the figure had reached 69 million tonnes, which represents 12 per cent of consumption. In many ways, China was beginning to resemble the European Union: just about self-sufficient in the grains eaten directly by people, but relying more and more on world markets for the maize and soybeans needed to feed animals. The appetite of Chinese diners for chickens and pigs was eroding the country's hard won self-sufficiency.

Unsurprisingly, this caused a run-up in the value of soybeans in 2007 and 2008. But the effects were not confined to this crop. Soybeans grow in climates that are well suited to maize. Farmers decide on the relative allocation of land to each based on prevailing prices – there is competition for acreage. Therefore, a rise in soybean prices causes farmers to shift away from maize, which reduces the supply of that crop and causes its price to rise as well. Moreover, an increase in soybean prices encourages farmers who are raising pigs, chicken or cattle to use alternative animal feeds, such as maize or wheat, which also forces up their prices. Because of the substitutability of crops, by both the grower and the consumer, changes in the price of one agricultural commodity can affect many others. China's entry into soybean markets, therefore, sent out ripples far and wide.

What of other fast-developing Asian countries? Have they followed China up the carnivorous food chain? In the case of India, the answer is no. For religious or cultural reasons, one-third of the population are strict vegetarians: the amount of meat consumed per person is about one-tenth of that in China. As a result, the country does not import significant quantities of soybeans or other animal feed. For three years, between 2003 and 2005, Indian grain production did fall beneath the level of consumption, mainly because of drought. This led to a temporary halt in all grain exports in 2007 and, as we shall see in a later chapter, this was one factor in driving up wheat and rice prices. But India began exporting grains again the next year. Overall, during the last decade India has never been a net importer of grains and, on average, has exported about 7 million tonnes each year. The country has managed to maintain its food self-sufficiency during a period of rapid economic growth. (Its one weakness is for palm oil, an energy-rich vegetable oil derived from the fruit of tropical palm trees that is mostly used for cooking. Indian imports grew from under 1 million tonnes in 1995 to more than 7 million tonnes in 2011, about one-seventh of the world's total production.)

But other Asian countries have followed China's lead, albeit on a smaller scale. Imports of grains and oilseeds into Indonesia, Bangladesh, the Philippines and Malaysia, four countries with a combined population of 500 million, more than doubled between the 1990s and mid-2000s. These countries now regularly ship in 25 million tonnes each year, about 40 per cent of the total flowing into China. Looking at the Asian region as a whole, even if we exclude rich importers such as Japan and South Korea, it is clear that a structural food deficit has emerged over the past decade. The year 2000 was the last time in which domestic production of staple crops matched consumption. The populous developing countries of Asia, which had successfully used the tools of the Green Revolution to wean themselves off import dependence from the 1970s onwards, were losing the battle for self-sufficiency. No longer able to sit on the sidelines of world markets, they had no choice but to hold their noses and take the plunge.

The biofuel surge

In the past, the first place these Asian countries would have turned to buy food would have been the USA. Instead, most of the extra supply came from South America, in particular Brazil and Argentina. The grassland around Buenos Aires, home to the famous *gaucho* cowboys, was ploughed up and turned into a soybean monoculture in response to the rising prices. Why did the North Americans take a back seat? Because just as the developing Asian countries began to enter world food markets the USA was turning inwards. It had found a new use for its agricultural surplus – converting it into fuel.

Maize is full of starch, which can be broken into sugars, fermented and then distilled into ethanol (another name for alcohol). The ethanol can then be blended with petrol to produce a fuel that works in vehicles. Although Americans have been toying with this technology since the oil crisis of the 1970s, ethanol became a major industry when the US Congress passed the Independence and Security Act in 2007. This law mandated the use of 164 billion litres of renewable fuel by 2022, with up to 68 billion litres to come from maize. Coupled with rising oil prices, this triggered a wave of investment in ethanol production facilities. In 2008 one-quarter of the maize crop was used to make ethanol. By 2010 ethanol production in the USA had topped 60 billion litres, up from a mere 7 billion litres ten years earlier. In 2011 four out of every ten bushels of maize ended up in fuel tanks. Maize is by far the most important component of American agriculture, accounting for almost four-fifths of the country's total grain crop. In just a few years, therefore, the ethanol industry had changed the game of American agriculture completely.

The emergence of this new source of demand inevitably caused maize prices to rise. Between 2002 and 2006 the average price of a tonne of maize at a Louisiana port was around $107. In June 2008 the price hit $208. After a brief dip, prices started an upward march in the summer of 2010 and reached a new high of $332 two years later. Because the USA is by far the biggest producer, the American price tends to set the world price. Moreover, demand for maize has a knock-on effect on other crops. American farmers reduced the acreage planted for soybeans to focus on maize (even though soybean prices were also rising). The Corn Belt expanded a notch or two, pushing north and west into areas that traditionally grew wheat. The rising price of maize dragged up the prices of all animal feed grains, and caused meat prices to rise too. The effects could be seen on every American supermarket shelf.

The USA has long been the breadbasket of the world, supplying about one-third of all internationally traded grains. What impact did the new biofuels policies have on American exports? Remarkably, the answer is not much. Between 2007 and 2011 the USA exported (on average) about 90 million tonnes of grain each year, which was a little higher than the average for the preceding ten years. The new demand for maize was largely met by increased domestic production. The USA achieved record harvests in 2008 and 2010 and now grows about 50 per cent more maize than in the 1990s. This indicates just how productive American farmers can be if the price is right.

However, there is another way of interpreting these figures. Even though world prices were at all-time highs, and even though international buyers were frantically searching for shipments, American exports hardly budged. This is in stark contrast to the last food crisis in the 1970s, when the USA increased its grain exports by two-thirds in just one year (between 1972 and 1973) and was exporting almost three times as much by 1981. Then, the USA had acted as the world's swing producer, ramping up production to satisfy global demand. In recent years, the USA has been unable to fulfil this role because any spare capacity has been used to supply its biofuels industry. Like the dog that didn't bark in the Sherlock Holmes story, the true significance of the American trade figures is what *didn't* happen.

US biofuels policies have been strongly criticised for driving up the price of food, while delivering few environmental benefits. (Because of the energy-intensive way that maize is grown, switching from regular petrol to ethanol does not reduce greenhouse gas emissions much.) Jean Ziegler, the UN Special Rapporteur on food, called support for biofuels a 'crime against humanity'. The British environmentalist George Monbiot wrote that 'biofuels could kill more people than the Iraq war'. Others have questioned why the US government is giving $4 billion a year in subsidies to the ethanol industry when it produces such dubious benefits. The high level panel of experts of the Committee on World Food Security, an inter-governmental talking shop, claimed that it was 'incoherent' for the government to provide such massive public support for biofuels when it was otherwise trying to reduce farm subsidies.

This misses the point. US biofuels policies have nothing to do with the environment, nor with feeding the poor. To a minor extent they are driven by a desire for energy security, as so much of the USA's oil comes from abroad. But the primary objective of the biofuels policy is to provide financial support to American farmers. It is the latest in the long line of attempts to find uses for the country's grain surpluses. First grains were fed to animals; then scientists came up with derivatives like high fructose maize syrup. Grain has always been exported but demand waxes and wanes, and the prices on offer are not always attractive. In contrast, a domestic biofuels industry can absorb all the grains that

American farmers produce. Under this logic, a higher maize price is not a problem; it is a sign of success. Ultimately, the biofuels subsidies and mandates are a product of the political configuration of the US Congress, where thinly populated agricultural states are over-represented and farm lobbies wield considerable power.

Of course, the USA is not the only country to have supported the diversion of food to fuel. Since the 1970s, Brazil has built up an impressive ethanol industry based on sugar, which is a more efficient feedstock than maize. Most Brazilian cars are adapted to run on either ethanol or petrol, and consumers switch between them depending on the relative price. The country produced 26 billion litres of ethanol in 2010. The European Union has focused on biodiesel, which is derived from the oils of rapeseed, soybeans, sunflower and oil palm. Thanks to a range of mandates, subsidies and import tariffs, the region produced more than 6 billion litres of biodiesel in 2007. The decision by local farmers to devote more land to rapeseed further increased European demand for soybeans and maize from abroad. Other countries setting targets for the development of biofuels include China, India, Indonesia, South Africa and Thailand.

Mandates and subsidies have been important for getting the biofuels industry off the ground, but at a certain point they don't matter any more. For every crop that can be used to make biofuels there is a break-even point at which it becomes cheaper than petroleum, even without any subsidies. So long as crude oil prices are high enough, food will be diverted to make biofuels as this is where the most profit lies. We have hitched our food markets to energy markets, without fully understanding the consequences.

There is no doubt that biofuels pushed up food prices over the last five years. Alongside population growth and changing diets in Asia, it is one of the demand factors that helps explains the recent tightness in world food markets. However, there were also supply factors at work. Critical agricultural regions suffered disruptions to production, which meant that supply could not keep up with demand. The most visible cause of disruption was an unusual series of extreme weather events.

Climate shocks

Russia smouldered during the summer of 2010. Temperatures exceeded a record 38°C. Wild fires spread through tinder-dry forests and bogs. 'Practically everything is burning,' President Dmitry Medvedev announced on television, wiping perspiration from his forehead. Thousands died from smoke-related illnesses in Moscow. More than 2,000 people drowned as they tried to keep cool by swimming in lakes or rivers. Russian agriculture, which had recently emerged from its post-Communist slumber to become a major supplier of grain to world markets, was devastated. The Russian grain harvest shrank from nearly 100 million tonnes to just over 60 million. In an attempt to control domestic food prices, the Russian government banned all grain exports. This threw global wheat markets into turmoil.

The Russian heatwave was just one of a number of extreme weather events to hammer world agriculture. Australia was one of the worst affected countries. Starting in 2003, it experienced its most severe drought in a century. Reservoirs emptied, soils baked, and the Murray-Darling River, which provides the bulk of Australian irrigation water, shrunk to a trickle. Wheat exports fell by one-third between 2002 and 2003, crept back towards normal levels for a couple of years, but then dropped by almost one-half from 2007 to 2008. Two years later, the drought broke in dramatic fashion and floods swept through eastern Australia. In February 2011, Cyclone Yasi flattened sugar cane fields in the northeastern state of Queensland, cutting sugar exports by a third. Australia is not the largest agricultural producer in the world but, thanks to its low population and massive land area, it normally exports most of what it produces – it is a top three exporter of wheat, beef, sugar and many other commodities. This gives it a disproportionate influence on world markets. The downturn in Australia production was one of the reasons why global wheat supplies were so scarce in 2008.

Other regions have had to grapple with similar extremes. In 2010 the Indus River Basin in Pakistan suffered its worst flooding in history. Approximately four-fifths of the country's land was submerged, damaging the country's wheat, rice and cotton crops. Heavy monsoon rains in Thailand in the autumn of 2011 inundated the fertile central plains, threatening crops. On the other side of the world, the Texas summer of 2011 was the hottest and driest on record for more than 100 years. Crops and pastures withered in the sun, dozens of wildfires broke out, and farmers suffered an estimated $5.2 billion in agricultural losses. A few months later drought hit the soybean lands of Brazil, Argentina, Uruguay and Paraguay, cutting the harvest by one-sixth.

The summer of 2011 was just a taster for the calamity that was to befall American farmers one year later. July 2012 was the hottest month ever recorded in the continental USA. From the Great Plains to the Midwest, the heartland of American agriculture, there was little rain for two months. The US Department of Agriculture declared natural disasters in 1,800 counties across 35 states, more than half of the country's total. The hot, dry weather destroyed one-sixth of the nation's maize crop and one-eighth of its soybeans. The price of maize surged by almost 60 per cent in just two months, and soybean prices reached record highs.

Almost every year since 2008, at least one weather event somewhere in the world has thrown food markets into a spin. Could the frequency of disruptions be more than coincidence? Despite the well-publicised efforts of a few sceptics, there is almost complete unanimity within the scientific community that climate change is happening and that it is caused by human emissions of carbon dioxide and other greenhouse gases. As well as bringing about long-term changes in temperature and precipitation, global warming is predicted to lead to an increase in extreme weather events. There will be more floods and droughts, more heatwaves and storms. Studies released in 2012 by the UK Met Office, the US National Oceanic and Atmospheric Administration and the Intergovernmental Panel on Climate Change all strengthened this conclusion. Changes in the frequency and severity of extreme weather events will probably have a much bigger impact on agriculture than changes in average climatic conditions, at least in the short term.

According to Professor Peter Hoppe of the giant insurance group Munich Re, the process has already begun. Munich Re maintains the world's most comprehensive natural catastrophe database. It reveals that the number of extreme weather events, such as windstorms and floods, has tripled since 1980. According to Professor Hoppe, the figures 'indicate a trend towards an increase in extreme weather events that can only be fully explained by climate change. It's as if the weather machine had changed up a gear.' The weather that repeatedly disrupted global food markets over the past five years may be a sign of things to come.

The Russian summer of 2010 was enough to convince President Dmitry Medvedev, who only a year before had dismissed global warming as a Western plot to thwart his country's development. 'What's happening with the planet's climate right now,' he told reporters, 'needs to be a wake-up call to all of us, meaning all heads of state, all heads of social organizations, in order to take a more energetic approach to countering the global changes to the climate.'

Natural constraints

Between 2008 and 2012 extreme weather events provided acute shocks to the global food system. This was an obvious cause of shortfalls in supply. Yet, there were also chronic maladies at work. We have already seen how the phenomenal yield growth of the 1960s, 1970s and 1980s tapered off in the 1990s. Sluggish yields meant that farmers struggled to keep up with increasing demand. Although lack of investment and changes in economic policy can partly explain this, farmers were also running into environmental and natural resource constraints. The modern agricultural revolution was slowing in some parts of the world and going into reverse in others.

It is not altogether surprising that crop yields in the most advanced systems started to plateau. Breeders have coaxed plants to focus their photosynthetic power on producing food, but there is only so much sunlight that one plant can absorb and only so much energy that the plant can divert to growing seeds before its roots, stems and leaves begin to suffer. So far, genetic engineering has not helped much. Genetically Modified Organisms (GMOs) can simplify farming operations, for example by cutting down on pesticide use, but they don't produce more food per hectare. This is why the US Department of Agriculture expects yields in the USA to continue to grow at only 1 per cent per year during the next decade, half the historical rate. The situation is worse for rice in Asia: scientists believe that rice yields in China, India and Indonesia are already as high as can be achieved. The high performance plants that farmers use today may be reaching their biological limits.

The modern agricultural revolution of the twentieth century was also based on the use of chemicals to eliminate weeds, insects and fungi. But nature has a defence against this sort of human interference – evolution. By the mid-1980s some 450 species had developed resistance to one or more insecticides, about 150 fungi and bacteria were resistant to fungicides, and nearly 50 weed species were resistant to herbicides. One of the most worrying recent developments is the appearance of weeds resistant to glyphosate, a herbicide that is widely used in combination with genetically modified maize, soybean and cotton. Just as the over-use of antibiotics led to the rise of drug-resistant supergerms, the ubiquitous use of glyphosate by American farmers has led to the emergence of tenacious superweeds. Scientists have to work harder and harder to come up with new chemicals when the old ones are no longer effective.

Some of this work is being conducted at Jealott's Hill, among the rolling fields of Berkshire, outside London. This is the high-tech laboratory of Syngenta, one of the world's leading plant science companies. Robot arms whiz from side to side, depositing tiny drops of chemicals on tray after tray of miniature plants, as white-coated scientists search for new compounds to fight pests. The Jealott's Hill storage facility contains over 1 million different compounds waiting to be tested. However, good compounds are becoming increasingly difficult to find, and tighter regulations make it more expensive to get new products to market. As a result, the Sygenta scientists now have to test around 100,000 compounds each year to develop one new product. Twenty years ago they would find a new product with every 10,000 tests. The crop protection companies, and the modern farmers who depend on them, are on an innovation treadmill, whose speed keeps increasing. This is one reason why the proportion of crops lost to pests (about one-third) has not changed since the 1970s, even though farmers are spending more and more on pesticides.

The resistance of pests to chemicals is nature's way of biting back. But there are more fundamental natural limits with which our food systems must cope. First and foremost, agriculture needs land. In populous and developed regions, such as Asia and Western Europe, there is little new land available for cultivation. Moreover, some countries appear to be losing agricultural land, as fields are buried under houses, factories and roads. Since the end of the Second World War, Japan, Taiwan and South Korea have all lost one-third of their arable area. Experts claim that China's arable land has shrunk by about 6 per cent over the past decade. Because cities tend to be located in fertile areas, their expansion often takes place at the expense of the most productive farmland.

A more insidious threat is land degradation. It happens inch by inch, soil particle by soil particle, sometimes so slowly that a farmer, like the metaphorical frog in boiling water, is unaware of what is happening until it is too late. Soils can lose their fertility as their composition and structure alter, or they can disappear altogether through the effects of wind or water erosion. Farmers are usually the cause of this destruction. Inappropriate management of livestock can strip the land of vegetation and turn semi-arid areas into desert; the clearing of forests for agriculture can make land susceptible to erosion; irrigation can deposit salts that make soils barren; excessive tillage, over-use of agro-chemicals, or failure to restore the nutrients extracted in harvests can lead to a loss of fertility. The result is a decline in yields or, in the worst case, complete abandonment of the land. The United Nations estimates that 12 million hectares of arable land become unusable each year, about 1 per cent of the world's cultivated area.

Perhaps the most pressing constraint on food production is water scarcity. Irrigation is crucial to the world's food supply: only 17 per cent of the world's land is irrigated but this land produces around 40 per cent of the world's food. Since the 1970s, thanks to the advent of powerful diesel and electric pumps, more and more of this water has been extracted from underground aquifers. Some of these aquifers are replenished every year. They can be sustainably exploited so long as the rate of extraction does not exceed the speed at which they refill. But other aquifers were formed thousands of years ago and are no longer replenished from above. This 'fossil water' is a finite resource; once it is gone it is gone.

Unfortunately, some of the water is going rather quickly. One of the largest aquifers in the world is the Ogallala, which stretches under the Great Plains of the USA. It provides about 30 per cent of the irrigation water used on American farms. But the water level is falling and some expect it to dry up completely in twenty-five years. On the North China Plain, which produces half of China's wheat, farmers rely on an aquifer that is dropping between three and six metres every year. In the Indian states of Punjab and Haryana, water tables are falling so much that well-drillers have to use modified oil-drilling technology to find water, sometimes drilling a whole kilometre underground. The World Bank estimates that 175 million people in India depend on grain produced by over-pumping; the figure for China is probably 130 million. Lester Brown, one of the pioneers of the American environmental movement, calls the boost in grain production that comes from depleting aquifers a 'water-based food bubble'.

In the Middle East, the bubbles are starting to burst. From Yemen to Jordan to Syria to Iraq, there has been a precipitous decline in domestic food production as water resources have dwindled. Consequently, the Middle East and North Africa have massively increased food imports in recent years, putting pressure on world markets.

Nowhere illustrates the problem like Saudi Arabia. During the 1980s the government embarked on an ambitious food self-sufficiency programme, tapping aquifers far beneath the ground so that wheat could be grown in the desert. It seemed to work. During the 1990s Saudi Arabia briefly (and bizarrely) became the world's sixth largest wheat exporter. But eventually the aquifers began to run out, placing the water supply of Saudi cities in jeopardy. In 2008 the government decided to phase out the irrigation programme. Wheat production is set to end entirely by 2016. As a result, Saudi Arabia is now a major wheat importer, buying in 2 million tonnes per year.

Of course, Saudi Arabia can well afford these food imports because of the spiralling price of oil. The rising price of energy is driving food prices higher too because modern food systems are fossil fuel intensive. A frequently quoted statistic is that it takes seven calories of energy to deliver one calorie of food to the dinner table in the USA. The figures are similar for the European Union. Nitrogen fertilisers are a big contributor, because about 80 per cent are made from natural gas through the Haber-Bosch process. Oil is used in the fuel that powers tractors, in the manufacture of agro-chemicals and in the mining and transport of phosphate and potassium. In the words of John Gray, a British political philosopher, 'intensive agriculture is the extraction of food from petroleum'.

Fossil fuel energy leapt in price in the mid-2000s, as demand increased for a finite and dwindling natural resource. Crude oil prices rose from less than $50 a barrel at the start of 2005 to a high of $145 in July 2008. After dropping to a low of $30 in December 2008, they rebounded to over $100 a year later and have stayed there since. This drove up the costs of agricultural inputs. The US Department of Agriculture calculates that between 2002 and 2008 the prices paid by farmers for fuel and fertilisers roughly tripled (even when adjusted for inflation). Fuel and fertilisers accounted for one-fifth of the total expenses of farms growing maize, soybean and wheat during this period, driving up the costs of production. This made a rise in food prices certain, as unless farmers were paid more they would not bother producing as much.

So far, I have concentrated on the production of food on land. Yet, the impact of ecological limits is even more apparent when we look at the harvesting of food from the seas. The latest FAO figures report that 80 per cent of marine fisheries are being fully exploited or over-exploited and, therefore, at risk of decline. Some have already collapsed, for example the Newfoundland cod and South American sardine fisheries. Globally, the total fish catch peaked in 1996 at an estimated 86 million tonnes and has since levelled out. This is clear proof that wild marine fisheries have reached a production threshold.

Instead, the world has come to rely more and more on aquaculture – the farming of fish, shrimp and other shellfish. In 2010, for the first time, over half of all fish produced for food was farmed rather than caught in the wild. But aquaculture faces ecological constraints too. Producing carnivorous fish such as salmon requires large amounts of fish meal and oil, which must be harvested from the seas. Aquaculture is susceptible to disease, which can lead to huge losses in production. For example, the Chilean salmon farming industry, the world's second largest supplier, collapsed in 2007 due to an outbreak of the Infectious Salmon Anaemia virus. The over-exploitation of wild fish stocks and the unsustainability of many aquaculture practices mean that it is difficult to keep up with demand. The one billion people who rely on fish for their main source of animal protein today may turn increasingly to the fruits of the land, which will put even more pressure on agriculture.

In many parts of the world, environmental and natural resource constraints are limiting the ability of modern food systems to increase supply. This argument has long been made by environmental campaigners, but it has recently been picked up by mainstream scientists and economists as well. The UK government's two-year study into the future of food and farming pulled no punches when it delivered its final report in January 2011:

> Many systems of food production are unsustainable. Without change, the global food system will continue to degrade the environment and compromise the world's capacity to produce food in the future, as well as contributing to climate change and the destruction of biodiversity... Nothing less is required than a redesign of the whole food system to bring sustainability to the fore.

The inexorable rise in demand for food, the biofuels surge, extreme weather events and natural constraints were all fundamental drivers of the world food crisis. They go a long way towards explaining why food supply struggled to keep up with demand during the first decade of the twenty-first century. They also changed how the world's five food blocs interacted with one another, disrupting a fragile equilibrium. Many of the fast-developing countries of Asia were losing their battle for self-sufficiency. China entered world food markets in a big way for the first time. The advanced breadbasket countries in North America and Europe, which would normally have responded to this new demand, turned inwards, preferring to convert food to biofuels in reaction to high energy prices. Another traditional exporter, Australia, struggled with biblical droughts and floods. This meant that world markets had to rely on the emerging agricultural powerhouses of Latin America and Asia, but there was a limit to how quickly they could increase production and, as we shall see later, they had a tendency to put the interests of domestic consumers ahead of foreign trading partners. The rich food importers were more dependent on trade than ever, as quixotic efforts such as the Saudi irrigation programme ran into an ecological sand-trap. These countries were still able to buy their way out of trouble, just, but turmoil on global markets gave them a shock they would not forget. As always, the greatest losers were the poor food importing countries, who were hit with massive price hikes that they could ill afford. The hunger, poverty and riots were concentrated in these countries. This is what turned volatility on commodity markets into a world food crisis. The tectonic plates of the global food system were shifting and some of the poorest countries were being ground up in the process.

But what of the future? Where will things go from here? All the factors that underpinned the food crisis are likely to intensify in coming decades, not weaken. The world's population will grow to over 9 billion by 2050; fossil fuels will get scarcer and more expensive; we are only beginning to see the impacts of climate change; and falling water tables and eroding soils, if unchecked, will eventually result in empty aquifers and barren lands. For some observers, the recent food crisis is the beginning of something much worse. Since 2008, there has been a steady stream of books and articles warning of the impending crash of the global food system, even of our civilisation. Malthus, the nineteenth-century prophet of population

THE WORLD FOOD CRISIS

collapse, is back in fashion. How scared should we be? Will we be able to feed everyone without wrecking the planet? This is the '9 billion person question' the next chapter will attempt to answer.

EXPANDING THE AGRICULTURAL FRONTIER
Amount of suitable uncultivated land available for agriculture, million hectares

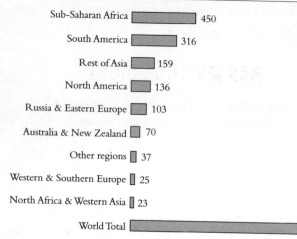

Region	million hectares
Sub-Saharan Africa	450
South America	316
Rest of Asia	159
North America	136
Russia & Eastern Europe	103
Australia & New Zealand	70
Other regions	37
Western & Southern Europe	25
North Africa & Western Asia	23
World Total	1319

Note: Estimates the area of uncultivated grassland and woodland suitable for rainfed agriculture, excluding all forests and protected areas. Total cultivated area today is 1.6 billion hectares.

THE YIELD GAP
Current yields per hectare compared to attainable yields, per cent

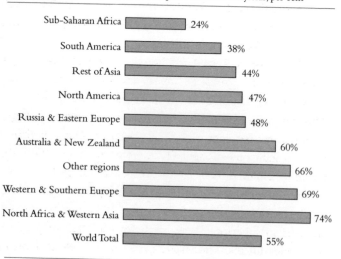

Region	per cent
Sub-Saharan Africa	24%
South America	38%
Rest of Asia	44%
North America	47%
Russia & Eastern Europe	48%
Australia & New Zealand	60%
Other regions	66%
Western & Southern Europe	69%
North Africa & Western Asia	74%
World Total	55%

Source: IIASA, GAEZ 2009

4

WAS MALTHUS RIGHT?

Population growth and carrying capacity – a
stock-take of the planet's food resources

For a nineteenth-century economist and clergyman, the Reverend Thomas Robert Malthus is surprisingly popular. You can buy T-shirts, coffee mugs, a jigsaw puzzle and shopping bags all adorned with the Malthus image. There are at least *three* death metal bands named after Malthus. Their music includes ditties such as 'Pestilent Desecration' and 'The Stench of Cadavers', which gives some indication of the gloomy ideas with which the man is associated.

Malthus owes his fame to a book he first published in 1798, *An Essay on the Principle of Population.* In it, he argued that growth in population always tends to outrun food production. This is because agricultural productivity only increases slowly, adding a few per cent each year, whereas human population tends to increase exponentially – the more people there are, the more children they have, who then go on to have more children. One plus one quickly equals eight. The balance is usually restored by disease, famine or war. 'The power of population is so superior to the power of the earth to produce subsistence for man,' he wrote, 'that premature death must in some shape or other visit the human race.' Malthus's arguments were influential in nineteenth-century Britain and were used to oppose intervention in Irish and Indian famines. These events could be interpreted as the checks needed to keep population within natural limits.

For 200 years, Malthusian fears have receded and resurfaced according to the preoccupations of the time. The last upsurge was in the late 1960s and early 1970s when world population was growing at its fastest. In 1967 William and Paul Paddock wrote an exclamatory book entitled *Famine 1975!* in which they predicted massive food shortages in India within a decade. They advised the USA against giving more food aid because it would only allow more children to be born who were certain to starve. A year later the American biologist Paul R. Ehrlich published his best-selling *The Population Bomb*. It began with a chilling statement: 'The battle to feed all of humanity is over. In the 1970s hundreds of millions of people will starve to death in spite of any crash programs embarked upon now.' The most extreme Malthusians predicted a 'Great Die-Off' in which 4 billion people would perish by the end of the century. The Malthusian outlook was given a more sophisticated presentation by the Club of Rome think tank, which used an early form of computer modelling to show that a rapidly growing population was about to run into the brick wall of finite natural resources. The resulting *Limits to Growth* report, released in 1972, sold 12 million copies in 30 languages.

However, for as long as there have been Malthusian warnings there have been equally strong ripostes from scientists and economists who have more faith in the human capacity for technological progress and social organisation. In the 1970s, debates raged between these 'Malthusians' and 'Cornucopians', 'eco-pessimists' and 'techno-optimists', 'doomsters' and 'boomsters'. The problem for the Malthusians is that they made specific predictions of what would happen in the near future. As time passed, it was obvious they had got it very wrong. For example, India in 1975, far from experiencing famine, was self-sufficient in food, even with a rising population. The first decade of the new millennium passed without an ecosystem collapse. Rather than experiencing a 'Great Die-Off', the world's population is now seven times greater than when Malthus wrote his treatise. People live longer and are better fed than before. Reality has repeatedly confounded the apocalyptic predictions – so far.

Nonetheless, forty years later, we are living through another revival of Malthusian fears. The mood change can be detected in the titles rolling off the printing presses: *The End of Food*, *Famine in the West*, *World on the Edge*, *Climate Change Peril*, *The Coming Famine*. Some of the earlier prophets of disaster have seized upon the recent food crisis as evidence that their predictions are finally coming true. Paul R. Ehrlich, now professor of population studies at Stanford University, is more pessimistic than ever, telling the *Guardian* newspaper that there is only a one in ten chance of avoiding a collapse of global civilisation. Lester Brown, one of the pioneers of the American environmental movement and a champion of population control in the 1970s, writes in his most recent book that 'if we continue with business as usual, civilizational collapse is no longer a matter of whether but when', mainly because of the difficulty of growing enough food. After being almost taboo for two decades, population control is starting to appear in the mainstream media as a valid subject for debate.

Neo-Malthusian arguments are based on the idea that we are using up the finite resources of our planet and approaching hard ecological limits. Figures are thrown around about how we are running out of land, water, biodiversity, fertiliser or fossil fuel. Climate change is cited as the great new threat, multiplying all the others. Some argue that mankind's environmental footprint is already so big that it would take one and a half earths to sustain current levels of consumption.

How seriously should we take these warnings? This chapter will start to answer this question. The first step is to assess the biophysical potential of our planet for food production. If the laws of biology and physics prevent us from growing enough food to satisfy everyone's nutritional needs we have a major problem, irrespective of how this food is distributed or priced. So, as you read through this chapter, put economic and political considerations to one side. Imagine that there are no borders, no economic disparities, no unequal power relationships within society. Instead, pretend that the planet is a single system that can be optimally managed to deliver food and other services for humanity. In this fantasy world, how much food can be sustainably produced? Do we have enough land, water, energy and climatic stability to feed 9 billion people by 2050? The good news is that scientists have been mapping, sampling and modelling the planet like never before, so we are now in a much better position to answer this question.

A Domesday Book for the twenty-first century

The notion of a 'crowded' planet has entered popular consciousness. It implies that all the good land is already being used and that there is little room for expansion. If there is any spare land it must be under forest and therefore cannot be touched, as deforestation would release greenhouse gases, destroy important biodiversity and alter rainfall patterns. Moreover, as we saw in the last chapter, people worry that we are *losing* precious farmland each year to urbanisation, industrialisation and environmental degradation. So are we running out of land?

The organisation best-placed to answer this question can be found in an eighteenth–century palace outside Vienna. The

International Institute for Applied Systems Analysis (IIASA) was founded during the Cold War with the aim of bringing scientists from the West and East together. After the collapse of the Soviet bloc, the institute broadened its membership and devoted itself to tackling big issues such as energy and climate change, food and water, poverty and equality. Inside its palatial headquarters, once a residence of the imperial Habsburg family, grand staircases lit by crystal chandeliers lead to rooms with stuccoed ceilings and walls covered in silk fabric. Outside the sash windows, a former royal deer park dotted with cherry blossom trees offers a soothing backdrop. However, the inhabitants are less interested in their surroundings than the results coming out of their powerful computers. Some 200 mathematicians, scientists, economists and engineers, bristling with PhDs, have been brought together, in an impressive assemblage of brainpower.

One of the most tenacious minds in IIASA belongs to a German mathematician named Günther Fischer. Over the past fifteen years, a team under his leadership has pulled together practically all the data that exists on soils, terrain and climate – the three factors that determine the suitability of a piece of land for agriculture. They put this data into a geographic information system and linked it to a model that calculates which crops can be grown (out of 280 different types) and what yields can be expected. Over the top, they then laid data on how the land is being used today. It was a heroic effort, requiring the integration of dozens of databases.

The resulting Global Agro-Ecological Zones computer model contains terabytes of data. In theory, a user can pick any one of the 2.2 million grid-cells on the world map, each representing an area no more than 10 kilometres by 10 kilometres, and discover how much food can be produced in that area under different farming systems. It is a sort of twenty-first-century version of the Domesday Book, the famous survey of all the land in England commissioned by William the Conqueror in 1086.

The IIASA model shows that about a quarter of the world's land mass (excluding Antarctica) is not productive: 22 per cent is occupied by desert, mountain, inland lakes or rivers, while 3 per cent is used for human settlement and infrastructure. Another 28 per cent of the land is under closed forest. About 35 per cent is covered by grassland or open woodland, much of which is used by pastoralists for grazing livestock. This means that approximately 12 per cent of the planet's land mass, or 1.6 billion hectares, is cultivated for agriculture. It is from this land that most of our food comes.

How much new land could be brought into cultivation? The conclusion of Günther Fischer and his team is that 3.1 billion hectares of additional, uncultivated land is agro-ecologically suitable for rain-fed crop production. That is, if properly cleared and prepared, and if brought under modern farming systems, this land has the right climate, soils and terrain to deliver acceptable yields, without having to rely on irrigation. If we exclude protected areas such as national parks, the figure drops to 2.7 billion hectares. But much of this area is under forest, so let's exclude this land as well. This still leaves 1.3 billion hectares of grassland and open woodland suitable for agricultural expansion, a large area equivalent to 80 per cent of all the crop fields today.

These figures disguise big regional disparities. Some of the most populous parts of the world are already maxed out. There is very little spare land in Southern Asia (especially India, Pakistan or Bangladesh), the Middle East or in Western Europe, and only small amounts available in China, the rest of East Asia and Southeast Asia. In contrast, North America could expand its cultivated area by more than half without encroaching on any forests. Indeed, the amount of cropland in the USA shrank by almost this much since 1950, as farmers intensified production on better land, so this would be simply reversing a half-century trend. The Russian Federation and Eastern Europe could also increase the amount of cropland by a similar proportion, as big areas fell out of production after the collapse of the Soviet Union. But the two regions with by far the biggest potential are South America and Africa. They contain almost 60 per cent of the suitable land identified by IIASA. They could triple the amount of land under crops without touching forests or protected areas. Without doubt, these two continents are the land banks for humanity.

The IIASA research shows that the world has not run out of farmland yet. If there was real food scarcity, if there was no better way to increase food production, the agricultural frontier could be expanded further. And this would not require clearing rainforests, ploughing unstable hillsides or 'mining' the soil in other short-term and unsustainable ways – these fragile lands have all been excluded from the analysis. IIASA's modern-day Domesday Book, therefore, does not support a doomsday conclusion.

Of course, the IIASA computer model only tells us what is biophysically possible. In the real world, actually bringing this land into production would pose an enormous social, economic and environmental challenge. Clearing the land of vegetation and preparing it for planting would require vast amounts of capital and labour. Many of these areas are remote, so billions of dollars would need to be invested in roads and railways. The IIASA model assumes a relatively sophisticated application of modern farming technologies to make this land workable, including fertilisers, pesticides and machinery, something which is out of reach of many farmers today. And there would be trade-offs. Even the clearing of grasslands and open woodlands, away from the forests, would affect the carbon balance, destroy biodiversity and deprive pastoralists of the grazing lands on which they depend.

This is why the abundance of fertile land on our planet, although reassuring, may be largely irrelevant. If possible, it would be better to get more food out of *existing* farmland. As we saw in Chapter Two, there is an enormous difference in productivity between the most advanced and least developed farming systems in the world. An Iowa corn farmer, or a Vietnamese rice grower, can produce ten times more grain per hectare of land than a poor farmer in East Africa. If a way could be found to bring the least productive farmers up to the level of the most productive, or even halfway towards this goal, the amount of food in the world would double or triple. As an added benefit, such an achievement could help tackle rural poverty in the poorest parts of the world.

Can the yield gap be closed? To answer this we first must understand what has caused it. If the cause is the biophysical environment, if nature has dealt these countries a losing hand in terms of soil, terrain and climate, then it may be difficult to do much about it. Is this the case? It is true that natural endowments differ from region to region. For example, Northwest Europe is blessed with fertile humus-rich soils, long periods of daylight during the summer growing season, and the influence of the warm Gulf Stream, which moderates the climate. At the other extreme, parts of Africa are cursed with nutrient-poor soils, variable rainfall, periodic heatwaves and the presence of virulent pests and diseases. Yet, it is important not to over-play this stereotype. Most populated parts of the world lie somewhere between these extremes. Many regions with low-yielding agriculture possess adequate soils and a good climate. Moreover, their natural constraints are such that they can be overcome with tried and tested farming techniques.

This is one of the most powerful insights to emerge from Günther Fischer's team in Austria. In the latest phase of their work, they have compared actual food production with the biophysical potential, as determined by local soils, terrain and climate. This allows them to estimate the 'yield gap' – the amount by which output could be increased under best practice management and production technologies.

The results show that no country achieves the maximum attainable yields. Western Europe and Eastern Asia get close to 90 per cent, which is probably the most that can be expected on working farms. Interestingly, North America only attains 70 per cent of its potential, which implies that there is still room for productivity increases there – the American agricultural revolution may not have run out of steam just yet. South America, Eastern Europe and Russia produce just under half of what they could on their existing farmland, pointing to even greater potential for improvement. But the region that stands out is sub-Saharan Africa, where yields are less than a quarter of what they could be, given the agro-ecological conditions. There are large areas of Africa which contain fertile soils, abundant rainfall and terrain suitable for productive agriculture. According to the IIASA work, maximum attainable yields in Africa are just as high as in North America or Europe. In theory, African farmers could triple their output without putting any new land under the plough.

This research demonstrates that the yield gap has more to do with the human environment than the natural environment. The unproductive state of agriculture in Africa and other poor regions is a product not of geography but of political, social and economic failures. The real reasons include poor infrastructure, dysfunctional markets, lack of knowledge and skills, limited access to finance and technology, unclear land rights, harmful regulations and tax regimes, unbalanced trade arrangements, and governmental systems that do not serve the interests of the rural poor. To quote Akin Adesina of the Alliance for a Green Revolution in Africa, the problems facing African farmers today are 'a result of missed opportunities and decisions made by governments and international institutions rather than a result of stubborn facts'.

The situation of agriculture in Africa and other poor regions is tragic, but looked at another way it is also a cause for great hope. If the problems are made by humans, not nature, they are amenable to human solution. These areas could double or triple the amount of food they produce. It is why IIASA and the United Nations' FAO expect that the amount of cultivated land in the world, despite the abundance of suitable unused areas, will only grow by 10 per cent between now and 2050. Instead, increased food production will overwhelmingly come from closing the yield gap on already cultivated land. To use the jargon, the best opportunity for agriculture is 'intensification' not 'extensification'.

So far, we have considered the planet's potential for food production under current climatic conditions. But what if the climate changes? Unfortunately, this is almost certain to happen. Over the past 200 years, humans have pumped carbon dioxide and other greenhouse gases into the atmosphere by burning fossil fuels and cutting down trees. The amount of CO_2 in the atmosphere today is 40 per cent higher than in the pre-industrial era. This traps heat in the atmosphere. The average temperature of the earth has already increased by 0.74 degrees Celsius during the last hundred years. Even if steps are taken to stabilise greenhouse gases now, it is almost inevitable that temperatures will rise by at least 2 degrees by the end of the century. If emissions are not controlled – and little has been achieved so far – temperatures could rise by 5 or 6 degrees.

What impact will climate change have on agriculture? This is one of the big questions in climate studies, one that super-computers all over the world are trying to answer. Considerable uncertainty remains. No one is sure about the quantity of greenhouse gases that will be in the atmosphere, how this will translate into surface temperatures, how this will affect precipitation, and how this will alter plant performance. One open question is to what extent plants will grow faster because of the greater amount of carbon dioxide in the air. In theory, this should boost photosynthesis in what is known as the 'CO$_2$ fertilisation effect'. Another challenge is assessing the impact of more extreme weather events, such as droughts and floods, or the change in distribution of pests and diseases. The computer models focus on average changes over long periods and cannot capture the effect of short-term shocks, even though the latter will probably have more impact on food production. And a lot will depend on what action farmers take to adapt to climate change, for example by switching crops or introducing new technologies.

However, if we look at the period between now and 2050, the broad conclusions are not as bleak as might be expected. Yes, agricultural production in the mid-latitudes and tropics is likely to be negatively affected because of higher temperatures and changed precipitation. Deltas and coastal areas will be threatened by sea level rise. Mountain and irrigated systems that rely on summer snowmelt are expected to experience long-term changes in water flows. (Marine fisheries may also be affected by changing ocean temperatures, rising sea levels and acidification.) But, on the other hand, the high latitudes, especially in the north – places such as Northern Europe, Canada and some parts of Russia – will experience increased agricultural productivity as higher temperatures lengthen the growing seasons and bring new land into cultivation. At a global level, if the CO_2 fertilisation effect kicks in, the positive and negative impacts may net out in the medium-term. The latest assessment of the Intergovernmental Panel on Climate Change, released in 2007, actually concluded that global productivity would increase slightly between now and 2050.

One of the reasons why the impact will be relatively small over the next forty years is that the planet is only expected to warm by about one degree during this time. Things will really heat up in the second half of this century, which will cause a lot more problems for agriculture. Indeed, the latest research indicates that the world is warming quicker than expected, which could bring forward some of these impacts. Tipping points, such as the disintegration of the Antarctic ice sheet, could lead to sudden accelerations. Therefore, although climate change should not prevent us from producing enough food between now and 2050, it is definitely something to be worried about. Feeding a world of 9 billion in 2100 could be a real challenge, if we continue on our current path.

To finity and beyond
The previous section assessed the potential of soils, terrain and climate for food production using 'modern' agricultural methods. But there are question marks over the sustainability of these methods. 'Sustainable' is one of the most rubbery words in the English language – it is stretched in every direction by a multitude of sinners and saints. Most simply, it means using natural resources in a way that does not jeopardise the ability of future generations to use those same resources. There are two charges levelled against agriculture. The first is that it consumes non-renewable resources – such as oil, natural gas, minerals and water – that will eventually run out. 'Peak Oil', 'Peak Nitrogen', 'Peak Phosphate' and 'Peak Water' are concepts that have provoked much hand-wringing in recent years. The

other charge is that agriculture destroys our environment by polluting water, shrinking biodiversity, clearing forests and pumping out greenhouse gases. These are 'externalities', in the sense that their costs are borne by all of society and not just by the farmer, although in the long run they may undermine the environment that the farmer depends on to produce food. For all these reasons, can modern farming systems continue to deliver?

Much of the concern focuses on the dependence of modern food systems on fossil fuels. The logic goes something like this: in industrialised nations it takes the equivalent of seven calories of energy to deliver one calorie of food to the eater; most of this energy is derived from fossil fuels; these fuels will eventually run out; therefore, our current food systems are in danger of collapse. An extreme version of this argument can be found in Dale Allen Pfeiffer's book *Eating Fossil Fuels: Oil, Food and the Coming Crisis in Agriculture*. He argues that in order to return to a system that relies on the energy provided by the sun each day, rather than the accumulated solar energy in fossil fuels, the world's population will have to fall to a sustainable carrying capacity of about 2 billion. In ultra-Malthusian fashion, he predicts a great human 'die-off'.

The rise in energy prices has certainly been a major factor behind the food price spikes of recent years. And, for crude oil at least, there are justifiable concerns about scarcity. No one expects oil to run out in the next fifty years, but it is likely to get more expensive. Yet, it is also important to understand what this really means for our food systems. Four-fifths of the energy consumed in food systems in North America or Europe is expended beyond the farmgate. It is used to transport, store, process, retail and cook food – your fridge and cooker play a big part. There is enormous scope for energy efficiency all along this food chain, as well as the potential to replace fossil fuel with renewable energy as a source of power. Delivery trucks could run on biofuels, machines could operate on clean electricity. If energy became truly scarce, some of the over-processing, the frivolous packaging and the flying of exotic products around the world could be eliminated. Diets in the wealthy countries would become less resplendent, more local, but people wouldn't starve; indeed, they would probably be healthier.

One-fifth of the energy is used on farms, some of it to power tractors and other machinery. Here, there are also alternatives to crude oil. When Henry Ford drove his first car it ran on ethanol made from crops. Rudolf Diesel fired up his nineteenth-century combustion engines with peanut oil. It is possible to imagine farms in which tractors run on biofuels grown on the same land as part of a self-sustaining energy system. Even if there were not enough biofuels to go around, and supplies of petroleum began to dwindle, it is likely that these supplies would be reserved for agriculture. How do we know? Because this is what happened during previous times of scarcity. During the Second World War, when petrol for civilians was rationed in Britain and the USA, farmers were given priority alongside the armed forces and emergency services. Today, agriculture is responsible for a modest 3 per cent of global energy consumption, so it should not be difficult to ensure a continuous supply for farmers long into the future.

The single greatest energy input in modern farming systems is nitrogen fertiliser. It is estimated that almost half the people on the earth are fed as a result of manufactured nitrogen fertiliser. There is no shortage of nitrogen in the air but it needs to be 'fixed'. This is done through the Haber-Bosch process, which mostly uses natural gas. Many 'doomsters' have latched on to this as the weak link in the global food system. The view was particularly prevalent in the USA in the early 2000s when experts predicted that domestic gas reserves would be gone within a few decades.

However, since then scarcity has turned to abundance because of widespread use of a new technology called hydraulic fracturing (or 'fracking') in which huge volumes of water and chemicals are injected at high pressure into dense shale rock to release hydrocarbons. Although environmental concerns remain about this technology, US natural gas production is up fourteen-fold since 2000. Reserves have been recalculated to more than 100 years of supply. At the time of writing, prices were just one-fifth of the peak reached in 2005.

Although supplies are less abundant in other regions – gas prices are three times higher in Europe and six times in Japan than the USA – at a global level the supply situation for natural gas looks much better than for crude oil. In addition, it should be remembered that only 4 per cent of the world's natural gas output is used to make fertiliser. As with crude oil, if there ever were a true shortage of natural gas, it is hard to believe that supplies would not be reserved for food production.

Yet, even if natural gas reserves were to be completely exhausted, nitrogen fertilisers would not disappear. This is because there are at least two other ways to produce these fertilisers. The Haber-Bosch process does not require natural gas per se. It just needs a reliable source of hydrogen. This could also be produced by electrolysis – passing an electric current through water – which could be powered by renewable sources such as wind turbines or solar panels. A completely different technology was developed by an eccentric Norwegian scientist named Kristian Birkeland more than a hundred years ago. While trying to develop an electromagnetic cannon for the military, he discovered that he could 'fix' atmospheric nitrogen by passing a super-hot electric arc through the air. He founded a company and built a factory beside a Norwegian waterfall to make use of hydropower. By 1908 the factory contained twenty-four electric furnaces all churning out fertiliser at full capacity. These furnaces continued to operate until 1934. The company later evolved into the modern chemical giant Norsk Hydro.

The Haber-Bosch process is not the only way to produce nitrogen fertiliser, just the cheapest. If natural gas ever ran out, we could turn to other technologies and power them with renewable or nuclear energy.

The other fertiliser critical to modern, high-input agriculture is phosphate. This input is more like a finite resource, as it is derived from mining deposits of phosphate rock. Two-thirds of global production comes from just three countries: China, the USA and Morocco. There are varying estimates of the size of phosphate reserves: the US Geological Survey estimates there are 100 years of consumption, whereas a more recent study by the International Fertilizer Development Center puts the figure closer to 400 years. There is no 'right' answer. Reserve estimates depend on the cost of extraction versus the market price; as prices rise, lower grade ores become commercially exploitable. In addition, phosphate does not disappear within the food system – it is relatively inert and most is eventually flushed into the sea. So, there may be opportunities to increase the capture and recycling of phosphorus from food, human and animal wastes. For all these reasons, phosphate fertilisers will not suddenly 'run out' in the next hundred years, although costs of production are likely to rise because of the need to turn to lower grade sources.

The most important 'input' for agriculture is not petroleum, nitrogen or phosphate. It is water. Over the past decade, the idea of 'Peak Water' has become a popular apocalyptic theme in the media. Agriculture, because it accounts for more than two-thirds of freshwater use, is seen as the chief culprit. The same statistics appear again and again: that it takes 1,300 litres to make a loaf of bread, 3,400 litres to grow 1 kilo of rice, 3,900 litres to rear a kilo of chicken, and anywhere between 15,000 and 100,000 litres to produce 1 kilo of beef. The implication is that here is another finite resource that humanity is remorselessly working its way through.

But this is a simplification. Water, like all matter, can neither be created nor destroyed. And, logically, one kilo of wheat or beef cannot contain more than one litre of water, as this is precisely what this much water weighs. So where does all the water go? Most of the water 'used' in agriculture is taken up by the roots of plants and transpired via their leaves as water vapour. A rule of thumb is that for every gram of biomass growth, half a litre of water is lost to the atmosphere by transpiration. If this moisture comes from rainwater stored in the soil, it is simply returned from whence it came, to fall somewhere else as rain. The same goes for animals grazing on pastures; most of the water contained in the grass they eat is returned to the pasture in the form of urine and dung. It is essential to view water in the context of the hydrological cycle, the constant shifting of H_2O molecules between the atmosphere, the soils, living organisms, freshwater systems and the sea. Water is not consumed in agriculture, just shifted to a different part of the cycle.

Rather than falling for dodgy statistics, we should focus on the real sustainability issues associated with the use of water in agriculture. The most critical relate to irrigation. Irrigation is vital to our food security, accounting for 40 per cent of total agricultural output today. As we have seen, several countries, including Libya, Egypt, Israel, Jordan, Saudi Arabia, Yemen and Uzbekistan, already withdraw more water than their total renewable resources. They are 'mining' water from fossil aquifers, or over-extracting water from rivers and lakes to the extent that they are in danger of ecosystem collapse.

Unsustainable extraction is also common in the North China Plain, around Mexico City, on the Indo-Gangetic Plain in India and in much of the western USA. In these parts of the world, there is little scope for increasing water extraction.

Yet, despite these regional shortages, which are only likely to get worse, there is no global scarcity of freshwater. Europe only withdraws 6 per cent of its renewable freshwater resources and Asia only 20 per cent. In many parts of the world, especially in Africa, there is scope to increase the amount of land under irrigation. The FAO estimates that globally little more than half of the land suitable for irrigation is currently irrigated. The problem is not a lack of water but that water is inaccessible because the right infrastructure is not in place. There are opportunities to increase the supply of water to farmers by investing in dams, canals and small-scale water conservation features.

Even in areas currently suffering from water stress, food production does not necessarily have to fall. The reason is that water is used so inefficiently. Little more than one-third of irrigation water is actually taken up by plants. The rest is lost to evaporation, run-off or ground seepage. The crudest methods of irrigation are the most prevalent: almost nine-tenths of the water is used for flood irrigation, which maximises the losses. Only 11 per cent of irrigation water goes through sprinklers, which are more efficient, and only 1 per cent through drip irrigation, the most efficient by far. 'Crop per drop', we get a lot less from our water than we should. And the reasons for this are mostly institutional and political, rather than technical or biophysical. In many schemes, water is too cheap or not priced at all, so farmers (and other users) have little incentive to preserve it. Institutions do not exist to manage watersheds well.

'Peak Oil', 'Peak Nitrogen', 'Peak Phosphate', 'Peak Water' – all these fears are overblown. The advocates of 'peak theory' have got ahead of themselves. Either the peak is not as imminent as claimed, or there are steps we can take to deal with resource scarcity. But what about the external impacts of our agricultural systems? How long can the environment continue to take a beating from our farmers?

The charge sheet against agriculture is long. For good reason, food writers frequently read from it. As mentioned in the previous chapter, unsustainable farming practices can lead to soil erosion and land degradation. The release of large quantities of fertiliser and pesticides can damage human health and create 'dead zones' in rivers, lakes and seas. The clearing of wild vegetation, the introduction of monocultures and the application of agro-chemicals wipes out biodiversity – apart from the odd meteor, agriculture is probably the greatest destroyer of species that the planet has ever seen. Deforestation and draining of wetlands can alter critical landscape-level ecosystem services such as flood control. Finally, although agriculture produces the food that keeps us alive it can also generate diseases and toxins that kill: outbreaks of Mad Cow Disease or E. coli are just some examples.

Agriculture is also a major cause of climate change. Farming activities are directly responsible for around 13 per cent of greenhouse gas emissions. The biggest source is the production and application of nitrogen fertilisers, which can lead to the release of nitrous oxide, a greenhouse gas 300 times more potent than carbon dioxide. The second largest source is livestock production, as digestion by ruminants and the decomposition of manure can produce large amounts of methane. Indirectly, agriculture can also be blamed for a large proportion of the 17 per cent of greenhouse gas emissions that comes from deforestation. So, altogether the production of food could account for close to one-third of man-made annual emissions, more than all the factories, cars or planes in the world. If we are to limit global warming it will be essential to reduce these emissions.

Many of these negative impacts are felt outside farms. They are 'externalities', whose costs are borne by society as a whole, or by future generations, and not by the farmer. But many will eventually erode the natural resources on which our food system depends. The production of greenhouse gases does not immediately hurt farmers but it is a significant cause of the global warming that will threaten farming in later decades. The run-off of nitrates and pesticides can reduce water quality for downstream farmers and destroy fisheries that are an important source of protein. The loss of biodiversity shrinks the genetic pool that scientists need to breed pest-resistant crops. As a result, agriculture risks undermining its own ecological foundations.

Because of the environmental damage it inflicts, there is a legitimate question about the sustainability of modern agriculture. Even if the 'peak theorists' are wrong, and there is enough oil, gas, phosphate and water to last until 2050, business as usual is probably not the answer. We need to find food systems that damage the environment less while using non-renewable resources more efficiently.

The good news is that alternatives exist. There are many examples of agricultural systems that produce fewer greenhouse gases, or even act as carbon sinks, that build soil fertility and that preserve watersheds. They also tend to consume less energy, minerals and water as inputs, which will address the issue of resource scarcity as well. At the same time, they produce large amounts of food at an affordable price and deliver good profits to the farmer. To use an ugly phrase, they are 'win-win-win'. These systems do not require new technology or major scientific breakthroughs. As the final chapter of this book will explore, they are being successfully implemented all around the world right now, albeit often on a small scale. The challenge will be to scale them up.

Fungible demand

So far, we have only looked at the supply side of the food equation. But what about demand? How much food will be needed to satisfy the world in 2050? Is there anything we can do to ease the strain?

There is no doubt that the growing demand for food represents a considerable challenge. The latest UN projections show that the human population is expected to reach 9.3 billion by 2050. Under a more extreme scenario, if birth rates do not fall as predicted, the population could even peak at 10.6 billion. Equally, research by the consulting firm McKinsey & Company shows that the size of the global middle class is likely to grow by 3 billion people between now and 2030. These newly wealthy consumers will want richer diets, in particular more meat and dairy products, which will have a multiplier effect on demand for grains. Meat consumption in Asia is still only 30 kilos per person, compared to 80 kilos in developed countries, so there could be a long way to go. In addition, bioenergy producers will continue to draw crops away from food markets.

It is generally assumed that increased demand will have to be directly matched by extra supply. As a result, the FAO estimates that the total supply of food will need to increase by 70 per cent between now and 2050. In other words, an additional billion tonnes of cereals and another 200 million tonnes of meat will need to be produced every year. In developing countries, it is assumed that food production will need to double.

These sound like big numbers, the sort that will place an enormous strain on agricultural systems. It is one of the major props in the Malthusian argument. However, it is important to place this extra demand in context. Demand for food is expected to grow at a slower rate than in the 1960s and 1970s, as the rate of population growth is slowing. When we remember that global food production tripled between 1950 and 2000 an increase of 70 per cent in forty years does not sound impossible. Moreover, at a biophysical and nutritional level, it is a mistake to regard this extra demand as something fixed, an absolute that the food system must deliver at all costs. This is because there are two big levers that could be pulled to change the demand side of the equation. Both would increase the *efficiency* of food use.

The first is reducing food waste. It is estimated that 30 per cent of all the food grown worldwide is lost or wasted before it reaches the consumer. In poor countries, most of the waste occurs during post-harvest storage, or as food is handled by traders, processors and retailers. Vegetables rot in sweltering, open markets; rickety grain stores are infiltrated by rodents. In contrast, most of the waste in rich countries occurs at the point of the consumer, or in shops or restaurants. Because food has become so cheap, it is not valued. Much ends up in the rubbish bin. Every single day in Britain, people throw away 4.4 million uneaten apples, 5.1 million potatoes and 1.6 million bananas.

There are simple ways in which this shocking amount of waste could be reduced. In developing countries, investment is needed in storage and transportation infrastructure, everything from metal grain silos to refrigerated trucks. In high-income countries, education campaigns and a shift away from 'best before' dates to more sophisticated food management tools have been shown to change consumer behaviour. There are great opportunities to reduce waste within fisheries by minimising the discard of non-target species ('by-catch') and limiting spoilage along the value chain. It should also be possible to recycle food waste back to farming and aquaculture, in the form of feed for animals and fish, or fertiliser for fields, thus helping to 'close the loop' on nutrient cycles.

Halving the amount of food waste is a perfectly achievable target. It would not only reduce the pressure on food supplies but would also save money. In this regard, it can be compared to the role of energy efficiency in energy policy – throwing away less food is the equivalent of putting insulation in your attic.

The second major lever that could be pulled to moderate demand involves changing the way we use crops. About one-third of the world's cereal production is used to feed animals. This is an inefficient way to produce food, as it takes many tonnes of grain to grow one tonne of meat. In many cases, it is also an unhealthy choice, contributing to rampant obesity in many industrialised countries, an epidemic that is estimated to cost $78 billion per year in the USA alone. Assuming that current trends continue, almost 1.5 billion tonnes of cereals will be used annually for animal feed by 2050. If, instead, these cereals were consumed directly by humans it would be enough to satisfy the calorie needs of 3.5 billion people. People would not have to give up meat and dairy entirely, but they would have to limit their consumption to animals that were raised on pasture or on recycled food wastes. Add to this the one-fifth of grains that are now used in the production of biofuels and there is an even larger potential reserve of food that could be diverted towards human consumption.

We grow enough food *today* to feed 9.3 billion people. It is just that a lot is wasted and a lot more is diverted towards animal feed and biofuels. This is why it is so shocking that 870 million people still go hungry. There has always been plenty of food to go around, but there are hundreds of millions of poor people who lack the purchasing power to lay a claim to it. Our pattern of food use is a function of political choices and economic disparities. Therefore, the ability to change is within human hands. We could pull the levers to moderate demand, thereby taking the pressure off supplies and allowing a fairer distribution of resources. This is yet another reason why, at a purely biophysical level, we should be able to feed a much larger population in 2050.

The Malthusian doomsday scenario does not stand up to scrutiny. All the science indicates that we have not reached the biophysical carrying capacity of the earth, so long as we use resources wisely. This is why practically every research organisation that has examined this question – from the FAO, to IIASA, to the Office of the Chief Scientist of the UK government, to university departments all over the world – has concluded that it will be possible to feed the world's population in 2050. The more alarming prophesies tend to come from environmentalists or single issue advocates who cherry-pick bits of research that fit their preconceptions and fail to consider competing evidence. In many cases, tendentious statistics are repeated so many times that they gain the appearance of truth, whereas a little digging reveals that they are based on shaky foundations. The more extreme the warning, the more likely it is to be picked up by the mainstream media looking for a good story. Sometimes the alarmists perform a service, by drawing attention to the unsustainability of aspects of modern farming. There is no doubt that our food systems need to change. However, by exaggerating the threats, the 'doomsters' can also polarise the debate and provide an excuse for supporters of the status quo to ignore their arguments altogether.

Nonetheless, just because we can feed 9 billion people in 2050 does not mean that we will. The global food system is failing to nourish 7 billion right now. In this chapter, we have focused on the biophysical potential of the planet for food production, setting to one side economic disparities and political boundaries. But this is, of course, a fantasy. Whether people eat or not has always depended on how food is distributed and whether it is affordable. Biophysical potential is a necessary but not sufficient condition. In the next few chapters we will look at how food will be priced and how it will be distributed across different regions. It is time to return to the real world.

THE REAL PRICE OF FOOD OVER THE LAST HUNDRED YEARS
(ADJUSTED FOR INFLATION)
Grilli-Yang Agricultural Food Commodity Real Price Index 1900–2010

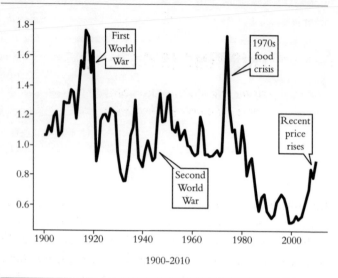

1900–2010

Source: IMF

5

THIS TIME IS DIFFERENT

*Is this the end of cheap food? Structural shifts,
price volatility and the 'new normal'*

If neo-Malthusians are guilty of exaggerating the risk of civilisational collapse, others seem intent to downplay the significance of the recent food crisis. A number of agricultural economists characterised it as a temporary blip and predicted that food prices would soon resume their long-term decline. This view was especially prevalent among those writing at the end of 2008 and during 2009, when the financial crisis caused a retreat in all commodity prices. For example, when the United Nations' FAO and the OECD issued their annual *Agricultural Outlook* for 2009 to 2018, they forecast that prices over the next decade would be only slightly higher than the historical average.

They could draw on history to support this view. It is often said that the recent volatility in food markets is unprecedented. But this is only because people have short memories. There were three periods of rapidly rising prices during the last century. The first was during the First World War. Thirty years later, prices rose strongly when many parts of the world were still recovering from the devastation of a second war. The third occasion was during the 1970s, when there was a combination of rising demand, extreme weather events, high oil prices and trade disruptions that bears an uncanny resemblance to the current era. World food prices more than doubled between 1971 and 1974 and kept rising until 1980. However, on each occasion price rises were followed by steep falls. For more than 100 years, the trend of world food prices, once adjusted for inflation, has been downwards.

This led to a theory that agricultural markets follow a cyclical pattern of boom and bust. 'World food crises are relatively rare events, occurring roughly three times a century,' according to Professor Peter Timmer, who has studied food markets for more than forty years at Harvard, Stanford, Cornell and the University of California. 'But they also tend to be regular events; every three decades or so, suggesting there is an underlying cyclical cause.' The theory is that a period of low prices deters investment in agriculture. This causes production to stall and inventories to run down. Eventually, there are shortages and food prices rise. This, in itself, is a cure, as the increased profitability of farming draws investment back in and stimulates new technologies. Eventually farmers cannot resist over-producing, which leads to a price collapse and the resumption of the slide towards ever cheaper food. According to this theory, the current rise in food prices is just the latest turn of the cycle.

'This time is different' has been described as the four most dangerous words in finance. It is right to be sceptical when someone starts talking about new paradigms. You should usually check your wallet. Nonetheless, sometimes there *are* discontinuities, diversions from the mean. An equally important phrase in investment is 'past performance is no guarantee of future results'. Could we be witnessing a structural change in the global food system, one that will make the high and volatile prices of the present the norm of the future?

The end of cheap food

Predicting the future price of anything is a risky business. When population pessimist Paul R. Ehrlich wagered a thousand dollars in 1980 that the prices of five commodities would rise over the coming decade, he famously lost. Yet, there are factors related to both the supply and demand of food that lead to the conclusion that the era of cheap food is probably over. Prices may not stay at record-breaking highs for ever but they are likely to reset to a level that is significantly higher than the average of the previous twenty years.

One reason is that, on the supply side, the cost of producing food is likely to go up. As we have seen, agricultural inputs such as fuel and fertiliser are not going to run out in the next fifty years, but they are almost certainly going to get more expensive. This is because their price is strongly influenced by the cost of crude oil and natural gas. Forecasting energy prices is an even more precarious pastime than predicting food prices, but there are few experts who believe that we will return to the cheap energy of the 1980s or 1990s. Because of demand from China, and the higher costs of extracting hydrocarbons from less accessible sources, crude oil at $100 a barrel increasingly looks like the 'new normal'. The latest prediction of the International Energy Agency is that prices will climb to $120 a barrel by 2035 (in today's dollars). If energy prices are high, the cost structure of agriculture will be elevated and this will eventually translate into higher food prices.

Another reason why the cost of food production is likely to stay high is that farmers will increasingly be forced to account for the negative environmental 'externalities' associated with agriculture. The 'true cost' of food, if these negative impacts are priced, often looks very different. For example, one study found that £100 of food from UK farms would really be 50 per cent more expensive if the environmental costs associated with greenhouse gas emissions, biodiversity loss, soil erosion and water pollution were included. The price of beef in Brazil would double because of the environmental costs associated with deforestation in the Amazon, much of which is carried out by ranchers. Farmed shrimp from Thailand should cost one-third more because aquaculture pollutes water and leads to the clearing of mangrove swamps that protect the coastline from storms.

Governments are slowly taking steps to force farmers to internalise some of these environmental costs. Taxes and regulations are being used to discourage harmful practices. Markets are being created to put a price on what was previously a free resource. No one is sure when a price will be put on carbon, but the policy signals point in this direction. The most immediate changes will probably occur in the management of water. In Australia and California, water trading schemes already require irrigators to pay a market price for each litre they use. In other dry regions, some form of water pricing or rationing will be needed to ensure more efficient use of this precious resource. Subsidies, for example the European Common Agricultural Policy, are also being reformed to encourage more sustainable practices. These are only baby steps, but their effect will be to raise costs for environmentally destructive farming systems and to encourage a shift to more sustainable practices. Eventually, the price of food will more closely reflect the true economic, social and environmental costs of production.

Higher operating costs due to expensive energy and tighter environmental policies will apply to agriculture everywhere. On top of this, there may be extra costs in those regions that will need to play a bigger role in the global food system in the future. In the last chapter, we saw that it should be possible for the supply of food to meet growing demand at a global level. But increased production in the established food bowls of

North America, Western Europe and Asia will not be enough. South America and Africa will need to step up their agricultural output as well.

Achieving productivity increases in these parts of the world will require considerable investment. Bringing new land into cultivation is an expensive, back-breaking task. Scrub needs to be cleared, soils prepared, drainage or irrigation put in place. New roads, railways, ports and entire settlements are often required. Moreover, achieving high yields in these areas can take more effort than in the traditional breadbaskets of the northern hemisphere. IIASA's research shows that South American and African farmland usually suffers from one or more biophysical constraints. The most common is a lack of soil nutrients, although other problems include erratic rainfall, poor soil structure and the presence of salts and other toxic compounds. Costly interventions may be needed to overcome these constraints.

The simple fact is that most of the world's best and accessible land is already being used. Most expansion will take place on more marginal or remote land. Farmers will only take on the hard work of ramping up production in these places if food prices are high enough to deliver an attractive return.

This dynamic can be seen in the story of the most active agricultural frontier in the world – the Cerrado of Brazil. The 'miracle of the Cerrado' illustrates the potential that exists to increase food yields in areas once thought barren. But, in economic terms, the picture is more complex. Cerrado farmland is not very fertile. As well as requiring industrial amounts of lime to reduce acidity, the fields need a constant application of fertilisers. This is high-cost agriculture. In 2008 when soybean prices hovered around $450 per tonne, farmers in the Cerrado state of Mato Grosso were spending almost a quarter of this on fertilisers – seven times more than soybean farmers in Iowa.

They spent the same amount to transport the soybeans to port, as their farms are 2,000 kilometres from the main port at Paranaguá, and the only way to get there is by truck. All in all, local farmers actually *lost* money on their soybean crop in 2008, even though global prices were sky high. In these marginal and remote areas, high food prices will be necessary to make agriculture profitable. Otherwise, farmers will not bother.

Higher input prices, the internalisation of environmental costs associated with farming, and the need to rely on more marginal land, will all act to increase the costs of food production in coming decades, with an inevitable impact on food prices. This is the supply-side argument. Just as important, there are demand-side factors that will pull prices up. The slow, steady rise in demand from a growing global population and a swelling middle class has already been noted – many other countries will be following China along the meat-eating, food-importing path. But there is one other factor whose effects we are beginning to feel: the growing importance of the bio-based economy.

We have already explored how biofuel demand played a role in driving up prices in recent years. The government mandates and subsidies that stimulated this demand are mostly still in place. Moreover, so long as oil is at $100 per barrel, biofuels take on an economic logic of their own, even without subsidies, as they can be cheaper than conventional fossil fuels. Most forecasts assume that biofuels will represent one-tenth of global transport fuels by 2030, perhaps even one-fifth by 2050. As a result, the FAO expects that 12 per cent of the world's grain, 16 per cent of vegetable oil and one-third of all sugar will be used to make biofuels in just ten years' time.

What effect will this have on prices? Biofuels demand will lead to a general rise in crop prices, as more buyers compete for supply: one study estimates that it will cause agricultural prices to rise by between 10 and 20 per cent above current levels. But biofuels demand will also stop prices from falling too low. This is because whenever the price of a feedstock (such as maize or sugar) falls below the break-even point that makes it competitive with crude oil, biofuel processors will step into the market, hoover up supply, and use it to produce fuel, thus driving prices back up. This will tend to establish a minimum price for these crops (which will, of course, shift up and down as the oil price changes). It will completely transform the dynamics of food markets, putting a floor under food prices. Instead of the boom and bust cycles of the last hundred years, we are likely to see the booms without the busts.

The relationship between food and energy prices can already be seen in some commodity markets. For sugar, it has been established for many years. Because of the highly developed local biofuel sector, Brazilian sugar mills switch between refining sugar for human consumption and distilling ethanol for cars depending on which is more profitable. Sugar prices in Brazil track crude oil prices on a weekly and even daily basis. This, in turn, drives world sugar prices, as Brazil is the biggest exporter.

The same type of relationship now links maize and oil prices. According to Soren Schroder, chief executive of the North America unit of the grain trader Bunge, whenever crude oil is at $100 a barrel, US maize will be priced at a minimum of $5.00 or $5.50 per bushel. This is because of the relative calorific values of the two commodities and the cost of converting each to vehicle fuel. 'The two are forever linked,' he says. 'Even if you didn't have mandates, there's an economic value of corn that is tied to the price of gasoline.'

Concerns about the increasingly intimate links between food and energy prices, and the effect they have on the poor, have propelled a search for 'second generation' biofuels. Rather than relying on foods such as maize, sugar or vegetable oil, these emerging technologies can make use of a wide range of non-food biomass: for example, wood, grasses, agricultural wastes or algae. Breaking down the lignin, hemicellulose and cellulose in this indigestible material often requires the use of complex enzymes and heat treatment processes. This is more expensive, and these technologies are not commercially viable yet. However, it is hoped that they will eventually supplant first generation biofuels. Visionaries speak of 'bio-refineries' that can convert large volumes of biomass into fuel, biogas, chemicals, pharmaceuticals and industrial materials – just like petrochemical refineries today. It is hoped that this will have less impact on food prices because the feedstocks can be grown on 'non-food' land.

Switching to second generation bioenergy certainly makes a lot of sense, on both environmental and food security grounds. However, the development of this technology has been slower than expected, so it is likely that food crops will provide the feedstocks for most biofuels for at least the next twenty years. Moreover, even second generation bioenergy will not be entirely disconnected from food markets. It is hoped that these feedstocks can be grown on marginal land, but experience shows that poor land equals low yields, so there will be pressure to use fertile land that is already cultivated. Farmers will tend to switch between food and fuel crops depending on the prices on offer. In other cases, bioenergy crops will occupy grazing lands, with implications for meat production. In addition, to achieve the best yields, these plants will require water and some means of restoring soil fertility and guarding against pests. Thus, indirectly, second generation biofuels will still compete with agriculture for land, water, fertilisers and other inputs, which will tend to preserve the link between food production and energy demand.

In many ways, the emergence of bioenergy is a return to old ways. For thousands of years, humans lived in a bio-based economy and drew on the land for many non-food uses. We harnessed draught animals for power, burned wood for heating, wove cotton or wool into textiles, and used timber or straw as building materials. In 1920, for example, it is estimated that more than one-quarter of all the arable land in the USA was used to grow feed for horses. The advent of fossil fuels changed everything. It reduced competition for land, as fuelwood was replaced by coal and oil, timber by steel, and cotton by synthetic fibres derived from petroleum. The most immediate dividend was the freeing up of the land that had supported all those horses; it could now be used to produce crops or livestock for human consumption (which is a major reason, often unrecognised, for the rapid increase in food production in the twentieth century). Now, this hydrocarbon era may be drawing to a close. Higher fossil fuel prices, combined with the need to limit carbon emissions, mean that societies will once again turn to biological resources. Rather than mining the fossilised energy stored underground, we will increasingly harvest current solar energy in the form of green-growing, carbon-neutral plants.

The impact of higher crop prices, caused by biofuels and other factors, will be concentrated on livestock producers who depend on grains and oilseeds. The multiplier effect of this production model has already been noted: it takes many kilos of feed to produce one kilo of chicken, pork or beef. Animal feed is typically the biggest cost for these operations, which at the best of times exist on thin profit margins. When the prices of grain and oilseeds soar, profits disappear. For example, one economist at Purdue University calculates that the American pork industry will suffer annual losses of $4 billion because of higher feed costs associated with the country's 2012 drought. The grain-fed animal production model, which emerged at a time when the world was overwhelmed by cheap grains and soybeans, does not look so clever now. These producers are caught between commodity prices they do not set (the price of meat) and input prices they cannot control (the price of maize or soybean). As a result, they are cutting back, which means meat prices are set to rise.

For all these supply and demand reasons, there are good grounds to believe that food prices will be a lot higher in the next twenty years than the last two decades, starting with crops but with an indirect effect on meat. One way to understand this is to think of a shift in the terms of trade between agriculture and the rest of the economy. During the twentieth century, technical progress and cheap energy led to massive productivity gains in farming and a boost in food production, especially in industrialised countries. The price of food fell relative to manufactured goods and services. Now, energy is no longer cheap, there are more demands for biological resources, and productivity gains in farming have slowed. The price of food (and land) is rising relative to, say, a computer or legal services. Of course, it is possible that some new technical breakthrough will open the path for another agricultural revolution. But none of the technologies currently being developed, including genetic modification, offer such transformational possibilities, so at the moment this is an unknown. There are also possible risks to food production – in terms of diseases and climate change – that could weigh in the other direction.

Interestingly, over the past three years a new consensus has emerged. Almost every public or private organisation to study the topic has concluded that we are witnessing a structural rise in food prices: they include, among others, the International Monetary Fund, IIASA, the International Food Policy Research Institute, Oxfam, Deutsche Bank and Goldman Sachs. The UK government's study on the future of food and farming agreed that 'the trend over the last century of low or falling food prices is likely to be at an end'. Even the experts at the FAO and OECD have changed their tune. Their latest *Agricultural Outlook 2011–2020* was released under the headline 'Higher agricultural commodities prices here to stay'.

A rollercoaster ride

When forecasting food prices, organisations like the FAO use complex computer models to estimate future supply and demand. These models assume gradual trends over time. What they are not good at is capturing the effect of shocks, volatility or non-linear changes. In the world of computer models, food prices rise or fall by a few per cent each year; they never double in six months. However, as recent events have shown, these sorts of whipsaw movements – in particular sudden price spikes – are a feature of real markets and can be hugely damaging. Unfortunately, price spikes are unlikely to disappear. Indeed, they may become more frequent.

Why? The first thing to note is that commodity markets, even in the best of times, are inherently more volatile than other markets. Not only that, but price fluctuations are asymmetric: price increases tend to be more sudden than price falls. The reason is the role played by stocks. The main agricultural products – wheat, rice, maize, soybeans – are storable commodities. When prices fall, traders build up their stocks, adding to demand and causing prices to stabilise. In theory, this process of stock building can go on indefinitely – there is no upper limit to how big stocks can get. However, when prices rise, traders sell stored commodities into the market and allow inventories to fall. Eventually, if this process continues, there comes a point when there are no more stocks left. Prices then have to increase enough to ration demand, that is, to make people buy less. This can lead to dramatic price spikes because it takes a lot to force consumers to change their eating habits – economists speak of the low 'elasticity' of food demand. If supplies are really tight, a 'rational panic' can drive prices to feverish levels, as everyone scrambles to secure supplies before they run out. The commodity rollercoaster often defies the laws of gravity, hurtling up the inclines and descending at a more leisurely pace.

The changing nature of food demand may accentuate this market behaviour. Demand becomes more inelastic as people get richer. If food prices rise, poor people who spend most of their income on food are forced to switch to cheaper staples or, in the worst case, to eat less. Richer people, for whom food accounts for a small share of monthly expenditure, often decide to pay more, rather than consume less. As more people in the world reach the income levels of the affluent middle classes, the inelasticity of food demand will become more pronounced. In a world where 2 billion are wealthy and 5 billion are poor, a relatively small increase in food prices can force the 5 billion to adjust their consumption, which may be enough to bring supply and demand back into equilibrium. (The rich, of course, probably will not change their behaviour at all.) But if there are 5 billion wealthy people and only 2 billion poor, and there is a supply shortfall, prices will have to increase much more to force enough people to eat differently. (The poor, of course, will suffer terribly in the process.) More extreme price spikes on global food markets may, therefore, be a perverse consequence of a reduction in global poverty.

The deepening linkages between food markets and energy markets also create the potential for new shocks, on both the supply and demand side. Sudden increases in oil and gas prices will affect the price of agricultural inputs such as fuel and fertiliser and, therefore, the cost of producing food. If oil prices jump, the break-even point for the conversion of crops into biofuels will change, causing more of these crops to be diverted from food markets and driving their prices higher. An oil crisis, sparked by conflict in the Middle East for instance, is likely to become a food crisis too.

Increasing climate volatility due to global warming will probably have the biggest effect on the stability of food supplies in future decades. Lately, scientists have started to fill a gap in our knowledge by attempting to model the impact of droughts and floods, rather than just gradual changes in average temperatures or precipitation. The results are frightening. Research by the Institute of Development Studies showed that extreme weather events – in regions such as the USA, South America, South Asia or Africa – could cause prices to rise as much in a single year as in two decades of steady increases. In another study, the International Food Policy Research Institute (IFPRI) looked at the implications of a drought in India between 2030 and 2035. They found that it would place a huge strain on global markets, drive up the price of rice, wheat and maize, and cause an extra 1 million children around the world to become malnourished.

The impact of climate volatility may be magnified by the changing nature of trade in food. Thirty years ago, two-thirds of all grain exports came from the traditional breadbaskets of North America and Western Europe. These regions have unusually stable climates. Crop production usually fluctu-ates only slightly from year to year. This was why the 2012 drought in the USA was so noteworthy – you have to go back almost twenty-five years to find a comparable shortfall in the American harvest. Now, because of the diversion of crops to biofuels and the growth in international demand, North America and Western Europe account for little more than 45 per cent of traded grains. Their share is set to decline further. Instead, the world has come to rely more and more on new sources of supply.

One of the most important is the Black Sea region, which comprises Ukraine, parts of Russia and northwest Kazakhstan. As we have seen, by 2009 these countries had emerged as major suppliers to world grain markets but a heatwave the following year decimated the harvest and led to a cessation of all exports. The point is that there is nothing new about this. At various times over the past 150 years, a run of bumper crops has put Russia in the position of becoming a major exporter. But the country has just as regularly suffered spectacular crop failures. This happened in 1890–91, in 1920–21 and again in the late 1920s and 1930s (although political events played a role too). In 1946 drought and famine caused 2 million deaths. Poor harvests between 1972 and 1975 forced the Soviet Union to buy heavily from abroad, helping to drive up prices. At the time of writing, Russia and Ukraine were in drought again and the harvest was down by one-third. The climate in this part of the world is simply more variable than in North America or Western Europe. Cereal yields tend to fluctuate greatly from year to year. Increased dependence on exports from this region is likely to lead to more turbulence in global markets.

Commodity markets, by their nature, are more volatile than other markets. But in the coming decades, reliance on new breadbaskets, climate change, the linkages between food and energy markets and the effect of the expanding global middle class will all tend to increase this volatility. Food will not only be more expensive than before: violent price spikes may become a more frequent occurrence. Hang on for a wilder ride.

How can the world best deal with volatility in food markets? The obvious answer is trade. Trade can allow food to move from regions with agricultural surpluses to those with deficits. A crop failure in one place can be offset by abundance elsewhere. As IFPRI notes, 'international trade flows provide a balancing mechanism for world agricultural markets'. Trade may also be an antidote to higher food prices, as it helps ensure that food is produced in countries with the lowest costs of production. Most agricultural economists call for the removal of trade barriers and the freeing up of global food markets, so that supply and demand can find their equilibrium in the most efficient way, just like in the economic models.

The problem is that when food prices doubled and supplies ran short during the recent food crisis, the world lurched in the opposite direction. When free markets should have had their finest hour, they almost seized up. Governments intervened more than ever before to protect domestic interests. Financial speculators swamped commodity markets, distorting price formation. Countries and businesses tried to bypass the market altogether by grabbing farmland and establishing captive supply chains. These developments will be the subject of the next four chapters. They are new and unexpected phenomena, born out of the transition from an era of low and falling food prices to one of high and volatile prices. But they may well be a sign of things to come.

COUNTRIES IMPOSING FOOD EXPORT BANS OR RESTRICTIONS,
2008 – 2010

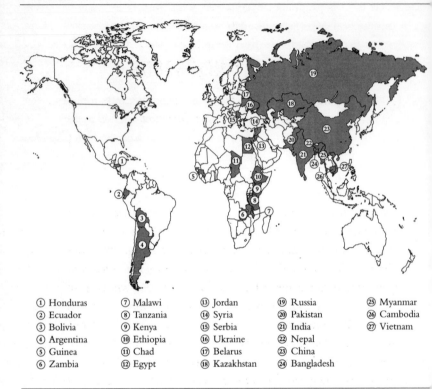

① Honduras   ⑦ Malawi   ⑬ Jordan   ⑲ Russia   ㉕ Myanmar
② Ecuador   ⑧ Tanzania ⑭ Syria   ⑳ Pakistan   ㉖ Cambodia
③ Bolivia   ⑨ Kenya   ⑮ Serbia   ㉑ India   ㉗ Vietnam
④ Argentina ⑩ Ethiopia ⑯ Ukraine   ㉒ Nepal
⑤ Guinea   ⑪ Chad   ⑰ Belarus   ㉓ China
⑥ Zambia   ⑫ Egypt   ⑱ Kazakhstan ㉔ Bangladesh

Source: R. Sharma, 'Food export restrictions', FAO Commodity and Trade Policy Research Working Paper No.32, 201

6

STARVE THY NEIGHBOUR

*Export bans, panic purchases and why countries
are stuck in a Prisoner's Dilemma*

Imagine that you and an accomplice have been arrested for
robbing a bank. You are being held in separate cells and have no
way of communicating with each other. A police officer strides
through the door and makes you an offer. 'If you confess and
your accomplice denies taking part in the crime, I will drop all
charges against you and use your evidence to make sure that
he spends the maximum five years in jail. On the other hand,
if you stay silent but your partner confesses, you will do five
years while he goes free. If you both confess, you will both go
to jail for a reduced sentence of three years. However, if you
both deny the charges I will have to settle for token sentences
for firearms possession and both of you will be out of jail in a
year. Now, what do you want to do?'

This is the classic 'Prisoner's Dilemma', first developed in
the 1950s by the Rand Corporation as part of efforts to use
game theory to inform nuclear strategy. Since then, the puzzle
has been the subject of more than a thousand academic articles.
Psychologists, economists, lawyers and evolutionary biologists
have been absorbed by its logical paradoxes. The dilemma arises
because, so long as you are not sure what your accomplice will

do, you are better off confessing than remaining silent. If you confess, and he denies the charges, you go free – a big win. If you both confess you go to jail for three years. This is not a great outcome, but it is a lot better than the 'sucker's payoff' you would receive if you remained silent and he betrayed you. However, the outcome obtained when you both confess is worse than the outcome had you both remained silent. If you both trusted each other to present a united front against the forces of the law, you would be better off. But without this trust it is rational to 'rat' on the other guy first.

The Prisoner's Dilemma throws light on why individuals and society may end up not cooperating, even though it is in their best interests to do so. In the 1980s, it was used to explain why the USA and the EU competed with each other to subsidise food exports, even though this drove down prices on world markets and generated less revenue for both. Since 2007 countries have found themselves in a different sort of Prisoner's Dilemma, one shaped by food scarcity and rising prices. Food exporters have restricted the amount of food leaving their countries in an attempt to reduce domestic prices, while food importers have cut tariffs and panic purchased in order to build up their stocks. These measures have only intensified the crisis, straining world markets and driving prices even higher. Trapped in a Prisoner's Dilemma, countries have decided to pursue their own interests instead of cooperating in a way that would maximise global welfare.

Export bans and import surges
Nowhere was this more evident than in the rice markets of 2008. Rice is consumed by about half the people in the world, mostly in Asia, where nine-tenths of the crop is produced. In many Asian languages the words for 'food' and 'rice' are identical. Only about 7 per cent of harvested rice is traded

across borders, which makes the world rice market a very 'thin' market. Moreover, it is an asymmetric market, as, though rice is imported by many countries, just five nations – Thailand, Vietnam, the USA, India and Pakistan – typically account for 80 per cent of rice exports in any one year. Therefore, a variation in production in one or two countries can have a major impact on world rice prices.

Known as the 'diplomatic crop', rice has long been considered too important by governments to be left to the market. Governments, especially in Asia, purchase crops from local farmers, hold large reserves and attempt to control domestic prices. State agencies either directly import and export, or exercise a strict control over private traders through the use of licences, quotas, tariffs and taxes. You cannot pick up a newspaper and easily discover the price at which rice is trading in the world market; information is tightly held by market participants. The world rice market is a thin, murky and imperfect one that can be suddenly thrown into turmoil by a change in government policy or even the rumour of such a change.

One man who has devoted his life to understanding these complexities is Tom Slayton. Mild-mannered, with a drooping grey moustache, Slayton becomes animated when the subject turns to his favourite crop. He spent thirteen years working on rice policy with the US Department of Agriculture, first in Indonesia and then in Washington DC, before tiring of government bureaucracy and moving to the USA Rice Millers' Association. When it became clear that no one understood what was happening in the Asian markets, he decided to fill the gap by starting *Rice Trader*, a weekly publication that every trader relied on to find out what their competitors were doing.

After selling the business in 2006, Slayton worked as a consultant and occasionally appeared on business television whenever rice made the news. In a normal year, this was not often. But in the first half of 2008 a conflagration swept through the international rice market. The prices quoted in Thailand trebled in four months, there was real concern over whether enough rice would be available at any price, and the media was full of stories of the 'Asian rice crisis'. Few people were better placed to interpret these events than Tom Slayton. Over the following months he worked the phones with his old contacts and carried out a forensic analysis to discover the causes of the crisis. His conclusion? 'The fire was man-made.'

The crisis had its origins in India. The Indian government ment operates a Public Distribution System that offers food – mostly wheat and rice – to poor people at subsidised prices. In 2006 a drought led to a shortfall in the Indian wheat crop, causing wheat prices to rise. The government tried to fill the gap by buying more rice. At the same time, other countries switched from wheat to rice, which led to a greater foreign demand for Indian rice exports. The price of rice in India rose sharply during 2007. This was a pressing political issue, as state and national elections were looming and voters tend to punish their leaders for high food prices. In October 2007 the Indian government banned rice exports (excluding Basmati rice, a niche product); three weeks later it replaced this with a minimum export price set well above the prevailing world price; it then reimposed the outright ban in April 2008. As India had been the source for one-sixth of the world's rice exports in 2007, this left a large hole in the market.

Initially, the world's second largest rice exporter, Vietnam, rushed into the opening. As is befitting a technically Communist state, the Vietnamese rice industry is directed by the government ment. It sets export quotas and high minimum export prices to ensure adequate local stocks and diverts most trading activity to two state-owned enterprises (the 'Vinafoods'). The Vinafoods took advantage of the high world prices to seal a number of lucrative deals with other countries at the end of 2007. But they were too greedy. They promised to export more rice than Vietnamese farmers could easily supply. Local stocks dwindled and prices rose – during one weekend prices in Ho Chi Minh City doubled and markets were practically emptied of stocks. In the first half of 2008 the Vietnamese government reversed course by tightening export restrictions and only allowing a small number of export deals. This further stressed world markets.

As prices rose, a number of smaller rice exporters followed suit. Cambodia banned exports for two months; Brazil banned the sale of government stocks; Pakistan raised the minimum price that had to be paid before rice could leave the country; Egypt banned exports in January 2008 (and still had the ban in place in 2012). China, which normally shipped about 1 million tonnes of rice per year, did not officially ban exports, but it slowed the issuance of export permits and raised export taxes so that during the critical period of spring 2008 very little rice left the country.

None of these countries had a physical shortage of rice. Their goal was to limit the rise of domestic prices and the only way to do this, the only way to prevent rice flowing out to increasingly desperate world markets, was to restrict exports. The complete collapse of the rice trade was only prevented by the stance of Thailand, the world's largest exporter. It did not restrict exports and eventually cashed in on the high prices. However, the Thai government delayed releasing its own stocks, and some unfortunate public hints by ministers that they were considering export restrictions sent shudders through the market.

The export restrictions imposed by India, Vietnam and smaller producers explain the constraints in rice supply in the first half of 2008. The situation was made worse by panic buying among rice importers. With the media full of stories about a crisis, rice importers such as Malaysia, Nigeria, Oman and Iran tried to buy more than usual, dropping import tariffs to facilitate this process. Saudi Arabia went even further, introducing an import subsidy of almost $300 per tonne: in effect, the government paid importers to bring in rice in the hope that this would lower domestic prices. Rice was squirrelled away in warehouses all over the world, just in case. The panic was intensified because the previous decade of low and stable food prices – together with the advice given by the FAO, the World Bank and most Western economists – had prompted many countries to allow their reserves to run down. Soaring rice prices led to a self-fulfilling dynamic as countries rushed to increase their stocks before prices rose any further, thus creating a spike in demand at exactly the time when supplies were low.

One country more than any other sprayed petrol on the over-heating market – the Philippines. Although an early beneficiary of the Green Revolution, the country had lost its self-sufficiency and in a typical year was the world's largest rice importer. Rice supplies ran low in the early part of 2008 because of poor agriculture policies and mismanagement of stocks. From then on, the actions of the government helped to stoke a sense of panic. President Arroyo personally greeted vessels carrying rice as they sailed into Manila and launched a crusade against 'hoarders' and 'speculators', some of whom were arraigned in court in high profile trials. The media reported that the army was using armoured cars to deliver rice from warehouses to the poor in Manila. Government officials went on TV urging people to eat less rice, which only convinced people to go out and buy even more. The actions of millions of consumers caused a run on rice, emptying shops of most stocks.

In response, the National Food Authority went on an aggressive buying spree in global markets. It announced a target to import 2.2 million tonnes in one year (the most since 1998). Within the first four months of 2008 it imported more than the entire previous year. Moreover, it did so with little regard to price. It issued monthly 'mega' tenders with conditions that excluded most bidders apart from Vietnam's Vinafoods. Prices pole-vaulted with each tender, until on 17 April 2008 the National Food Authority agreed to pay $1,320 per tonne for Vietnamese rice, more than three times the price it had paid just four months earlier. The Indonesian government and the World Bank urged the Filipinos to scrap these tenders, as each time they set a new benchmark for the market, making rice more expensive for everyone else.

Panic and greed, fear and expectation were driving the world rice market in the middle of 2008, not the fundamentals. From his home on a quiet street lined with cherry blossoms in Arlington, Virginia, Tom Slayton helped to prick the bubble. One day he called up a frequent collaborator, Professor Peter Timmer. 'Peter, there's a million and a half tons of high-quality rice sitting in Japan,' he said. These stockpiles existed because, under the rules of the World Trade Organization, Japan was forced to import quantities of mostly US long-grain rice each year. It is a variety unpopular with Japanese consumers, so most of it ended up untouched in warehouses. It could not be re-exported without American permission. Slayton and Timmer lobbied for Japan to be allowed to release this rice to the world market. On 9 May they released a paper titled 'Unwanted Rice in Japan Can Solve the Rice Crisis – If Washington and Tokyo Act'. On 13 May 2008 the US government gave its approval to the proposal. Although little Japanese rice was ever re-exported, the announcement in itself helped to change market sentiment, especially as it was followed by news of a record world rice crop. By the end of 2008 rice prices had halved (although they still remain more than twice the historical average).

There are supply and demand reasons that explain why rice prices should have risen to an extent in the first half of

2008. But there is now a consensus that export restrictions and import surges were the prime causes of the excessive price spikes. A series of government decisions, although perhaps rational in their own terms, led to collective panic.

Rice was not the only food subject to this sort of government behaviour. The same pattern could be seen in the market for wheat, which is second only to rice as a food staple for the world. Wheat prices began to rise in 2006 because of drought in Australia, rising energy prices and the steady march of demand. In an effort to control domestic prices, five of the top ten wheat exporters imposed some sort of export restrictions during 2007 and 2008. Ukraine kicked things off after suffering a mild drought: between July 2007 and March 2008 the country exported virtually no wheat at all. Around the same time, India banned exports after the failure of its monsoon caused a sharp drop in its wheat harvest. Importers turned to Russia and Kazakhstan, which caused a run-down of their stocks, prompting both of these countries to impose export restraints in early 2008. In response to rising prices at home, Argentina increased its export tax on wheat and intermittently suspended new export deals. There was a contagion effect, as the actions of one country forced prices higher and pushed world demand on to a smaller number of exporters. The USA stepped into the gap and increased its exports to North Africa and the Middle East. Wheat is not used for American biofuels, so here was an occasion when the country *could* act as supplier of last resort. But this came at the expense of a rapid decrease in its stocks, which caused wheat prices to reach new highs in the spring of 2008.

The next crisis in wheat markets, two years later, can also be traced to government action. The heatwave that struck Russia in the summer of 2010 slashed the country's wheat crop by one-third and caused an immediate jump in domestic wheat prices. In order to protect consumers and local meat producers, the Russian government instituted a grain export ban in August that lasted for the next eleven months. The price of wheat on world markets shot up by 60 per cent. Inevitably, other countries followed suit. Ukraine, Argentina, Pakistan, Macedonia and Serbia all placed new controls on the export of wheat. India maintained the export ban that had been in place since 2007. Major importers such as Egypt, which usually bought half its wheat from Russia, scrambled to fill broken contracts. (Egypt could hardly complain as it maintained its own ban on rice exports throughout this period.)

The same dynamic played out in East Africa in 2011 when drought parched large areas of Kenya and threatened famine in Somalia. Ethiopia banned maize exports in March 2011 due to rising domestic prices. The Tanzanian government took similar action because higher prices in neighbouring countries were drawing stocks away. Even Malawi, which had briefly become a breadbasket for the region thanks to a large-scale subsidy programme, halted exports at the end of the year. The Secretariat of the East African Community pleaded with member states 'to remove barriers that hinder movement of food across the borders' and 'to cooperate with fellow member states to alleviate suffering in the region'. Widespread famine was only avoided in the Horn of Africa because of a massive humanitarian response by the international community.

Recent events demonstrate how ready food exporters are to slap on export taxes, export quotas or outright bans to protect domestic consumers, whenever prices rise too much. A survey by the FAO of 105 countries found that 33 imposed some sort of export restrictions during 2008 (with the highest proportion in Asia). Conversely, when markets are tight, food importers are prone to engage in panic purchasing and stock building because of fear that supplies will get scarcer. More subtly, countries with high import tariffs often reduce them at a time of high prices to encourage imports: when the European Union did this in 2008 it led to a huge surge in maize imports at exactly the time when global supplies were tight.

Economists describe these types of trade measures as 'pro-cyclical': they drive rising prices higher and falling prices lower. One study found that nationalistic policies were responsible for 45 per cent of the increase in rice prices in 2008, with the comparable estimate for wheat prices being 30 per cent. There were good reasons for food prices to move to a higher equilibrium, but the way countries manipulated trade helps to explain why prices overshot the way they did.

From the standpoint of individual governments, these actions can be perfectly rational. If only one country takes protectionist measures, there is a good chance it will be able to stabilise domestic food prices, while having only a limited impact on the rest of the world. On the other hand, if one country does not adjust its trade policies, while all others do, the free trader risks letting foreigners buy up its food reserves while domestic prices rage out of control. How can a government, especially in a developing country, justify this to its people? Trade policies are the only means available to developing countries to protect themselves from international price instability and the superior purchasing power of richer countries.

The problem is that if one country imposes an export ban, or starts panic buying, it is likely to set off a domino effect, with many other countries joining in. This can drive global prices even higher, which has a tendency to rebound on the country that took the original protectionist action. Food exporters find that they cannot insulate their domestic economy completely from world markets – commodities find a way across borders, for example through smuggling. Farmers lose out on the higher world prices (and may be unable to regain export markets when the restrictions are lifted). Food importers eventually deplete their stocks and may have to re-enter world markets when they are at feverish levels. And a terrible price is exacted on those countries that do not have the wealth or power to protect their citizens from the ravages of price spikes. People talk of 'beggar thy neighbour' trade policies. These are literally 'starve thy neighbour' policies.

Collectively, a competitive world of export bans and import surges is not in everyone's best interests. If countries refrained from such actions, food prices would never reach such dangerous highs in the first place. But this requires trust and cooperation, two other commodities in short supply. It is a classic Prisoner's Dilemma.

The failure of food governance

One way out of the Prisoner's Dilemma is to create rules and institutions that strengthen trust between participants or impose punishments should one betray the other. Take the example given at the start of this chapter. If the two prisoners shared a thieves' code of honour, or if there was a threat that a crime boss would exact a terrible revenge if either 'ratted' on the other, both prisoners might choose to remain silent when questioned, not least because they would be confident that the other would do the same. International trade rules and institutions are supposed to instil similar restraint. Instead of engaging in 'beggar thy neighbour' (or 'starve thy neighbour') competition, countries are supposed to cooperate with one another to achieve better collective outcomes – and be subject to sanctions should they choose to go it alone.

An open, rule-based food trade system has been the dream of mainstream economists for decades. These economists are as appalled by the export bans and taxes of recent years as they were by the European and American subsidies and tariffs of the 1980s and 1990s. According to standard economic models, restrictions on trade lessen efficiency and welfare. This is the official position of most intergovernmental agencies that focus on agriculture – the FAO, the World Bank, the International Fund for Agricultural Development, the International Food Policy Research Institute, the Organisation for Economic Co-operation and Development and the World Trade Organization. There is a touching faith in these institutions that politicians will eventually come to their senses, stop pursuing short-sighted trade policies and begin cooperating with one another to improve 'global food governance'.

The problem is that the history of the last hundred years points towards a different conclusion. Trade in food has never been free; governance of the global food system has been especially weak; and nations have pursued food policies according to their own interests, with little regard for the impact on other countries.

This was the reality encountered by Sir John Boyd Orr, the first Director-General of the UN Food and Agriculture Organization, when he attempted to introduce an ambitious scheme for organising the global food system after the Second World War. There never was a more propitious time. The Allied war effort had engendered a confidence in what could be achieved through state planning and cooperation, as well as great optimism for the new world order that would be created once the fighting stopped. At a UN Conference on Food and Agriculture convened by President Franklin D. Roosevelt at Hot Springs, Virginia, in 1943, the representatives declared their 'belief that the goal of freedom from want of food, suitable and adequate for the health and strength of all peoples can be achieved'. The FAO was established at a subsequent conference in Quebec in 1945.

A determined Scotsman, Boyd Orr had devoted his career to improving standards of nutrition among the poor. He had initially studied for a career in the church but then turned to science, qualifying as a doctor and establishing a world-class research institute in Aberdeen. His studies of the dietary deficiencies of schoolchildren in Scotland in the 1920s were instrumental in persuading the government to start a nationwide programme of free school milk – leading Winston Churchill to comment 'there is no finer investment than putting milk in babies'. Orr, whose only son was killed while serving in the Royal Air Force, believed that a just food system was the least the Allied nations owed to the millions who had given their lives in the Second World War. In his opinion, the world was at a crossroads, faced with the choice between 'cooperation for mutual benefit' or 'a drift back to nationalistic policies leading to economic conflict'.

In his first action as Director-General of the FAO, Boyd Orr put forward a proposal for a powerful World Food Board. The Board would stabilise commodity prices by holding buffer stocks, selling when prices were high and buying when prices were low. Stable prices would provide an incentive for farmers in developed countries to maximise production. At the same time, the Board would make cheap credit available to poor countries so they could improve their agricultural sectors. And, in the short term, the Board would relieve hunger around the world by handing out food aid or allowing poor countries to buy food on concessionary terms. This would be a global food system carefully managed in the interests of humanity. It has been described as 'one of the boldest and most imaginative plans for international action ever put forward'.

It was far too bold for the great powers. According to Boyd Orr, Britain opposed the scheme because it 'might have lost her advantage of cheap food imports'; the US 'thought that she could do better for herself as a world power through bilateral aid to other countries'; and the USSR was 'cynically suspicious'. The proposal was quietly sabotaged as it made its way through UN committees. Bitterly disappointed, Boyd Orr quit the FAO in 1948 and returned to Scotland. His idealism and tenacity were recognised a year later when he received the Nobel Peace Prize and a seat in the House of Lords, but this was scant consolation for the failure of what should have been the culmination of his life's work.

Over the next twenty years, various reincarnations of the Boyd Orr proposals were put forward by FAO staff and national governments. None was adopted. The food trade system continued to be fragmented, lightly governed and distorted by the surpluses and export subsidies of the USA and other developed regions.

There was a renewed effort to bring some order to the global food system in the early 1970s when surplus turned to scarcity and high food prices caused havoc. The showpiece event was the World Food Summit organised by the United Nations in November 1974. Held over twelve days in Rome, it was attended by delegates and observers from 131 countries, 26 UN bodies, 25 intergovernmental organisations, 161 non-governmental organisations and numerous liberation movements. *Time* magazine described it as 'the first concerted global effort in history to confront the problem of hunger'. The US Secretary of State, Henry Kissinger, gave a rousing keynote address, urging governments to 'accept the goal that within a decade no child will go to bed hungry'. However, the US Agriculture Secretary, Earl L. Butz, was less keen on radical reform and blocked proposals for a strong World Food Authority and an international system of grain reserves. Although a few tangible programmes did emerge, the diary of a senior FAO official who played a key role in the conference reveals many people's disillusionment with the outcome. Sartaj Aziz wrote that the event had brought out 'the selfish and sordid features of the world. Everyone was playing politics. The human or the moral angle was not important ... except in making speeches.'

The decline in food prices in the 1980s pushed the question of food governance off the political agenda. There was another World Food Summit in 1996, which pledged to halve the number of malnourished people by 2015 (another target that will probably be missed), but it attracted less attention than the 1974 jamboree. Instead, attention turned to trade. Under the 'Washington Consensus', the International Monetary Fund and World Bank pressed developing countries to open up to free trade. Agriculture had been kept out of the General Agreement on Tariffs and Trade (GATT), which governed international trade up until the 1990s. But it was brought into the Uruguay Round of negotiations that culminated in the establishment of the World Trade Organization in 1995. Under the subsequent Agreement on Agriculture many countries were obliged to decrease their import tariffs and to change the nature of their trade distortions – even as agricultural subsidies increased in rich countries. The playing field was still tilted in one direction.

Under the Doha Round of WTO negotiations, which began in 2001, the USA and other food exporters pressed for a more comprehensive deal on food trade. But there was strong opposition. On the streets, this was personified by South Korean farmer Lee Kyung Hae. He stabbed himself through the heart outside trade talks in Cancun while wearing a sign that read 'WTO Kills Farmers'. Inside the negotiating hall, India led the resistance of developing countries. The Doha process collapsed. Nicknamed the 'Zombie Round', it was revived on more than one occasion during the 2000s, but each time the creature had less flesh on the bone and staggered forward with less conviction.

This was the poisonous governance environment that existed when the 'World Food Crisis' attracted political attention in 2008. The response of the Director-General of the FAO, Jacques Diouf? Hold another conference. It was like the 1970s all over again. Heads of government from all 192 countries were invited to a World Food Summit in Rome in November 2009, which was preceded by separate events for representatives from NGOs and the private sector. On the eve of the summit, the FAO Director-General began a twenty-four-hour hunger strike in solidarity with the millions suffering from chronic malnutrition. Instead of Henry Kissinger, Pope Benedict XVI opened the summit, urging governments not to treat hunger in the poorest countries as 'a matter of resigned regret'.

These were fine words but the results were predictably disappointing. Less than one-third of the invited heads of state and government turned up. President Berlusconi was the only leader from the club of rich countries (the G8) to attend, but then he had little choice as he was the host. Rich countries watered down the draft declaration, removing a hunger reduction target and a commitment to boost agricultural aid. Many participants left after the first day, and media interest waned. An event held by Libyan leader Muammar Gaddafi – who recruited 200 Italian women through a hostess agency and tried to convert them to Islam – ended up grabbing most headlines. Little was achieved except for pious statements and the devouring of much fine Italian food by conference attendees. 'We had all told Diouf not to organise this summit,' an EU diplomat ruefully told Reuters.

The WTO system proved just as ineffectual when it came to controlling the 'starve thy neighbour' trade policies that were rampant during this period. The disciplines of the Agreement on Agriculture (such that existed) were designed for an era of agricultural surpluses and cheap food. Their objective was to limit the use of import tariffs and export subsidies. They had little to say about the sort of trade distortions – such as export bans and import subsidies – that emerged during a time of food scarcity and high prices. Indeed, WTO rules gave explicit authorisation to countries to impose export restrictions during times of crisis, so long as they notified their trading partners about what they were doing. Suggestions that the Doha Round could be used to introduce stronger rules on export bans bordered on the delusional, given the parlous health of the WTO negotiations.

Instead, all eyes turned to the new governance kid on the block – the G20. The G20 consists of twenty of the largest countries in economic size, with some adjustments to achieve representation across different continents. It gained prominence in 2008 when it was clear that the G8 would not be able to solve the global financial crisis on their own (largely because they had caused it). In a world of shifting economic power, it was essential to include large developing countries such as China, India and Brazil. When President Sarkozy of France chaired the G20 Summit in 2011, he made the food crisis one of his priorities. A number of radical proposals were floated but after the usual process of dilution the only schemes to emerge were measures to improve information gathering and an agreement that food supplies for humanitarian purposes would be protected from export bans. The USA and EU pressed for countries to sign up to a code of conduct that would restrict the use of nationalistic trade policies, but developing countries such as India and China were opposed. Yet again, advocates of better food governance were disappointed.

The failure to agree rules that would free countries from the Prisoner's Dilemma is hardly surprising. The world is suffering from a broader 'global governance deficit' – as can be seen in stalled talks on climate change and many other international issues. Moreover, the outcome of the G20 talks is entirely consistent with seventy years of failed attempts to introduce any rational or just organisation of the world's food systems – what one commentator has called 'the graveyard of aspirations'. There is a general disillusionment among experts who have devoted

careers to this thankless task. 'Yes, we have a World Trade Organization. Yes, we talk a lot about globalisation and international trade
liberalisation,' the former head of IFPRI Per Pinstrup-Andersen
said in a candid speech on 21 November 2011. 'But when push
comes to shove each government looks after its own.'

Food politics as Realpolitik

The obvious paucity of global food governance, despite all the
rhetoric since 2008, has made countries even more determined
to go their own way. There has been a further shift away from
free trade and towards a more managed system – with governments poised to intervene at any hint of crisis.

Among food importers, there is renewed emphasis on
'self-sufficiency'. The Philippines government has announced
massive spending to achieve the goal of rice self-sufficiency.
China has raised import tariffs and farm subsidies with the
result that its domestic food prices are even more isolated
from world prices. The value of agricultural subsidies in
China increased six-fold between 2008 and 2010, reaching
$147 billion. This is more than any other country in the world
– subsidies in the European Union and the USA for the same
year amounted to $100 billion and $25 billion respectively.
The fast-growing middle income countries of the world are
matching, or surpassing, the rich countries in their willingness
to subsidise agriculture and distort trade.

Populous, middle income countries are also building up
their food reserves to unprecedented levels, so that they have
more protection in case another food crisis erupts. In India,
even though harvests have been quite good in recent years,
little grain reached world markets as the government snapped
up surpluses for its stocks. Vast piles of wheat and rice, covered
in tattered tarpaulins, are a common sight along the highways
of the Punjab. Plenty rots each year.

China has also moved to hold back surpluses from export markets, and opportunistically purchased grain from abroad, propping up international prices. For example, after maize prices dipped in October 2011, the state-owned company that manages Chinese food reserves swooped to buy more than 2 million tonnes of maize and soybeans from the USA and Argentina. Just twenty years ago, most of the world's food stocks were held by the USA. Now they sit in China. It is estimated that the country holds three-quarters of the world's reserves of rice and maize, and half of all wheat stocks. No one knows exactly how big Chinese food reserves are because this information is guarded as a state secret.

Other countries are following a similar course. Saudi Arabia, Algeria and Indonesia all made unusually big purchases of wheat or rice in early 2011 to build up their stocks. South Korea, Egypt, Saudi Arabia, the United Arab Emirates, Nigeria and Angola all announced plans to build or increase strategic grain reserves. Gigantic new grain silos are rising on coastlines and river banks all over the world. These state-controlled larders are insurance against a recurrence of the world food crisis.

Should prices rise too high, a range of export controls remain within the armoury of food exporters. After the most recent drought cut harvests in the Black Sea region, Ukraine moved to ban wheat exports in November 2012. Russia did not formally ban exports but it has allowed domestic prices to rise, which has diverted grains to the local market. The amount of grain exported through the Black Sea slowed to a trickle by the end of 2012.

Some exporters, inspired by how oil producers united to create OPEC, are also toying with ways to ensure that prices never again fall too low. At the height of the rice crisis in 2008, the Thai government spooked markets by floating the idea that Thailand, Vietnam, Cambodia and Burma should come together to create a rice exporter cartel – an 'Organization of Rice Exporting Countries' or OREC. The goal would be to elevate the global price for rice, while reducing competition between exporters. The proposal was enthusiastically welcomed by Cambodia's prime minister, only to be dropped after an international outcry. For a number of years, Russian officials have talked openly about their desire to create a 'grain OPEC' alongside Ukraine and Kazakhstan. Because such a cartel would control one-quarter of the world's wheat exports, it might be in a position to influence global prices. The use of natural resources as a political weapon is a standard part of Kremlin foreign policy, as evidenced by manipulation of gas supplies to neighbouring countries. Grain exports fall naturally into this box of tricks.

In some ways, these initiatives take inspiration from long-standing efforts by developed countries to maximise the value of their food exports. Until a few years ago, farmers in Canada and Australia were compelled to market their wheat through state boards. The theory was that this would allow these countries to negotiate better export deals. In New Zealand, the majority of dairy farmers still sell their milk through Fonterra, a farmer-owned company that successfully extracts high prices from foreign buyers. The difference with the schemes floated by Cambodia and Russia is that the latter would bring together countries, not just individual farmers within a country.

In the end, few of these international price-fixing schemes are likely to get off the ground because of practical and political difficulties. Nonetheless, this sort of talk does not exactly instil confidence in the ability of markets to provide food security. One group to take notice is the Samsung Economic Research Institute, an arm of the giant Samsung conglomerate and one of the most prominent think tanks in South Korea. The mundane world of food is not a typical subject for its research, but in April 2011 it issued a sixteen-page report titled 'New Food

Strategies in the Age of Global Food Crises'. It started with a bald statement: 'the world's food supply is currently in transition from an era of persistent surpluses to one of chronic shortages and imbalances'. It warned that food producing countries could 'weaponize' food through export restrictions. As a result, the Institute recommended that South Korea – which imports three-quarters of its grain – should invest heavily in increasing domestic production and in securing supplies from abroad through channels that it could control. This report is the clearest articulation of the fear among food importing countries that markets can no longer be relied on. Interestingly, there is not a single reference to the WTO or other global governance mechanisms as a possible solution to increased resource competition. When faced with a Prisoner's Dilemma, the authors are in no doubt that South Korea should pursue its own interests, as they assume that other nations will do exactly the same.

The events of the last five years demonstrate the willingness of governments to intervene in food markets when national interests are at stake. *The Economist*, the *Wall Street Journal* and other bastions of neo-liberal economic thinking are aghast at the way governments are behaving. 'Access to resources is becoming fiercely contentious,' the *Wall Street Journal* intoned in July 2011. 'The world economies need clear rules to avoid undue competition that could spark new trade wars.' *The Economist* warned of an 'insidious' trend: 'a turn away from trade, markets and efficiency'. The assumption is that if only governments got out of the way, and let private markets take care of food, everything would work much better. But are private markets so efficient? Can we trust them to set the right prices? Or might financial speculators and commodity traders also be to blame for driving up food prices in recent years? Is someone making a killing out of food?

THE SPECTACULAR GROWTH OF COMMODITY SPECULATION
Futures & options contracts outstanding on commodity exchanges, millions of contracts

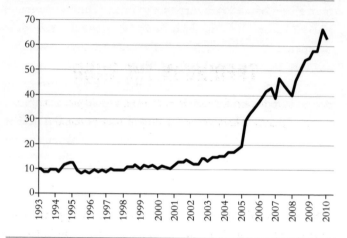

Source: Bank for International Settlements, Quarterly Review, March 2011

7

TRADING IN THE WIND

*Are financial speculators to blame for higher food
prices? Shadows and reality in futures markets*

The names of commodity speculators rarely appear in the
mainstream press. They are a secretive group, preferring to
operate in the shadows. But in the summer of 2010 British
newspapers were full of stories about how one trader, Anthony
Ward, had stealthily amassed a vast hoard of cocoa beans and
sent prices through the roof. Journalists gleefully nicknamed
him 'Chocfinger' after the villain in the James Bond film who
tries to manipulate the gold market by exploding a nuclear
bomb in the bullion depository at Fort Knox.

Ward has chocolate in his veins. Born into an English
upper-class military family, he attended Marlborough College,
one of England's elite private boarding schools. Soon after
leaving school he went to work as an apprentice at the
commodities firm E. F. Hutton. There, he began to trade cocoa.
Deals were brokered in the wood-panelled dining rooms of
London in between occasional trips to the cocoa-growing
districts of West Africa. Ward progressed rapidly, ending up
at Phibro, the commodities arm of Salomon Smith Barney,
where he rose to head cocoa and coffee trading. In 1998
he co-founded Armajaro, a trading house and hedge fund

that specialises in tropical commodities. Determined to get an edge, every year Ward would send staff to count cocoa pods on trees in Ivory Coast so that he could forecast the size of the crop. Now in his early fifties, Ward is widely regarded as the most influential player in the market: 'Anthony is the best cocoa trader,' according to a rival trader, 'most people do not have his appetite for risk.'

Drawing on all his years of experience, Ward launched an audacious bid to corner the cocoa market at the end of 2009. Convinced that prices would rise because of strong Asian demand and the ageing of African cocoa trees, he began buying up cocoa futures on the London commodities exchange, paying around £2,150 a tonne. To everyone's surprise, when the contract matured, he took physical delivery. This was a mountain of beans, the biggest delivery on the exchange in fourteen years. One imaginative journalist calculated that it was enough to make 5.3 billion chocolate bars. Ward's actions set the cocoa market boiling. The price surged to a thirty-three-year high of £2,732, making the Armajaro delivery worth £650 million.

Chocolate manufacturers cried foul. A group of mostly German companies wrote a letter to the London commodity exchange complaining that the market was being distorted by financial speculators and could no longer be used for its original purpose – helping genuine buyers and sellers to reduce risk. 'From the moment a market becomes purely a vehicle for speculation, it loses its usefulness,' they warned. Jürgen Steinemann, chief executive of the world's largest chocolate manufacturer, Zurich-based Barry Callebaut, declared that hedge funds were 'driving prices into unpredictability and creating volatility'.

The nexus where food meets finance has always been controversial. For millennia, societies have periodically rounded on 'food speculators'. In 386 BC, a group of Athenian grain merchants was tried for the capital crime of 'hoarding and collusion'. In the thirteenth century, St Thomas Aquinas condemned the 'buying of goods in the market with the intention to resell them at a higher price'. Three hundred years later, the first futures market for grain emerged in Amsterdam, but it was suppressed because of fear that manipulation of food prices would lead to social unrest. *Windhandel* – 'trading in the wind' – came to be the Dutch expression denouncing speculation.

The most important futures exchange today, the Chicago Board of Trade, was set up in 1848, but it has been the subject of repeated investigations by a suspicious Congress almost ever since. 'It is against the law to run a gambling house anywhere within the United States of America,' one Senator thundered in 1921, 'but today, under the cloak of business respectability, we are permitting the biggest gambling hell in the world to be operated on the Chicago Board of Trade.'

When food prices spiked in 2008, commodity markets were the focus of political attention once again. French President Nicolas Sarkozy used his leadership of the G20 process to launch a crusade against food speculators, accusing them of 'extortion and pillaging'. In certain sections of the media it became an accepted fact that speculators were to blame for the rise in food prices, profiting at the expense of the world's poor. Anthony Ward's forays in the cocoa market were presented as symptomatic of a wave of financial speculation sweeping across all food markets.

People who bet on food prices make an easy scapegoat. Yet, as we have seen, there were many reasons for food to become more expensive – constrained supply, rising demand, distortive trade policies. Perhaps commodity markets were setting prices correctly and efficiently, given these realities? Or have private markets become a source of volatility in themselves?

The financialisation of commodities

To answer these questions we have to first understand how commodity markets work. Even agricultural economists struggle with this, perhaps because traders are reluctant to reveal the inner workings of their business. The crucial point is that there are two quite distinct markets: a physical market in which commodities are actually delivered and exchanged; and a virtual market that deals in promises to buy or sell commodities at some point in the future. Both play a role in setting food prices.

The physical market for commodities – often called the 'cash' or 'spot' market – consists of thousands of individual deals struck by farmers, merchants, processors, importers and government agencies all over the world. A maize farmer in Iowa, after completing a harvest, goes to his local grain silo operator and agrees to sell his crop at a published rate. A Swiss chocolate manufacturer approaches a Ghanaian export company and negotiates a price to buy 50,000 tonnes of green cocoa beans. Indonesia's state food agency issues a tender for rice to be delivered to Jakarta in three months' time and then picks the best offer from competing grain traders. There can be thousands of different prices for the same commodity according to the time of year, differences in quality and quantity, and variations in transportation and storage costs. Prices will be very different, say, in rural Zambia compared to a shop in Zurich. Although regular surveys can reveal some of the prices agreed in local cash markets, there is never a single global spot price for wheat, rice, cocoa, beef or any other commodity.

Virtual markets based on promises first emerged in centres of physical trade such as Chicago, London or Amsterdam. Farmers and traders found that relying on spot transactions led to tremendous volatility: prices would plummet if all the farmers brought their goods to market after a harvest; conversely, prices would leap during times of scarcity. A farmer never knew what price he was going to receive for a crop before he reached town. 'Forward' contracts helped solve this problem. A farmer or trader could agree with a counterparty to sell a commodity at a fixed price at some point in the future, thus locking in the price. Forward contracts reduced the risk of dealing in food commodities over time.

The next evolution was to turn the forward contract into a standardised financial instrument that could be traded among third parties – a commodity 'future'. A futures contract is a promise to buy ('go long') or sell ('go short') a fixed quantity of a commodity at a certain price at some date in the future. The contract will specify the physical characteristics of the commodity and a delivery point, usually a major trading port. However, only a tiny proportion of these contracts are ever settled by delivery of physical goods. In most cases, they are settled for cash. (This is why Anthony Ward's action of holding a contract until expiry, and forcing counterparts to deliver physical cocoa beans, caused such a stir.) If the value of the futures contract has gone up since it was agreed – usually because spot prices have also gone up during that period – the seller has to pay the difference to the buyer. If prices have gone down, the buyer has to pay the seller. Rather than waiting until the delivery date, these payments are made continually throughout the life of the contract through a process called 'margin calls'. The last payment is made on the date of settlement and the contract then expires.

Futures contracts can either be agreed directly between two parties ('over the counter', which allows customised terms), or they can be traded on an exchange. The exchange brings many potential buyers and sellers together. It facilitates prices discovery, as the prices at which the contracts trade are published. Specialist clearing houses ensure that obligations are not reneged on.

A small number of exchanges around the world dominate the trade in futures, each specialising in different commodities. The Chicago Board of Trade is a centre for maize, soybeans and soft red winter wheat. The Kansas City Board of Trade is a specialised exchange for hard red winter wheat (the predominant local variety). NYSE LIFFE in London deals in tropical commodities such as cocoa, sugar and coffee, while its sister exchange in Paris focuses on milling wheat, malted barley and maize futures for European delivery. In China, futures markets for maize, wheat and sugar have more recently emerged in Dalian and Zhengzhou.

Futures markets and physical markets are, therefore, distinct. One deals in paper, the other in real goods. But the two are linked. The price on a futures market should reflect the price at which commodities are actually bought and sold, and vice versa, once the cost of storing and financing the commodity (the 'cost of carry') is taken into account. If this is not the case, there should be an opportunity to make a risk-free profit (known as arbitrage) by forcing the delivery of the physical goods. For example, if the price of a futures contract is too high relative to the spot price – that is, someone is willing to pay you a lot more in the future than the commodity is worth now – you could buy the physical commodity immediately, agree to sell the same amount via a futures contract, and wait until the expiry date; after paying the costs of storage, you would have made a guaranteed profit. Similarly, if a futures contract was undervalued, you could sell the commodity on the physical market immediately at a high price and buy it back at the lower price in a month or two via the futures market. The actions of arbitragers tend to restore the correct relationship between spot and futures prices. This is why both prices converge as a futures contract comes closer to maturity.

Futures markets are like the shadows in Plato's Cave. In Plato's parable, prisoners chained in a cave cannot see the real things passing in front of a fire behind them, only shadows projected on a wall in front of them. In the same way, futures contracts reflect the reality of what is happening in physical markets but they are not this reality. The great advantage is that they provide standardised prices that are clearly visible. This is why newspapers quote the prices of futures traded on public exchanges when they talk about changes in world food prices. When they say 'the price of maize has gone up 10 per cent' they mean that the price of the futures contract that is closest to maturity has changed by this amount. Because of the difficulty of tracking thousands of physical deals, the shadows are sometimes all that can be seen.

Futures markets attract two types of players. On the one hand, commercial actors who buy and sell physical commodities use futures to safeguard, or 'hedge', against price fluctuations. For example, if the owner of a grain silo in Kansas buys a wheat crop in August, and expects to sell it two months later, he can immediately sell a futures contract for October delivery to lock in his profit. If the cash price of wheat falls during this period, the value of his physical stock will decline but the value of his futures contract will rise. Conversely, if spot prices rise over the following two months, the value of his futures contract will fall but this will be offset by the increase in the worth of his physical stock. He neither has the excitement of price gains nor the terror of price falls. He can sleep more soundly at night.

On the other hand, there are various non-commercial actors who trade commodities futures solely to profit from changes in their price. These financial speculators are usually taking on risk, not hedging it. They are betting that commodities will get cheaper or more expensive and that the market has not yet recognised this. Or, they are taking advantage of risk-free arbitrage opportunities, such as the ones described above, if they are lucky enough to discover them. Their profits come at the expense of the other participants – this is a zero sum game. Yet, the others may not mind because the speculators play a vital role in the functioning of the market. They provide liquidity, stepping in to buy and sell futures when commercial actors may be unwilling. A healthy futures market requires the right balance between commercial and speculative players.

What worries many people is the way this balance has shifted. For decades, commodity futures were an esoteric corner of the financial landscape, dominated by tribes of men in coloured polyester jackets with their own language and rituals. The big banks and investment houses mostly left them alone. 'Until seven or eight years ago the industry was considered to be very conservative,' one Rabobank trader acknowledged. 'It was seen as boring.' This began to change after a wave of deregulation raised limits on the size of bets that an individual firm could lay. For example, position limits for maize futures were increased from 600 contracts per trader in the 1980s to 22,000 by 2005. One company could now amass a position on 2.78 million tonnes of maize – enough to fill fifty-five Panamax-sized vessels. Restrictions on trading in 'over the counter' markets were also eased. This prompted bigger financial institutions to step in.

At the same time, research emerged indicating that commodity futures could provide investors with attractive returns that were uncorrelated to other asset classes, while also providing a hedge against inflation. Investment banks, always enthusiastic proponents of financial innovation so long as it generates plenty of fees, created commodity index funds to invest in a basket of commodities primarily via the futures markets. These index funds were offered to pension funds, insurance companies, wealthy individuals and, eventually, to everyone. The emergence of Exchange Traded Funds (ETFs) made it even easier for normal savers to take a bet on commodity prices. Agricultural commodities were bundled into these index funds and ETFs, alongside oil, natural gas, metals and minerals.

Between 2005 and 2008 the amount of money invested in commodity index funds increased from $46 billion to $250 billion. The flood receded for a while when the financial crisis hit, but as commodity prices rebounded, while most other asset classes struggled, a tide of money flowed back in, both to index funds and to more nimble hedge funds that could bet either way on prices. According to Barclays Capital, the value of commodity-related assets under management peaked at $450 billion in April 2011. Of this, over $100 billion was invested in agricultural commodities. The big investment banks also got involved, with JPMorgan, Citi, UBS and Deutsche Bank all beefing up their agriculture trading desks.

Futures markets went into overdrive. Because buying or selling futures contracts requires a relatively small down payment (less than 10 per cent), and financial players often use debt to bolster their firepower, every extra dollar in assets under management translates into even bigger increases in activity on futures markets. Between 2000 and 2010 the number of outstanding futures and options contracts on commodity exchanges increased six-fold. The value of contracts changing hands 'over the counter' was fourteen times higher in 2008 than ten years before. Food commodities were just one part of this speculative frenzy but they were carried along by the wave. To take just one example – soft red wheat futures on the Chicago Board of Trade – the volume of trade in this contract in 2009 was the equivalent of trading the entire year's harvest each day, every day, for the whole year.

Since the financial crisis that struck in 2008, commodity futures markets have been subsumed within the binary 'risk-on/ risk-off' trade that dominates much investment activity. When investors fear a relapse into recession or the explosion of a new economic crisis, there is a gigantic sucking sound as they pull their money out of riskier assets (including commodities), causing prices to fall, and then pile into safe assets, which rise in value. If there are a few positive news stories, investors switch from safe assets to riskier ones, sending prices the other way. The trend has been accentuated by exchange traded funds which track commodities but are listed on stock exchanges, thereby intertwining commodity and stock markets more closely.

Not only that, but agricultural commodities are now also targets for the 'algorithmic' or 'high frequency' trading machines that increasingly dominate financial markets. These high-powered computers analyse market activity and activate trading strategies based on past price developments or the anticipated reactions of other traders to market developments. Rather than taking a long-term view, they move in and out of positions in a fraction of a second, exploiting tiny price discrepancies. High frequency trading firms vie with each other to get the fastest electronic connection to the major exchanges, as this can provide an edge. It is a remarkable statistic that fully half of all stock market activity in New York, and one-third in Europe, is now carried out by these high frequency traders. With the gradual introduction of full electronic trading on exchange platforms since 2005, they are also active on commodity futures markets. The newest breed of food speculators do not just use computers to bet on prices; they *are* computers. It is the final step in what the UN Conference on Trade and Development (UNCTAD) has called the 'financialisation of commodities'.

Boxing with shadows

Commodities have become just another asset class for financial investors in search of return. Futures markets are their point of entry. This has transformed how futures markets work. But does this matter? Has it had any effect on the real cost of food, that is, on prices in the physical or spot markets?

According to some economists the answer is 'no'. They argue that the financialisation of futures markets does not have any effect on physical prices. The reason is that all this money is not chasing after a finite amount of commodity. Instead, it is being used to enter into contracts that are a bet on future prices. These paper contracts are rarely settled for anything except cash. There is no limit to the number that can be signed, so long as there are enough willing buyers or sellers on the other side. Therefore, increased demand for futures contracts should not affect their price. And, according to efficient market theory, if the price for a particular contract was ever pushed beyond its 'true' value, willing buyers or sellers would immediately step in and take advantage, as the mis-pricing would allow them to make a risk-free profit through arbitrage. This is what keeps markets efficient in the first place.

This is a nice theory. It has even been backed up by some empirical research. After crunching data on the 2006 to 2008 period, a number of studies, often using a statistical technique called the Granger Causality Test, concluded that there was no correlation between the amount of activity in futures markets and changes in prices. Other studies pointed out that food

147

commodities for which futures markets do not exist have often experienced as much price volatility as those for which derivatives are available: the onions market is a famous example, as onion futures were banned by the US government in 1958 because of excess volatility. The consensus opinion among economists and leading institutions such as FAO and the OECD is that there is no clear proof that futures speculation causes higher or more volatile food prices. 'More research is needed,' is the usual conclusion. 'Until then we shouldn't blame the speculators.'

These fence-sitting studies have been embraced by investment houses such as Goldman Sachs, which dismiss fears about financial speculation as 'misinformed'. 'Rather than destabilising futures markets,' according to Goldman Sachs spokesman Lucas van Praag, 'commodity index funds provide them with a stable pool of capital, improving farmers' ability to insure themselves against the risks inherent in agricultural prices.'

Yet, there are many dissenters who have come to a different judgement. The more extreme among them blame speculators for *all* the increases in food prices in recent years. This is wrong. As we have seen in previous chapters, there were good reasons why food prices rose, not least because demand was high and supplies were tight. But serious economists have also analysed the data and shown that increased speculation in futures markets *has* affected price levels to an extent. For example, one study by Christopher Gilbert of the University of Trento in Italy argued that index-based investments were responsible for about 10 per cent of the rise in grain prices in the first half of 2008.

The hunt for causality in statistics is notoriously difficult. The Granger test, if mis-applied, can be used to show that Christmas cards cause Christmas! Moreover, economists' understanding of the functioning of commodity markets is often poor, and their models usually fail to capture the real dynamics that drive prices. Rather than relying on fancy econometrics, we might be better to ask the traders who are active in the markets day to day. What do they think of the wall of speculative capital that has flooded into commodity markets over the past five years?

One of the people best-qualified to answer is Ann Berg. The product of a marriage between a US Army officer who served in Europe during the Second World War and an Englishwoman who decrypted ciphers for her country's secret service, Berg was brought up to defy convention. After graduating from a small liberal arts college in Minnesota, she joined the commodities firm Louis Dreyfus and became the first woman grain exporter in the USA. In 1982 she became a member of the Chicago Board of Trade, where she made a living for eighteen years as an independent futures trader. She was elected to its Board of Directors as its first female Full Member. But the raising of position limits and the entry of banking behemoths forced her out of the market, as her pockets were not deep enough to compete. Since then, she has advised the United Nations and foreign governments, revealing the inner workings of the commodity markets and warning of the dangers of excessive speculation. One journalist called her 'a force-ten gale blowing through the Windy City of Chicago'. She is the sort of person for whom the phrase 'poacher turned gamekeeper' was invented.

In a number of incisive articles, Berg has pointed out the flaws in the theory that speculative capital has little impact on commodity markets. The problem is that index funds, when they accept new capital, only buy futures contracts – they have what is called a 'long-only bias', always betting that prices will go up. In theory, sellers should emerge to take advantage of these new market participants, keeping the supply and demand of futures in balance. However, this ignores the constraints that exist on the side of potential sellers. The amount of money at the disposal of index funds may be so large that potential sellers may lack the capital to match them. The volume of contracts may be so great that there are insufficient physical stocks to allow arbitragers to make risk-free profits on divergences between futures and spot prices. As a result, a sudden influx of 'long-only' money could disrupt the market and cause futures prices to temporarily spike. Similarly, a decision by investors to pull their money out of index funds could lead to the dumping of large numbers of futures contracts back on the market, which could cause prices to plunge.

If the flow of investment into commodity index funds, and thereby into futures markets, was based on real understanding of the fundamentals of food supply and demand then it could play a useful role in setting prices at the right level. But this is not what drives much behaviour. Most investors in commodity funds are ignorant of the dynamics of real agricultural markets. Decisions to allocate capital to the commodity asset class are increasingly taken in response to changes in macro indicators, such as GDP growth in China or the willingness of the US Federal Reserve to print money. This has little to do with wheat yields in Australia. Moreover, food makes up a tiny proportion of the commodities baskets that comprise most index funds. Investors are much more likely to be making a bet on future oil or metal prices, rather than an informed decision on soybeans or maize. Yet, for every dollar put into a commodity index fund, a certain amount will be placed into agricultural commodities. Food is dragged along for the ride.

Of course, not all speculative capital is so naïve. Alongside index funds there are much nimbler hedge fund managers who analyse the market and take positions on whether prices will go up or down. They may be buyers of futures contracts one day, and sellers the next. This is the sort of neutral speculative activity that, in theory, should provide helpful liquidity to the market and perhaps even help reveal correct prices. However, the work of behavioural economists tends to confirm that all financial markets are prone to irrational exuberances and panics because of the cognitive biases of human traders. Commodity markets are no exception. Speculators follow trends. They enthusiastically participate in bubbles and then flee when the bubbles burst. They stick together and follow the herd, which can be perfectly rational because acting against the majority, even if supported by the fundamentals, can lead to large losses. And the biggest career risk in finance is not losing money per se, but losing money when others are not. Rather than looking at the fundamentals, traders look at each other. One trader in food markets was upfront about his strategy in 2008: 'I kept buying in the futures market as prices were going up as there would surely be one more fool out there who would pay even more.'

High frequency and algorithmic trading takes this to the extreme. The computers do not bother with real developments in the supply and demand of food but focus 100 per cent on the activities of other traders, looking for trends and opportunities. They try to use superior technical capabilities to gain insights into the order books of the marketplace and then trade 'in front' of these orders, a quasi-illegal practice called front running. Ann Berg calls it 'parasitical trading'. Taking it one step further, some funds try to decipher the algorithms that other funds use by analysing rival trades. They then use this to guess how other funds will react to a piece of news and construct trades to take advantage. The end result is a commodities market that is increasingly self-referential, responding to signals it creates itself.

In private, many commodity traders confirm Ann Berg's analysis. UNCTAD produced a hard-hitting report on the subject of commodity speculation in 2011, much of it based on confidential interviews with market participants. There was a consensus that financial traders cannot move prices in the long run, but can cause substantial volatility and price distortions in the short run. One grain trader complained that 'outside money' from financial investors had introduced a 'Wall Street mentality' into the futures markets. There was widespread concern about algorithmic trading as it could reinforce herding behaviour: 'they all behave like lemmings,' one person commented. A US Senate Sub-Committee investigation into volatility in wheat markets in 2008 reported similar findings.

For all these reasons, it is hard to avoid the conclusion that excessive, uninformed speculation in commodities futures increases price volatility. Over the past five years, the influx of financial players into commodity markets has driven the highs higher and the lows lower, perhaps by 10 or 20 per cent. To a poor food importing country, or a consumer in one of these countries, this is enough to hurt. Even Goldman Sachs, departing from its usual script, admitted in another report that 'without question increased fund flow into commodities has boosted prices'.

In smaller markets, there is compelling evidence that speculators can affect prices even more, at least for short periods. There is a long history of speculators trying to 'corner' or 'squeeze' particular commodity markets, usually by buying up futures and hoarding stocks when there was a perceived shortage, with the goal of driving prices up even further (although not always with great success). Anthony 'Chocfinger' Ward's massive position in the cocoa market in 2010 certainly rocked the market. There have been a number of other examples in recent years. For instance, the London market for robusta, the lower-quality bean used mainly in instant coffee, saw squeezes in 2006, 2007, 2009 and again in 2012, as hedge funds and trading houses amassed huge positions in individual contracts, driving prices to temporary highs. The frequency of these incidents appears to have increased since holders of large amounts of investment capital began hunting for new territories in which to dabble.

Excessive price volatility is one thing. What is perhaps more damaging – and what may eventually drive real hedgers away from futures markets altogether – is the divergence between futures prices and those in the physical or spot market. As we have seen earlier, futures markets were set up to serve the needs of holders of commodities. Like the shadows in Plato's Cave, futures prices are supposed to reflect the day-to-day inter-actions between farmers, traders and food users. Yet, in recent years this has not always been the case. Prices for delivery of grain six months out have not reflected the physical price after taking into account the costs of storage and finance. The flood of money into commodities has caused a situation where futures prices are consistently higher than spot prices (what the market calls 'contango'). More tellingly, prices have not always fully converged as a futures contract approaches the date of delivery. It is as if the shadows have taken on a life of their own and gone walkabout.

The wheat market in the USA provides a clear example, one probed by a US Senate Sub-Committee. They found that the difference between futures and spot prices, which was historically around 25 cents per bushel, widened to between $1.50 and $2.00 during 2008. There was also a much bigger gap between the cash and futures price at contract expiration at the delivery location in Chicago. This sort of divergence creates risk for buyers and sellers of real commodities. A farmer holding a stock of grain sells a futures contract because he expects the price to move in tandem with his physical asset. If, in contrast, the futures price changes while the value of his stock does not, he may lose money. And, because of regular margin calls, he will have to fork out this cash immediately, which can place a strain on his finances. Futures markets that get hijacked by financial speculators no longer allow commercial users to hedge their risks; they can simply add new and highly complex forms of risk.

Defenders of increased financial speculation in commodity markets argue that it increases liquidity, reduces the costs of hedging and makes these markets work more efficiently. However, for many traditional buyers and sellers of commodities, the cost of hedging on futures markets has actually gone up, while its efficacy has decreased. This is not a good deal. As a result, some are deserting the markets altogether. Evidence reported by the Kansas City Board of Trade pointed to a reduction in long-term hedging by commercial users at the beginning of 2008, caused by higher market volatility. One grain trader told UNCTAD that the Chicago exchange had turned into 'a casino' with a number of physical traders moving away from it because 'hedging does not make sense, when it is riskier to hedge than not to hedge'. Futures exchanges for smaller agricultural commodities, such as cocoa, coffee or sugar, are seeing participants leave because of perceived market manipulation. As one sugar trader puts it, more clients seem 'bored of being with the wrong end of a squeeze'.

The gyrations in food prices since 2008 have led to calls to tighten regulation of commodity markets. The French, with their traditional suspicion of Anglo-Saxon financiers, have been at the forefront. Ironically, futures markets in the

European Union are much less regulated and transparent than those in the USA, where the Commodities Futures Trading Commission has long imposed some control. (Anthony Ward's intervention in the cocoa market might have landed him in jail on the other side of the Atlantic.) The outcry has led the NYSE LIFFE authorities to introduce new limits on the number of contracts a single trader can hold in the London and Paris markets, which should bring them up to American standards – and make Chocfinger-style squeezes a thing of the past. Within the USA, the Chicago Board of Trade has introduced new rules requiring traders to submit more data on their trades. In response to public criticism, some investment banks, mostly in Germany, have declared that they will no longer offer index funds that include food commodities.

However, in general, financial institutions have been successful in stalling far-reaching reforms. In October 2012 Wall Street lobbyists won a court battle against the Commodities Futures Trading Commission, preventing it from introducing tighter limits on the number of positions a single firm could hold. Commodity exchanges have taken steps to woo more speculators, for example by extending opening hours and facilitating high frequency trading. There is a shift underway from futures contracts that can be settled by physical delivery to ones that can be settled by cash only. The ability to force a counterpart to deliver physical goods was one of the few things that kept futures markets honest; a departure from this will further weaken the ties between futures and physical prices. The exchanges, all controlled by private companies, back these moves because they are intent on maximising trading volumes – this is what drives their profits. Financial institutions are the most lucrative customers because they carry out the most trades. The interests of buyers and sellers of real commodities come second.

The financialisation of commodities marches on. As a result, commodity markets are becoming more and more correlated with other financial assets. The original argument for investing in commodity futures was that they had no connection with equities, bonds or real estate and, therefore, provided diversification. But new research by two economists at Princeton University shows that from 2005 onwards the prices of wheat, soybeans, live cattle and many other commodities have tended to move together and in line with all other asset classes. They trace this to the growing role of index funds, pointing out that Chinese commodity markets – which are off-limits to Western financial capital – do not exhibit the same correlation. A more recent study by UNCTAD reveals that this heightened correlation extends to very short periods, including 5-minute, 10-second and 1-second intervals. These co-movements did not exist before 2008. The cause, it seems, is high frequency traders moving in and out of all these markets at lightning speed. It is hard to see what this has to do with the fundamentals of food supply and demand.

In a fairy tale called 'The Shadow', Hans Christian Andersen tells the story of how a writer's shadow wanders off one night and takes on a life of its own. As time passes, the shadow becomes richer, sturdier and more powerful, while the writer gets poorer, weaker and paler. Eventually, they agree to switch positions: the former shadow becomes the master and the fading writer pretends to be *his* shadow. Something similar is happening in commodity markets. Futures prices are becoming more and more disconnected from the growing and buying of food in the real world. The shadow markets are taking on a life of their own and starting to dominate the physical trade in food. Indeed, for most financial investors, the shadows have become the only reality that matters. This will only accentuate the volatility of food prices.

BOOM YEARS FOR THE BIG COMMODITY TRADING HOUSES
Combined revenues of ABCD commodity firms, $ billion

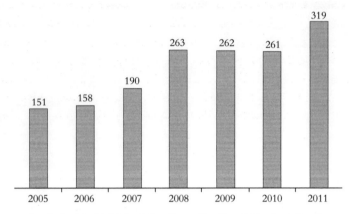

A = Archer Daniels Midland, B = Bunge, C = Cargill, D = Louis Dreyfus

Source: Company reports and press interviews

MARKET DOMINANCE IN THE GLOBAL FOOD SYSTEM
Share of international grain trade handled by ABCDs and Glencore

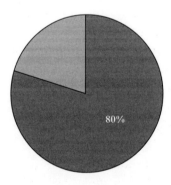

80%

Source: Berne Declaration, Commodities: Switzerland's most dangerous business, 2011; Glencore company documents

8

STIRRING THE ALPHABET SOUP

The ABCD of commodity trading – established companies, new competitors and the race to secure supply chains

Futures markets play a role in determining the price you pay for food. But you cannot eat a paper futures contract. Far more important are physical markets, where real agricultural commodities are bought and sold. Historically, the international trade in food has been dominated by a small number of multinational corporations. The top four, known by their initials as the 'ABCDs', are Cargill, Archer Daniels Midland (ADM), Louis Dreyfus and Bunge, in order of size. Recently, they have been joined by a 'G', a Swiss-based company called Glencore that is active in oil, metals and minerals as well as food. These companies have built up networks of logistics, storage, finance and marketing that stretch into almost all the countries of the world. They, not financial speculators, are the true powers behind the global food system.

The commodity trading houses are also famously secretive. Two – Cargill and Louis Dreyfus – are private companies, still mostly owned by the founding families. As a result, they have few obligations to publish data. Glencore was the most secretive of the bunch until it listed on public markets in 2011 and had to disclose thousands of pages of information – an event that provided a fascinating insight into the commodity trader's toolbox. Even the publicly listed companies do their best to shield their trades from prying eyes. Information is their most precious commodity.

Perhaps because of their traditional secrecy, the commodity houses have long been suspected of exercising a malign influence. They have been accused of manipulating food prices, squeezing farmers and consumers, avoiding taxes, and using their financial clout to get politicians on their side. They have been an easy target for critics of globalisation and corporate power. Are these criticisms justified? What role will the commodity traders play in the global food system of the future? Whose interests will they serve? Like the rest of the global food system, the business of food is changing, in ways that could affect everyone.

Rootless capitalists

The ABCDs epitomise the modern transnational corporation. They operate in the cracks between states, having long outgrown their countries of origin. The company with the longest lineage, Bunge, best illustrates this rootless capitalism. Founded in Amsterdam in 1818 it moved to Belgium in 1859, and then to Argentina in the late nineteenth century, following the emergence of that region as a major food exporter. This provided the base for expansion into Brazil and North America during the twentieth century under the leadership of the Born and Hirsch families. After two siblings were kidnapped by left-wing Argentinian terrorists in 1974 – and a $60 million ransom was paid, the largest on record at the time – the families scattered to Brazil and Spain, before establishing a parent company for the group in Bermuda. Bunge eventually listed on the New York Stock Exchange in 2001, moving its headquarters to White Plains, New York. It still has many assets in South America, especially in the sugar industry.

The largest European food trader, Louis Dreyfus, has a similar global reach. Léopold Louis-Dreyfus began his enterprise in 1850 by driving cartloads of wheat from his family farm in Alsace across the border to Switzerland. He moved to Paris after Alsace was ceded to Germany following the Franco-Prussian War. Over the next few decades, the French business was built around the import of grains from Russia and the Danube River. Because the family was Jewish, the company's assets were confiscated by the Nazi-controlled administration in Paris during the Second World War, but its American arm kept the corporate flame alive and the firm sprung back to life after 1945. By 2010 Louis Dreyfus was the largest trader of cotton and rice in the world, and the second largest trader of wheat, maize and sugar, with 35,000 employees spread across 55 countries.

Archer Daniels Midland, based in Illinois, USA, has always been a food processor as much as a food trader, pioneering the transformation of basic crops into flour, oils, starch, sweeteners, animal feed, and the obscure ingredients found in processed foods – it practically invented the veggie burger in the 1960s as a way to turn cheap soy protein into a higher value consumer product. More recently, it has moved into biofuels, producing large quantities of ethanol in the USA and Brazil. The company maintains storage and transport facilities around the world and now has around 30,000 employees in 75 countries.

The largest trading house, Minneapolis-based Cargill, has its roots in the pioneer farmlands of the American Midwest. Starting in 1865 with a simple grain storage facility, it followed the expansion of the railroads and built up a network of grain silos and transportation assets throughout the USA. From the 1950s, as the world became ever more dependent on

American food exports, the company went global, establishing a major trading centre in Switzerland. By 2011 it had 139,000 employees in 65 countries and generated revenues of almost $120 billion. The *Financial Times* refers to Cargill as 'one of the hidden companies of the global economy… the equivalent of ExxonMobil for the agricultural market'.

The commodity trading houses have been willing to buy from anywhere and sell to anyone, hunting out profitable trades wherever they could be found. For example, in 1972, at the height of the Cold War, American firms such as Cargill helped Soviet agricultural agents to procure shiploads of wheat while the US government unknowingly footed part of the bill through a farm subsidy programme. Company executives were hauled in front of a Congressional hearing for their part in what was called the 'Great Grain Robbery'. The traders have also aggressively pursued deals with developing countries, resorting to bribes where necessary. In his book *Merchants of Grain*, which first shone a light on the industry, Dan Morgan conjures up a vision of 'villas sprouting up in Swiss resort towns, inhabited by Romanians, Iranians, Koreans, Mexicans, and Filipinos – all owing their life of leisure to nothing more than one lucrative encounter in the bowels of some seedy bureaucracy with the local agent of some multinational company'.

The recent upstart in the grain trade, Glencore, epitomises this buccaneering spirit. Glencore was founded in the 1970s by Marc Rich, an American commodity trader who fled to Switzerland rather than face federal charges of tax evasion. (He was notoriously pardoned by Bill Clinton on the President's last day in office in 2001.) Rich rose to prominence by championing 'combat trading', high-risk deal-making in countries facing turmoil. He sold oil to apartheid South Africa while that country was under UN sanctions; he bought up mines in conflict-ridden Zaire; he was embroiled in the 'Oil for Food' scandal in Iraq; and he traded oil for the Ayatollahs when Iran was blacklisted by the USA. Glencore's agriculture business was built on forays into the countries of the former Soviet Union, another region that requires a high tolerance for risk and legal ambiguity.

It is no accident that Glencore chose Switzerland as its base of operations. Cargill started the trend, establishing a Swiss subsidiary in 1956 to import grains and oilseeds from North America. ADM, Bunge and Louis Dreyfus all have trading centres in Switzerland as well. Obviously, this choice is not driven by the presence of deep-water ports or abundant local harvests. A principal reason is tax – the Swiss authorities offer very generous tax rates for this sort of trading business. The commodity houses are notorious for using webs of companies to shuffle profits to jurisdictions where they will be taxed the least. The exchequers of countries where food is produced or consumed receive less as a result. The ability to exploit different tax systems is one of the chief advantages of multinational corporations, a by-product of globalisation that benefits business executives and shareholders at the expense of the humble taxpayer.

Apart from tax avoidance and a willingness to do business with unsavoury regimes, the chief complaint about the commodity traders is that they are so dominant. The global food system resembles an hourglass. There are hundreds of millions of farmers growing food on many different farms; at the other end of the supply chain there are hundreds of millions of consumers. But there is a pinch-point in the middle, as much of this food passes through the hands of a few large firms. Exact figures are hard to come by, but it is estimated that the ABCD firms and Glencore handle more than four-fifths of the world's total trade in grains and oilseeds.

In some regions, individual firms control a large part of the market. For example, Bunge's ubiquitous operations in South America earned it a sinister local nickname – 'El Pulpo' or 'The Octopus'.

This sort of market dominance can be dangerous for others. Whenever there are many sellers and just one buyer, or many buyers and just one seller, the one can drive a hard bargain with the many. Economists call this monopsony or monopoly power. The Samsung Economic Research Institute, in its report on South Korea's food security, noted the danger of relying on such powerful intermediaries. It described the international grain market as 'subject to an oligopoly of the four major global grain conglomerates: Cargill, Archer Daniels Midland, LDC, and Bunge'. It warned that 'at times, the four grain majors have encroached on consumer welfare by exerting their influence on agricultural producers, or by creating an oligopoly regime'.

The dominance of these companies over the global food system has served them well in recent years. The combined revenues of the ABCD firms rose from $150 billion in 2005 to a whopping $318 billion in 2011. Within Glencore, agriculture contributed two and a half times more to total profits between 2008 and 2010 compared to the previous three years.

The leap in revenues and profits was partly due to the increased volume of food trade. Higher food prices helped too, as the companies could earn their typical 2–3 per cent trading margins on deals that were worth a lot more. But these firms have also benefited from the volatility of food markets. This is because their position at the fulcrum of the global food system provides them with two important assets: control over a large proportion of the world's privately held stocks, and insider information on the state of agricultural supply and demand. They have the best idea of who is buying, who is selling, where food is scarce and where it is abundant. This opens up some wonderful profit-making opportunities.

In physical or spot markets, it allows the multinational commodity firms to arbitrage across space, buying food *where* it is cheap and selling it in places where people will pay a higher price. Or they can arbitrage across time, buying food *when* it is cheap and storing it until prices rise, or promising to sell food in the future when they know they can accumulate stocks for a lower price in the intervening period. The more volatile prices are, the better. It confuses everyone else about the real value of a commodity. Indeed, Deutsche Bank's main report on Glencore at the time of the company's float was titled 'The Value in Volatility, Initiating with a Buy'. 'The key way in which Glencore generates profits from its marketing activities,' the report summed up, 'is exploiting fragmented and volatile markets, which give rise to arbitrage opportunities.'

The commodity trading houses are also some of the most active players in futures markets. They use futures to hedge their own risk, buying or selling contracts to cover their positions in physical markets. But they are also well positioned to take advantage of those risk-free arbitrage opportunities that sometimes emerge – as we saw in the last chapter – when futures prices diverge from physical prices. Because they control such a large proportion of food stocks and storage facilities, they can make promises to buy or sell commodities in the future without being exposed to the same risk as purely financial speculators. The data shows that between 2006 and 2011 physical traders acted as counterparties to the financial speculators flooding the market, usually taking a 'short' position (that is, they were sellers of futures). Futures markets are a zero sum game; for every participant that makes money from a trade, another must lose money. The commodity trading houses have usually been on the winning side. Over the last five years there has been a steady transfer of money from naïve financial investors to the wily insiders who control the trade in food.

On occasion, the commodity houses also use their superior information to take speculative positions on whether prices will rise or fall. They normally keep these trades well hidden. But one example emerged when Glencore briefed bankers in preparation for its public listing. A subsequent UBS report, intended only for potential investors, was leaked to the press. It revealed how during the spring and summer of 2010 Glencore received advance warning from its farms in Russia of the impacts of the deepening drought. This prompted the company to buy maize and wheat futures ('going long') in order to benefit from a later rise in prices. What is interesting is that Yury Ognev, the head of Glencore's Russian grain unit, simultaneously urged the Russian government to impose an export ban, something that was sure to cause a price rise. Russia took this action on 5 August, duly sending the price of the cereal more than 15 per cent higher in two days. Glencore was accused of having manipulated wheat markets (and policymakers) to its advantage.

Because of stories like this, the commodity houses are easy targets for those unhappy at corporate dominance of food. Critics have cast them into the same pit as financial speculators, accusing them of driving up prices. The British charity Oxfam complained that companies like Glencore were 'profiting from the misery and suffering of poor people who are worst hit by high and volatile food prices', adding that 'if we are going to fix the ailing food system then traders must be part of the cure'. One critic, the academic Raj Patel, refers darkly to 'the corporations that have controlled [the food system] for centuries, and who crack the supply chain like a whip'.

At times, the commodity houses have not done themselves any favours through their lack of transparency, tax avoidance and willingness to flirt with corporate misbehaviour. Yet, the criticisms can be overdone. These companies play an important role in facilitating the physical trade in food. Buying, processing, moving and selling food across borders does not happen by itself. The commodity traders have invested billions in developing the grain elevators, warehouses, railways, trucks and ships needed. For example, Cargill operates 32 grain elevators along US rivers, sends 8,217 barges full of grain down these rivers each year, charters around 350 vessels on the world's oceans at any one time, and loads and discharges bulk goods in more than 6,000 ports around the world. Although the scandals and daring trades attract the most publicity, much of the work of these companies is boring logistics – sourcing stock, arranging shipments, clearing customs. They provide the pipes through which the world's food can flow. This puts them in a very different category to financial speculators.

As well as managing the flow of food commodities across space, the commodity houses also smooth the supply and demand of food across time. They are willing to buy harvests from farmers during times of plenty, when customers may not be immediately available, and to take orders from importers when supplies are tight. By doing so, they take on risk. For example, although Glencore benefited from the Russian government's decision to impose an export ban, this event caused one of its rivals, ADM, to suffer losses of between $100 million and $200 million. The company had signed a deal to supply 1.5 billion tonnes of wheat three days before the export ban was announced and was then forced to buy from French and German markets at much higher prices to meet its obligations. What ADM did not do was renege on its contract, even though it was guaranteed to generate huge losses. The commodity houses invariably deliver on their promises to buy or sell at a specified price, which makes them reliable counter-parties for other actors in the global food system.

There is a legitimate debate to be had about the lopsided nature of the global food system and the role of trade. But so long as there are some countries with food deficits, and other countries with food surpluses, there will be a need for inter-mediaries such as the ABCDs to facilitate trade between them. To paraphrase Voltaire's quip about the existence of God, if the commodity houses did not exist, it would be necessary to invent them. And because they are private corporations they will seek to make a profit at the expense of others. Buying low and selling high is what traders do.

Profit-seeking behaviour is in itself not a problem, so long as there is sufficient competition between the trading firms to prevent oligopolistic behaviour and excessive margins. Further-more, the stateless nature of these companies has some positive features. They are willing to source food from wherever it is abundant and sell food to whoever can afford it. They are not susceptible to control by governments. There are no special favours. Food importers know where they stand – the highest bidder wins. Ruthless competition between rootless capitalists is one way to ensure that food markets are open to everyone on an equal basis, so long as they have the cash.

The race to the gate
We may have witnessed the high point of ABCD dominance over the global food system. This is because new challengers are rising in the East. Traditionally, Asian countries (with the possible exception of Japan) were happy to turn to the established American and European trading firms to arrange their food imports. But Asian firms now see an opportunity to take over this function. On the face of it, this should be

just the sort of competition that the industry needs to keep its more exploitative tendencies in check. However, the new Asian pretenders are pursuing different business models and are subject to greater influence by governments worried about food security. What effect will this have on the functioning of food markets?

Three of the biggest challengers to emerge from Asia over the last two decades are Noble, Olam and Wilmar. Thanks to their initials, they have gained their own nickname in the financial press – the 'NOW' group.

Noble, founded in 1987 and headquartered in Hong Kong, has revenues of $56 billion and 10,000 employees. China's sovereign wealth fund, the China Investment Corporation, is the second largest shareholder, holding 15 per cent. The company is active along the entire food supply chain, from production to delivery. It sources from low cost producers such as Brazil, Australia and Indonesia and supplies high growth markets like China, India and the Middle East. It is the largest importer of grains into Saudi Arabia and handles 10 per cent of South American soybeans. Noble models itself closely on the ABCDs, trades many of the same commodities and is staffed by many former ABCD employees – its chief executive used to work at Louis Dreyfus. It has even established itself in Switzerland, from where it trades cocoa, coffee and precious metals. It is often compared to Glencore because of its diversification across agriculture, energy and metals.

Olam and Wilmar are somewhat different, in that they focus less on temperate crops such as wheat or maize and more on tropical commodities. For example, Wilmar is the world's largest trader of palm oil and owns many plantations in Indonesia and Malaysia.

Olam began as a tiny venture in 1989 exporting cashews from Nigeria. It was founded by Sunny Verghese, a bespectacled

Indian businessman who learnt his trade the hard way, having been appointed as boss of a Nigerian cotton plantation at the age of twenty-six. In 1995 the company moved its headquarters to Singapore to take advantage of Asian markets. Olam has built a leadership position in niche commodities such as cocoa, coffee, cashews, sesame, cotton and timber. It prides itself on embedding staff in production regions and sourcing commodities directly from more than a million small farmers. As a rite of passage, up-and-coming executives are sent to work in remote corners of the world – what Sunny Verghese calls a posting in the 'bush' – so they can learn about the risks of commodity trading first-hand.

The NOW companies have shown a willingness to roll up their sleeves and get involved in poorer parts of Africa and Southeast Asia, which the ABCDs have tended to neglect. Fuelled by abundant Asian capital, and well positioned to take advantage of growing import demand from China and India, they are expanding rapidly. A Cargill executive will tend to worry more about these fast-growing upstarts than competition from its established rivals, ADM, Bunge or Louis Dreyfus.

Recent years have also seen the resurgence of long-established Asian players – the giant Japanese trading houses. Companies such as Mitsubishi, Mitsui, Sumitomo, Itochu and Marubeni, known as the *sogo shosha*, are the Godzillas of the Japanese economy, involved in everything from commodity production and trading to manufacturing and banking. Following the food crisis of the early 1970s, the trading houses were encouraged by the Japanese government to establish supply chains abroad. Now, thanks to another food crisis, they are on the march again.

In 2012 Marubeni swooped to acquire US grain merchant Gavilon. Based in Omaha, Nebraska, Gavilon was one of the few mid-sized independents left in the business, controlling the third-largest network of grain storage facilities in the USA. It normally sold its stocks to ADM, Cargill or other exporters – whichever offered the best price. The $3.6 billion acquisition will allow Marubeni to integrate a Gavilon supply chain that reaches deep into the American Midwest with its own export facility in Portland, Oregon. Marubeni is Japan's leading grain trader and the next largest grain trader in the world after the ABCDs and Glencore. According to chief executive Teruo Asada, the company shipped more than twice as much grain in 2010 as five years earlier, much of it to China, where Marubeni has gained an edge over rivals by signing a supply deal with Sinograin, the state enterprise responsible for managing China's food reserves.

Mitsui is another Japanese trading house looking to bolster its presence in food markets. In 2007 it took a minority stake in the Swiss-based company Multigrain AG, completing a takeover of the company in 2011. Multigrain grows soybeans, cotton and corn in Brazil and owns five harbour facilities and two flour mills in the country. Mitsui also looked at other farming regions. In 2009 representatives of Mitsui were exploring agriculture investments in Central Asia, Central America and Eastern Europe. Their preferred model was to offer inputs and machinery to farmers in exchange for the right to buy harvests. They explained that it was not only good business; it would also satisfy the Japanese government's desire to strengthen national food security by gaining a firmer control over supplies.

This is exactly the motivation of the newest entry into the global commodity trade – South Korea. Concern about the country's reliance on the ABCD companies and the Japanese *sogo shosha* led to some bold moves after the market turmoil of 2008. 'We must get our direct purchases up from zero, reducing reliance on the big trading companies,' one government official said. Breaking this monopoly would be no easy task. 'They've been controlling the whole gamut from production to sales for so long,' said Park Hwan-il, a research fellow at Samsung Economic Research Institute. Yet, South Korean policymakers and business leaders, acting together in a way that is common in Asia, decided to give it a go.

The state-owned Korea Agro-Fisheries Trade Corp. took the lead, putting up over half the initial investment. It will be responsible for procuring wheat, maize and beans – the goal is to purchase 30 per cent of Korea's grain needs by 2020. Three other companies will take charge of marketing and transportation. The consortium began by establishing a grain trading unit in Chicago, the traditional nerve centre of the American commodity complex. A subsidiary, aT Grain Company, was accepted as a member of the US Grains Council on 1 March 2012. Their plan is to acquire grain elevators in the USA, purchase harvests from farmers or local storage companies, and then ship the commodities to South Korea, bypassing the global commodity houses. 'Should it work out,' one official of Korea Agro-Fisheries Trade Corp. boasted, 'we will be able to help stabilise staple grains at less volatile prices.'

And what about China, whose growing imports are causing such ripples across the global food system? Perhaps because of the fragile state of US–Chinese relations, China has not tried to copy South Korea's aggressive attempt to build up a direct grain purchasing capacity in North America. It has been happy to make its purchases of American maize and soybeans through the ABCD companies or the Japanese trading houses. But in other parts of the world, Chinese companies have taken steps to acquire control over supplies.

China has been most ambitious in South America. This region is the source of most of its soybeans, a commodity for which it has an insatiable appetite. The Chongqing Grain Group has agreed to build an industrial complex for soybean processing in Brazil's Bahia state, reportedly planning to invest up to $2.4 billion. China's Sanhe Hopefull Grain & Oil announced plans to put $7.5 billion into soybean processing facilities in the Brazilian state of Goiás, in exchange for an annual supply of 6 million tonnes. This includes building a new railroad. Many of these Chinese companies are state-owned or closely tied to Communist party officials.

Kory Melby, a US agricultural consultant who lives in Brazil, said he has received calls from Chinese food companies wanting to partner with Brazilian grain merchants. 'The Chinese are forming partnerships with mega-producers so everybody feels nice and calm,' he said. 'Instead of trying to buy land directly, they are saying, "Here's $10 million at below-market interest rate. You go buy more land. You go buy equipment. You go do what you do well. But we have the option of setting a price and getting paid back in soybeans if we need them."'

Chinese companies may not be looking to acquire farmland in Brazil, but plenty of the Asian trading firms are. In the past, the ABCDs shunned the production of commodities – farming – because it was seen as capital-intensive, unprofitable and risky. The rising Asian trading firms are not content to copy this traditional business model. They are much more willing to go all the way upstream and to actually grow the commodities they sell.

Olam is perhaps the most active. In Nigeria, it has commenced work on a $90 million rice farm covering 10,000 hectares of irrigated land in Nasarawa State. According to the state governor, 'it is going to be the largest rice farm in Africa, fully mechanised'. In Gabon it has formed a joint venture with the government to develop a 50,000 hectare oil palm plantation, part of $250 million in total spending. In Brazil, Olam is investing a similar amount to acquire and develop an integrated sugar cane company called Usina Açucareira Passos. Overall, in the last few years Olam has made 24 investments in upstream activities and now farms 400,000 hectares worldwide, an area equal to almost twice the size of Luxembourg.

The Japanese *sogo shosha* are also on the hunt for farmland. When Mitsui acquired Swiss-based Multigrain, it gained control of 116,000 hectares of soybean fields in Brazil – equivalent to 2 per cent of Japan's own cultivated area. Mitsui said the purpose of the deal was 'to ensure stable supplies of grains from Brazil for the Asian market' at a time of escalating 'global competition for crop land'. Some of the Chinese companies investing in soybean processing facilities in Brazil are also seeking to acquire large areas of land elsewhere on which to grow the crop. The Chongqing Grain Group, for example, announced a project worth US$1.2 billion to grow soybeans, corn and cotton in Argentina.

All the activities of the Asian food traders in recent years have one thing in common – a desire to secure full control of supply chains, from the land to the end user. Rather than buying commodities in the open market, or relying on a series of intermediaries, these companies seek to own all the steps that are involved in getting food from farm to fork. As Noble explains on its website, its strategy is 'building integrated supply chains in key commodity sectors and controlling the critical stages of the supply process'. Sunny Verghese describes Olam as an 'integrated supply chain manager'. Vertical integration is the name of the game.

How are the incumbent American and European commodity houses responding to this challenge? By pursuing the same strategies – consolidation and vertical integration.

Buoyed by cash reserves after a few good years, the ABCDs and Glencore are in the market for whatever independent operators are left. The biggest deal so far has been Glencore's $6 billion acquisition of Canadian grain handler Viterra. (Glencore had to fend off rival bids from both ADM and Bunge.) Viterra was an attractive target because the Canadian government is ending the monopoly of the Canadian Wheat Board over the marketing of wheat and barley from the prairie provinces of western Canada, which should allow Viterra to increase its market share. Viterra also comes with substantial grain operations in Australia and the USA. The acquisition will act as a beachhead for further expansion into the USA and give Glencore access to a reliable source of grain outside the Black Sea region. It will advance the firm's goal of becoming a true global player in food markets.

After its failed bid in Canada, ADM is determined to acquire Australia's largest grain handler. It has launched a $2.8 billion bid for GrainCorp, a company that was privatised by the Australian government in 1992. GrainCorp owns 280 grain elevators in key farming regions and controls the bulk of Australia's east coast grain ports. It is an attractive target because ADM wants to procure more grain outside its American home base. The recent dismantling of the Australian Wheat Board has opened up the country for integration into the supply chains of the global commodity firms.

The American and European commodity houses are also showing a greater willingness to get involved in food production. Glencore has acquired 280,000 hectares of farmland in Russia and Ukraine – it was from these properties that it got advanced warning of the developing drought in 2010. Louis Dreyfus has large land holdings in Brazil, Russia and Ukraine. Bunge has acquired sugar cane plantations in Brazil to source feedstock for its local sugar and ethanol mills.

Cargill operates oil palm plantations in Indonesia and is looking to expand its activities to West Africa. There has been a fundamental shift in strategy within these firms, leading to a much greater willingness to take the final step back along the supply chain.

The food crisis has set off a scramble to control resources among private companies, some of which are discreetly backed by governments. In the past, when food was cheap and abundant, trading firms were happy to play a middleman role, dipping into local markets to buy what they needed. But now they want to control supply chains as much as possible. This is partly because there is more money to be made upstream – farming is a much more profitable business than before. But it is also due to concerns over the reliability of supply. This can become a self-fulfilling process, as companies feel compelled to take action when they see competitors lock up resources. According to Ray Goldberg, Harvard Business School professor emeritus of agriculture and business, the focus of all firms today is: 'how do we maintain our supplies in a potential supply-shortage world?' The race to the farmgate is on.

What impact will these changes have on the functioning of the global food system? In theory, the emergence of new players should increase competition – widening the neck of the hour glass, reducing opportunities for monopsony or monopoly behaviour and keeping trading margins in check. This should benefit farmers (who can demand higher prices) and consumers (who will benefit from lower margins). This is the theory. But in reality many of the moves by the commodity traders are designed to *reduce* competition. Their goal is to build captive supply chains, vertically integrated from the land to the consumer. Instead of one big hourglass, we may end up with a row of slender champagne glasses, each controlled by a different commodity firm.

A lack of competition could allow multinational companies to accumulate more profits, at the expense of farmers and consumers. If a single company controls all the storage and transport facilities in a farming region, it will be able to dictate prices to farmers. Similarly, if a customer only has access to one trading company that customer is at risk of a squeeze. In an interview with the *Financial Times*, Olam chief executive Sunny Verghese spoke candidly about one of the motivations for consolidation within the industry. 'You want to create choke points,' he explained. 'You don't want to add capacity and reduce industry profitability. You'd like to take out existing capacity and continue to operate these choke points.' Policymakers will need to keep an eye on the wave of acquisitions and mergers to ensure that there is sufficient competition in local markets. This may require government intervention and the use of anti-trust legislation to prevent consolidation or to force the break-up of monopolies.

Another risk of vertically integrated food supply chains is that they create more opportunities for tax avoidance. Companies can use mis-pricing to shift profits to where the tax burden is smallest. Let us assume, for example, that a company grows a commodity in Country A at a cost of $100 and sells it in Country B for $400. Both of these countries have corporate tax rates of 30 per cent. If the company made a direct sale, it should end up paying $90 in taxes (30 per cent of $300) in one of these jurisdictions. But if it hired some clever accountants and set up a shell company in an off-shore jurisdiction with no corporate tax, it could buy the commodity from its subsidiary in Country A at an artificially low price (say $105) and sell it to its subsidiary in Country B at an inflated cost (say $395), minimising profits in both those jurisdictions and booking almost all the profit in the low-tax location. This sort of trickery is rampant. A recent report on illicit financial flows from Africa concluded that more than 60 per cent of the $2 trillion that departed the continent over the last forty years was associated with tax evasion through mis-pricing (compared to only 3 per cent from bribery and corruption of public officials). The backward integration of agricultural value chains may mean that developing countries, with weak tax enforcement, miss out on the full value of their production.

Backward integration of supply chains, although it may affect the distribution of economic benefits, need not affect people's ability to eat, so long as there is enough food to go around. But what would happen if there was a genuine food crisis, one where supplies ran critically short? Powerful food importing countries are taking steps to establish vertically integrated supply chains so that they will have a first claim on them. They believe this will give them some insurance should a major crisis hit. This may have implications for countries that do not have their own trading infrastructure. Even if they have the cash to buy food, there may be no one to take their order. Some of the changes that are taking place in the structure of commodity trading could cause food markets to become more fragmented, more residual. If food production is locked up in captive supply chains, there will be less to go around for everyone else.

As we have seen, owning and operating farmland is the ultimate form of vertical integration. It allows companies to control every step of the chain from the germination of a seed to the delivery of processed foods to the end consumer. The examples given in this chapter are part of a much larger trend of foreign acquisition of farmland, especially in developing countries. Many call them 'land grabs'. It is the most controversial and dangerous phenomenon to emerge as a result of the recent food crisis, one that has echoes of darker colonial eras. Where will this trend lead?

THE NEW SCRAMBLE FOR AFRICA

Reported foreign land deals in Africa – top 10 target countries, million hectares

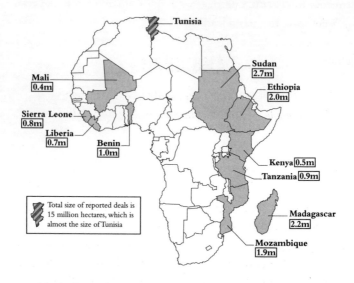

Tunisia

Sudan
2.7m

Ethiopia
2.0m

Mali
0.4m

Sierra Leone
0.8m

Liberia
0.7m

Benin
1.0m

Kenya 0.5m

Tanzania 0.9m

Madagascar
2.2m

Mozambique
1.9m

Total size of reported deals is 15 million hectares, which is almost the size of Tunisia

Note: Covers 372 deals. Excludes domestic deals where identified. Data is drawn from media reports and may contain errors
Source: Land Matrix database, accessed 27 July 2012.

9

LAND GRABS

Foreign investment in farmland and the new
scramble for Africa. Win-win or dangerous folly?

On 26 January 2009 a curious rice ceremony took place in one
of the air-conditioned palaces of Riyadh. With great fanfare,
King Abdullah bin Abdul Aziz of Saudi Arabia was presented
with a bowl of cooked rice. It was part of the first crop from a
farm in Ethiopia that had been established by Saudi investors
under the auspices of the King Abdullah Initiative for Saudi
Agricultural Investment Abroad. Spooked by the near-collapse
of world food markets in 2008, and running out of water at
home, the oil-rich Arab state had decided to acquire land in
other countries to grow food. The king liked the quality of the
rice and exhorted the assembled ministers and businessmen to
redouble their efforts.

The man presenting the rice was Sheikh Mohammed Al
Amoudi. Listed by Forbes as the world's sixty-third richest
person, he has a grin like Yogi Bear and is known for his
extravagant parties. Born in Ethiopia, he moved to Saudi Arabia,
gained Saudi citizenship and made a fortune in construction
and real estate – he is sometimes described as the world's
richest black man. But he retained close connections with the
ruling party in Ethiopia and built up a business empire there

spanning hotels, mines, construction and agriculture. When the Saudi government decided to funnel hundreds of millions of dollars towards acquiring farmland abroad, Ethiopia, with its fertile western valleys fed by the Blue Nile, was a prime target. Sheikh Al Amoudi was the natural person to lead the charge.

The Ethiopian government could not have been more welcoming. 'Why attractive?' reads one of the glossy posters produced by its investment promotion office. 'Vast, fertile, irrigable land at low rent. Abundant water resources. Cheap labour. Warmest hospitality.' Prime Minister Meles Zenawi, the country's autocratic ruler, was a former Marxist rebel who had firmly converted to capitalist enterprise. Even though 8 million Ethiopians suffer from chronic food shortages, he was 'very eager' to promote large-scale commercial agriculture in the country. His officials claimed that Ethiopia had 74 million hectares of land suitable for arable farming but only one-fifth was being cultivated. As a result, they made 4 million hectares available to investors. Legally, the government has the power to give away this territory as all Ethiopian farmland was nationalised by the Communists in the late 1970s. Native farmers use it under licence, so their rights are fragile.

Sheikh Al Amoudi was granted 10,000 hectares for sixty years in a remote, impoverished region called Gambella in the west of the country, a bumpy fifteen hours' drive from the capital. The plan was to use water from a nearby dam that had been constructed by Soviet engineers as part of a cotton-growing scheme that never materialised. But this was just the start. Over the next ten years, Almoudi hoped to acquire a total of 500,000 hectares across the country. This is a massive area, a quarter the size of Wales. He set up a new company, Saudi Star Agricultural Development, to pursue this goal, promising to invest more than $3 billion and to create 10,000 jobs. To cement his insider status, he appointed a former Ethiopian government minister as chief executive of the new company.

In 2009 giant Volvo trucks and Massey Ferguson tractors began trundling along the dusty roads of Gambella. Saudi Star put in a single order for agricultural machinery with Caterpillar worth $80 million. Land was cleared, and work began on a twenty-mile canal that would carry irrigation water to the property. Engineers and agronomists were brought in from Pakistan. The company started planting rice, using a highly mechanised, input-intensive form of agriculture. This must have been bewildering to the locals who peered through the new gates under the watchful eye of armed guards.

The Ethiopian government insists that the land given to Saudi Star was 'empty'. But this was not the case. Local Anuak people used it for shifting cultivation, while nomadic Nuer pastoralists grazed their animals in the area. There was a highly developed system of customary rights, under which families knew what land belonged to whom. In addition, several small villages had to be cleared to make way for the new irrigation canal.

Omot Ochan, a member of the local Anuak tribe, is just one person who was affected. Lean and tall, he lives in a straw hut on the margins of the Saudi Star property, by the remains of what was once a sizable village. As bare-breasted women cooked fish on an open fire behind, Omot described how two years earlier the company began chopping down the forest. 'Nobody came to tell us what was happening.' The bees, from which he used to make honey, disappeared, as did the animals his family hunted. Now they only had fish to sell, but he feared that the fish would go too once the Saudis drained the wetland. 'This land belonged to our father,' Omot bitterly said. 'All round here is ours.' He pointed to a distant tree that marked the boundary with the next village. 'When my father died, he said don't leave the land. We made a promise. We can't give it to the foreigners.'

Saudi Star has stepped into a complex inter-tribal conflict in Gambella. The hot, swampy region has always been geographically and ethnically distinct from highland Ethiopia. In the past, the Ethiopian state waged war against Anuak separatists and encouraged highlanders to settle in the region. More recently, the government has tried to clear the Anuak and the Nuer from their land and concentrate them in new settlements, through a programme known as 'villagization'. Although the government denies any link between this policy and the leasing of land to foreigners, this is contradicted by the statements of local officials. One farmer recounted how government officials told his village: 'We will invite investors who will grow cash crops. You do not use the land well. It is lying idle.' The Anuak see the arrival of companies like Saudi Star as yet another step in a process of internal colonisation.

Journalists from around the world, and NGOs such as New York-based Human Rights Watch, have drawn attention to events in this isolated corner of Ethiopia. Observers warned that the sullen resentment of the Anuaks could explode into violence. Sure enough, on 28 April 2012 gunmen opened fire on a group of Saudi Star workers, killing two Pakistanis and three Ethiopians. According to some reports, the farm offices of Saudi Star were ransacked. An organisation called Solidarity Movement for a New Ethiopia issued a statement saying that this was an inevitable reaction to 'the long term leasing of agricultural land in Ethiopia to foreign investors and regime cronies for next to nothing'. The Anuak are willing to fight to defend their rights, the group said. 'This should not come as a shock to anyone.'

The story of the Saudi farm in Ethiopia is just one example of a trend that is playing out all around the world. Since 2008 the media has been full of stories about 'land grabs'. Everyone from Bob Geldof to the late Colonel Gaddafi has spoken out about the menace, warning that it could lead to neo-colonial exploitation. In an absorbing recent book called *The Land-grabbers*, journalist Fred Pearce warns that it is of more threat to the poor of the world than climate change. Just how wide-spread is this phenomenon? Is it all bad? Or could foreign investment in agriculture play a positive role in increasing food security, as the Ethiopian President believed? What does it mean for the future of the world's food system? There is as much hype as reality in media coverage of this topic but, away from the headlines, there is no doubt that something important is going on.

The global land rush

There have been wildly differing estimates of the scale at which farmland is being acquired. In a much-delayed 2010 report the World Bank came up with a figure of 56 million hectares, bigger than the size of Spain. The British aid agency Oxfam trumped this a year later, saying that investors were looking to acquire 227 million hectares, an area one and a half times the size of Alaska. The latest census, prepared by an international coalition of researchers and NGOs as part of the Land Matrix database – and available online – documents 924 deals covering 47 million hectares of land.

There are many problems with these estimates. Reliable sources of data are hard to find because so many of these deals are wrapped in secrecy. The World Bank talks of 'an aston-ishing lack of awareness of what is happening on the ground even by the public sector institutions mandated to control this phenomenon' – which are strong words for a normally cautious institution. Most of the surveys quoted above rely on press reports, with little independent verification. The problem is that journalists looking for stories and activists with a drum to beat have sometimes turned rumour into fact, conjecture into certainty. A stray comment by a government official or an investor about the desire to do something – maybe, in the future, *inshallah* – gets turned into a confirmed mega deal involving a million hectares. You should not believe everything you read in the papers.

It should also be remembered that these figures contain many *domestic* deals, that is, land acquisitions by companies or individuals within their own country. At least 300 of the 924 land deals listed in the Land Matrix database are purely domestic. This is not to say that local land grabs are any less worrying than international ones. An Anuak villager in Gambella does not much care whether his ancestral land is taken by a Saudi sheikh or a cotton farmer from highland Ethiopia – the impact is much the same. In Cambodia local businessmen tied to corrupt officials have obtained large concessions for new sugar plantations, driving local farmers from their land, sometimes violently. In addition, local deal-makers may be acting as a front for foreign corporations or simply positioning themselves to flip their land to foreigners at some point in the future. Nonetheless, the focus of this chapter is on cross-border deals, as they reveal the most about how the global food system is changing.

Where are these international 'land grabs' taking place? Definitions also matter when answering this question. There has always been foreign investment in developed agricultural powerhouses such as the USA, Canada, Australia and New Zealand. For example, the US Department of Agriculture estimates that foreigners hold almost 2 per cent of American farm or forestland. Foreign acquisitions in these cases are mostly private transactions without government involvement. There are many willing sellers as farmers look to retire. The highly productive, export-oriented farming sectors of these countries are already integrated into global markets. A foreign acquisition may entail a change in ownership but little else.

Foreign acquisitions of farmland in Brazil and Argentina share many of these characteristics. Foreigners are usually buying into large-scale corporate farming enterprises, not pushing indigenous tribes or peasants off the land. (The locals have probably done this already.) There may be a question about whether it makes economic sense to allow foreign interests to control such a strategic resource, but it is a stretch to call these 'land grabs'. They are transactions between financial equals and the land does not come cheap.

The majority of land deals, however, and the ones that have generated the most concern, look very different. They target poor developing countries where land is cheap or can be obtained for free. They involve a radical change in the nature of land rights, usually a transfer from government or local communities to a foreign company in the form of a long-term lease. Host governments are usually heavily involved as they often hold the rights to the land. And the goal of these deals is to effect a transformation in how the land is used, for example by ploughing up grassland or clearing forest, and planting crops. Often, the ultimate goal is to integrate land that has been used for local subsistence into global commodity supply chains.

Although some of these deals have taken place in Asia – there have been substantial acquisitions in Indonesia, Cambodia and the Philippines – the prime target is Africa. The Land Matrix project identified 358 foreign land deals on the continent covering 15 million hectares – an area bigger than Greece. The number one country for foreign land acquisition is Sudan, where the government has been as welcoming as in neighbouring Ethiopia. Other important countries are

Madagascar, Ethiopia, Mozambique and Benin. Tanzania, Sierra Leone and Liberia are not far behind.

These are some of the poorest countries in the world. They all suffer from high levels of malnutrition and food insecurity. They have a history of corruption, conflict and poor governance. Rather than deterring foreign investors, this appears to be one of the attractions. The World Bank study concluded that investors were most likely to pursue land deals in countries with 'weak land governance' and 'poor recognition of local land rights' – which makes 'land grab' sound like an appropriate term after all.

So, who are the foreign investors doing deals in these countries? What motivates them? Perhaps the best way to approach this issue is to position the investors along a spectrum, where the two ends represent different motivations, as well as different sources of capital. At one end are governments of food importing countries worried about security of supply. At the other end are financial investors excited by the profits to be made from high food prices. In between are dozens of different actors who share these two motivations to varying degrees.

Governments of food importing countries in Asia and the Middle East, eager to grow food to ship home, are the engines of many of the land acquisitions. Officials clear a path in target countries by signing memoranda of understanding, agricultural cooperation frameworks or bilateral investment agreements. Political leaders fly in for handshakes and photo opportunities. Governments typically work through private companies to implement deals in foreign countries, but they provide support in the form of equity finance, cheap loans, guarantees or insurance. Cheap money and direct encouragement is enough to convince the private sector to take on projects abroad. This hybrid public–private model is a form of capitalism that is common in much of the developing world. And in many Arab countries it is hard to separate government from the private sector anyway because the same princes and sheikhs dominate both.

Saudi Arabia is one of the most active players in foreign land acquisition. As part of the King Abdullah Initiative for Saudi Agricultural Investment Abroad, the government created an $800 million fund for joint ventures with Saudi companies. Saudi Star is just one of many companies to benefit. Other partners include those firms that had been active in farming at home but now need something else to do because the pumping of domestic aquifers is being phased out. For example, the Hail Agricultural Development Company (HADCO) has begun a pilot project near the Nile in northern Sudan: the general manager explained that 'the area is big, the people are friendly' and 'they gave us the land almost free'. One of the most ambitious new ventures is the Foras International Investment Company, a joint venture involving the Saudi government, private investors and the Islamic Development Bank. Its '7x7' project aims to produce 7 million tonnes of rice on 700,000 hectares over 7 years by investing in Islamic countries such as Senegal, Mali, Sudan and Niger. To handle all these expected food imports, the Saudi government is building a new port at the Red Sea city of Jeddah.

Other Arab states looked at their deplenished larders in 2008 and took similar steps. Tiny Qatar, whose quarter of a million citizens have the highest per capita income in the world thanks to massive natural gas reserves, offered to build a deep-water port at the Tana River Delta in Kenya in exchange for cropland. It established diplomatic relations with Cambodia in 2008 so that it could discuss farming projects. More recently, it has tried to put a private sector face on its activities, using $1 billion from its sovereign wealth fund to create a new agricultural company, Hassad Food. This company has bought 250,000 hectares of prime farmland across Australia and is also looking at acquisitions in Brazil, Argentina, Uruguay, Sudan, Turkey, Cambodia, India, Pakistan and Georgia. By some estimates, Qatar now controls more land abroad than at home.

Almost every oil-rich Arab state has tried to get in on the action. Kuwait and Bahrain have been linked with land deals abroad. An official at the Ministry of Economy of the United Arab Emirates, which includes the emirates of Dubai and Abu Dhabi, spoke candidly in July 2012 about how 'the UAE has recently acquired and leased more than 1.5 million hectares of land suitable for plantation in Sudan, Eastern Europe and Asia, to maintain the country's food supplies in the face of progressively rising food prices'. And Libya, even as Colonel Gaddafi berated Western powers for their neo-colonial land grab, dusted off plans to develop a gigantic irrigated rice farm on the Niger River in Mali. In total, countries from the Middle East and North Africa are responsible for around one-sixth of the foreign land deals (by area) in the Land Matrix database.

Among the Asian countries, South Korea has been the boldest. Starting in 2009 the government allocated one-tenth of its agricultural budget to encourage Korean companies to acquire land abroad. 'Private companies will be in charge of investment,' a ministry official said, 'while the government and state-run corporation give technical support.' By March 2011, 60 companies were operating farms in 16 countries, mostly in eastern Russia, Southeast Asia and Brazil. For example, the world's largest shipbuilder, Hyundai Heavy Industries, operates a 10,000 hectare farm near Vladivostok in Russia. The government recently changed the metric it uses to assess food security from the 'self-sufficiency rate' – the amount of food grown at home – to the 'independence rate' – which also includes the amount grown by South Korean companies in other countries.

As far as officials are concerned, land acquired abroad might as well be Korean territory when it comes to measuring the security of food supply.

At the other end of the spectrum, far removed from officials worried about food security, investors with purely financial motives have been behind many land deals. The financial crash of 2008 devastated stock markets, bonds, commodity prices and real estate – all the standard asset classes for investment. The one sector that sailed through the crisis was agriculture. Buoyed by strong food prices, and attracting investment after decades of neglect, farm profits and land values rose. Investors wanted a piece of the action. Developing countries seemed to offer extra returns for those with an appetite for risk, as land was so cheap, even free. Investors familiar with the private equity model of buying struggling companies, turning them around and flipping them in a few years could see the parallel; in this case, they could acquire under-utilised land in poor countries, use their capital to introduce 'modern' farming techniques, and sell the productive enterprise later on for a big profit.

Pension funds, insurance companies and wealthy families, mostly from North America and Europe, queued up to spin this wheel. They acted through dozens of specialist investment funds. The *Wall Street Journal* counted forty-five private equity firms looking to raise over $2 billion to invest in African agriculture in 2010, with the largest number based in London. One of the most publicity-hungry was Emergent Asset Management, run by flame-haired Susan Payne, a former Goldman Sachs banker. 'Africa is the final frontier,' Payne explained after one investment conference. 'It's the one continent that remains relatively unexploited.' She told investors that investing in farmland in Africa would generate a return of 25 per cent annually – if true, certainly impressive in an era of near zero interest rates.

These investment funds are usually agnostic about whether their farms grow food for the local market or for export – whatever delivers the best price. In fact, in many developing countries it can be more profitable to sell in the domestic market, as tariffs and high transportation costs mean that local prices are higher than what the global commodity houses will pay at the nearest port.

Towards the middle of our spectrum, in between food-importing governments and purely financial investors, are global corporations looking for profit as well as security of supply. Land deals have been negotiated by the established commodity companies, in particular those that specialise in tropical plantation crops such as palm oil, sugar or rubber. These crops can be grown at scale. Considerable investment in processing facilities is needed to turn the raw material into a saleable product. Therefore, commodity corporates with large balance sheets can have an advantage when establishing new areas of production. We have already seen how Olam, Wilmar, Cargill, Glencore and Louis Dreyfus are stepping back along the supply chain, acquiring land and growing commodities. Many others are rushing to do the same thing.

One of the biggest pushes is coming from the large Asian palm oil producers. They are running out of space at home and turning to West Africa for expansion. In the biggest project to date, Malaysian company Sime Darby has allocated $800 million to develop a 200,000 hectare plantation in Liberia. 'It is increasingly difficult to acquire arable plantation land in Asia and thus it is imperative that new frontiers be sought to meet increasing demand,' said the company's chief executive, Ahmad Zubir Murshid. These companies have clear commercial motives but there is also a strategic element to their desire to acquire land. Worried about how to secure supplies in a resource-constrained world, they want to establish integrated supply chains ahead of the competition. Murshid added that one reason for doing the African deal was that Sime Darby would have 'first mover advantage over future entrants into Liberia in terms of securing choice land'.

Positioned closer to the purely financial end of the spectrum, there is a diverse group of companies that have studied the macro trends around food and believe they can make money by acquiring land in developing countries. We might call them 'commercial opportunists'. Many are new ventures. Swedish companies such as Black Earth Farming and Alpcot Agro have built up large holdings of land on the fertile soils of Russia and Ukraine. A flurry of biofuels companies emerged in 2005 and 2006 when governments in rich countries imposed mandates on the amount of fuel to be derived from biological material. Armed with ambitious prospectuses, small amounts of money and a few seedlings, these companies acquired concessions all over Africa and Asia, promising to grow vast quantities of jatropha, oil palm or sugar cane. Fifty companies, mostly from Britain, Italy, Germany, France and the USA, launched a hundred projects in more than twenty countries. As we shall see, few fared well.

This group of commercial operators also includes companies from emerging economies who see opportunity in the abundant lands and low yields of poorer countries. Brazilian firms are spreading into neighbouring Paraguay and Bolivia, clearing land and introducing mechanised farming. One of the largest Brazilian agribusinesses, SLC Agrícola, wants to recreate the 'miracle of the Cerrado' in lusophone Mozambique by growing soy and cotton. Of all the nationalities, Indian companies are perhaps the most numerous. They have been acquiring plots of land and setting up farming ventures to grow food for local markets and to export to India. East Africa is the main target: it is estimated that eighty Indian companies have invested more than $2 billion in land in Ethiopia alone. Unlike many European and American financiers, who jet in and out of projects and cannot quite give up the comforts of home, Indian entrepreneurs are willing to move to the most remote parts of the world, roll up their sleeves and make a real go of it – although this is still no guarantee of success.

Finally, this spectrum analysis would not be complete without a word on some of the most audacious, but probably least harmful, land grabbers. A few speculators have tried to lay claim to vast areas of land in the hope that they can one day turn their concessions into something valuable. They combine elements of nineteenth-century colonial adventurer, pantomime villain and Walter Mitty. It is not clear if they are exploiters of the poor, or if they are, in fact, being exploited by canny local elites who are happy to take their money and run. Nowhere has attracted them like the world's newest country, South Sudan, where it is claimed that 9 per cent of the land has been signed over to investment schemes. Few are more colourful than Philippe Heilberg of Jarch Capital.

Heilberg, a former New York commodity trader, first came to attention in 2009 when he announced to the world that he had leased 400,000 hectares of farmland in Unity State in South Sudan. His local business partner was the son of a former warlord, General Paulino Matip. The general was deputy commander of the Sudan People's Liberation Army, the national army in waiting. Although most land acquirers prefer to remain in the shadows, Heilberg sought the limelight, explaining his idiosyncratic business philosophy to the BBC and any journalist that would listen. *Rolling Stone* magazine ran a feature dubbing him the 'capitalist of chaos'. 'This is Africa,' Heilberg told the magazine. 'The whole place is like one big mafia. I'm like a mafia head.' He bragged to *Fortune* magazine that 'they can't change the laws on me, because I've got the guns ... As long as Gen. Matip is alive, my contract is good.' However, no one in Jarch Capital had any agricultural experience, and it was never clear how Heilberg intended to develop his massive concession. Both the governor of Unity State and the chairman of the South Sudan Land Commission said they had never heard of the deal. In 2012, following local protests, the President of South Sudan declared that land leases not authorised in the proper manner would be declared null and void. The Jarch project appears to have evaporated in the Sudanese heat. And Philippe Heilberg is no longer giving interviews.

You may have noticed that there is one country that has hardly appeared in this parade of land grabbers. I remember when I first started working on this book I fell into conversation with a man in a London pub. 'Ah yes, I have heard about these land grabs,' the citizen said as he put down his pint of ale. 'China is buying up farms in Africa, buying up the world.' I have had dozens of similar conversations since. Plenty of public officials seem to share this belief. Everybody knows that China is the world's chief land grabber, right?

This is where reality diverges the most from hype. Chinese firms have made some land acquisitions related to the commodities they import: soybean farms in Argentina, dairy farms in New Zealand, palm oil and rubber plantations in Southeast Asia. China's latest strategic plan for agricultural 'Going Out', released in early 2012, may herald a more aggressive strategy as it includes plans to create production bases in Brazil, Russia, the Philippines, Argentina and Canada. But China's activities in Africa have been limited. Although individual Chinese migrants and companies have been running small farms or livestock production units in Africa for many years, the official policy of the Chinese government is not to acquire large tracts of land. Rumours of mega-deals for millions of hectares of land in the Democratic Republic of Congo and Mozambique have been shown to be false when investigated. Instead, China has focused on running agricultural research stations to improve the productivity of local farmers – it has eleven training centres in Africa, employing more than 1,000 Chinese agricultural experts. The image of China as a rapacious grabber of African farmland says more about Western perceptions of China, and Western paranoia about China's economic rise, than it does about China itself.

Speculative deals that evaporate into thin air, Chinese deals that never existed – it is possible to exaggerate the extent of land grabs. Nonetheless, despite these caveats, there are still plenty of land deals out there that are all too real for the local communities affected. From the palaces of Riyadh to the glass towers of Wall Street, from the boardrooms of Mumbai to the trading floors of Singapore, a diverse group of states and companies are making large-scale acquisitions of farmland abroad, mostly in poor developing countries. It is impossible to put an exact figure on it, but there is no doubt that a large amount of land is involved. Overall, the hype is justified. The world has not seen cross-border land acquisition on this scale for at least a hundred years.

The nature of these deals is also different from before. For most of the twentieth century, foreign investment in agriculture in developing countries was confined to specialist cash crops that could only be grown in the tropics – rubber, tea, coffee, sugar, bananas. Even these sorts of investment were in decline since the 1960s, as newly independent states sought more control over their own resources. Now, land acquisition is back in vogue. Multinationals are rediscovering their love for the plantation business. Moreover, most land deals today focus not on tropical cash crops but on producing staple foods such as rice, wheat and maize. This is another feature that we have not seen since the wave of European colonisation in the nineteenth century.

Win-win or plain lose?

The proponents of large-scale land deals argue that they bring many benefits. The theory is that there are large areas of idle or under-utilised land in developing countries, barely producing any food. Foreign investors can provide the capital, technology, expertise and infrastructure needed to finally bring the agricultural revolutions of the twentieth century to these lands. This will produce more food for local markets, while generating a surplus that can be exported to the rest of the world. It will also create jobs for local communities, tax revenues for cash-strapped governments and better access to markets for small farmers as well. Most of the international organisations that deal with food security – such as the World Bank and FAO – have gone to great lengths to show how these deals, if done properly, can be 'win-win', delivering benefits for both foreign investors and target countries. They have invested a lot of time in developing a voluntary code to govern how these investments should be carried out.

However, the way in which many of these land deals have been designed and implemented makes it hard to see how local communities will benefit. As the story of Saudi Star in Gambella illustrates, it is a myth that there are vast areas of 'idle' or 'vacant' land in the world, suitable for cultivation. It is similar to the concept of *terra nullius* that past imperialists used to justify their occupation of distant territory, airbrushing indigenous people out of the picture. Almost all fertile land with adequate water is used by someone. It may look empty but this is probably because it is being left fallow as part of a shifting cultivation system, used by pastoralists to graze animals, or, in the case of woodland, used as a source of timber, wild food and medicines. The land may not be utilised to its full potential, compared with high–yield farming systems elsewhere, but it is not unused or unoccupied. When foreign developers take control of large areas of fertile land they are inevitably displacing someone.

Most of the claims to this type of land are undocumented and lie outside formal systems of land tenure. They take the form of customary rights, traditional rules for how communities, families or individuals can use land. These rights are well recognised at a local level even if they are absent from cadastral records in capital cities, where the land may be listed as belonging to the state. Up to 90 per cent of land in Africa is under this sort of customary tenure.

There are fair ways to negotiate the transfer of land between local communities and more powerful foreign investors. Prior consultation, free consent and fair compensation should all be involved. But many of the land deals taking place today do not follow these principles. They are often externally imposed by government officials who ignore customary land rights and make massive transfers at the stroke of a pen, or by local chiefs who have been seduced by the investor's chequebook and do not have the best interests of their people at heart. Many foreign investors engage in a sort of sham consultation with local people after the deal has been made – they have no intention of changing their plans. Or, in some cases, villagers only learn about land deals when the bulldozers arrive. The amount of compensation paid to local people for the loss of the land is usually minimal. If customary land rights are not recognised, host governments sometimes forcibly evict people without any compensation, calling them illegal 'squatters'.

The mantra of foreign investors is that it does not matter if local people lose access to the land as they can be employed in the new corporate farming operation. Better a secure, cash-paying job than the precarious existence of the subsistence farmer. This will also help transfer new farming skills to the host country and have lots of spillover benefits for the economy.

Unfortunately, it usually does not work this way. None of the grandiose claims about the creation of jobs have become a reality so far. Many large-scale agricultural projects never get from the planning phase to actual implementation – which makes job creation impossible. The highly mechanised, input-intensive farming system that most foreign investors want to introduce – replicating the norm in the USA or Brazil – is not likely to create much employment even when fully operational. And the few people employed need skills that local farmers usually do not have, which is why so many commercial farming projects in Africa use imported labour from Pakistan, India, South Africa, Zimbabwe or Australia. Local farmers who lose access to land are more likely to find themselves outside the fence looking in, rather than driving a million-dollar tractor and learning to farm like an Iowan. Local shopkeepers do not benefit much either, as foreign investors tend to rely on imported inputs and machinery, rather than spending money in the country.

Land grabs can also cause considerable environmental damage. The clearing of forests for new oil palm plantations in West Africa has led to flooding and soil erosion in surrounding areas. Cambodian farmers downstream from new sugar plantations have found their crops and animals poisoned by chemicals. Industrial farming systems can destroy soil fertility: indeed, because they do not own the land, yet receive huge concession areas, land grabbers are almost encouraged to mine the soil before moving on to a new plot. Perhaps the most contentious issue is water. It has been rightly pointed out that many of the recent deals are more 'water grabs' than land grabs.

A large number involve drawing water from rivers or lakes for irrigation, or draining wetlands. This can have a negative impact on downstream users. For example, large-scale irrigated rice projects on the Niger River, funded by Libya, China and the USA, aim to triple the amount of water extracted. This will dry and shrink the Niger Delta downstream, a gigantic wetland in the desert that supports hundreds of thousands of fishers, farmers and cattle herders. All food production carries environmental risk but foreign schemes in countries with weak governments are more likely than most to ignore environmental externalities.

Foreign land deals risk undermining the food security of poor rural communities in target countries. Governments and global corporations looking for security of supply intend to export as much of the food as possible – which means that local soil, water and nutrients will be exploited for the benefit of others. Even if the food is sold in local markets, communities displaced by the commercial farms may not be able to afford it. The loss of access to land and water may remove the only livelihood they have, and the economic spillover effects of the commercial farms may be limited. We saw in an earlier chapter how the amount of food produced is only a minor factor in determining whether people go hungry – it has much more to do with access to natural resources, the ability to earn income, and the distribution of wealth and power. Therefore, an approach that only focuses on maximising production may do little to enhance the food security of the poor. In fact, it may do more harm than good. The major World Bank report on the subject concludes that 'the risks associated with such investments are immense'.

The patent injustice of so many recent land deals has caused a vigorous backlash. The Anuak attack on farm workers in Ethiopia is just the most bloody example. In many developing countries, especially in Africa, land has cultural, sentimental and political meaning. It is a reminder of past dispossession, a symbol of present dignity and a source of future security. The threat of displacement has mobilised peasant groups and local communities to resist. Local opposition has been matched by a campaign by foreign journalists and NGOs to bring attention to this issue. Organisations such as GRAIN, The Oakland Institute, Oxfam, Welthungerhilfe and the International Land Coalition have written reports with attention-grabbing headlines. One journalist described how land grabbing was the 'hot button issue' at the World Food Summit hosted by the UN's FAO in Rome in November 2009. Every time there is an investment conference on the theme of agriculture it attracts a hardy band of protesters, condemning the land grabbers inside. This has been enough to scare many European and American financial institutions away from investing in agriculture in poor countries. The reputational risk is just too high.

Ironically, the campaigners may be doing these investors a favour. This is because many of these land deals are not only unjust; they also do not make economic sense. Local opposition is one reason. It is very difficult to implement a complex project across a large area of land in a remote part of the world if local people are actively opposed. Erecting fences and employing guards is expensive and ineffectual. Things go missing; machines are sabotaged; farmers drive their herds at night through newly planted fields. Physical attacks impede operations: one American farm owner in Ethiopia had to order a medical evacuation when his manager, whom he described as 'too aggressive in the culture', was hit on the back of the head with an axe. It is hard to grow food or to make money in that type of hostile environment.

Local opposition can also force host governments, who were once so welcoming to foreign investors, to change course. The determination of the President of South Sudan to cancel speculative land deals has already been noted. The Qatar project in the Tana River Delta in Kenya stalled after local pastoralists and environmental groups fought against it. In Madagascar, news that the Korean firm Daewoo Logistics had signed a deal to lease 1.3 million hectares of the country's arable land to grow maize and palm oil precipitated a coup that toppled the government. The first act of the new government was to cancel the Daewoo contract (and another deal involving an Indian company). The new minister for agriculture in Tanzania is taking a much harder line on foreign investment in land, stating that under-performing projects will be cancelled and higher rents charged. Foreign investors may think they have protection in the form of contracts and international investment agreements, but paper will not count for much if a regime changes.

There is also a more fundamental economic reason why many of the grandiose farming schemes are doomed to failure. Foreign investors tend to work from the same template. Their plan is to recreate mechanised, 'modern' farming systems on large areas of land in the developing world. The claim is that this will deliver 'economies of scale'. But there are some flaws in this thinking. The 'modern' farming systems of the USA, Brazil or Australia have developed in that way for a reason. Namely, capital in these countries is cheap compared to labour, which means that it makes sense to invest in labour-saving technology. Even still, more than 95 per cent of farms in these countries are run by owner-operators – they are still family farms – and average farm size is less than 200 hectares. This is because all the academic research shows that there are few economies of scale in agriculture. In fact, land management has *dis*economies of scale. The bigger the area the less a manager can know about microvariations in soil, vegetation and climate across it. A large area also means hiring staff who may not be as motivated as an owner-operator – supervising them is costly. The only economies of scale in agriculture tend to be in acquiring machinery and inputs such as fertilisers and chemicals (bigger operators can negotiate better prices), in obtaining finance and in marketing (more volume equals better bargaining power with buyers).

Conditions are very different in sub-Saharan Africa to the USA or Brazil. Land and labour are plentiful and cheap. Conversely, getting machinery and inputs to remote farms is extremely expensive – and the ability to order in bulk does not greatly lower the cost. Economies of scale may also not count for much when it comes to marketing crops, as the main obstacle is not the ability to negotiate a good price but the cost and feasibility of transport when there are no good roads, railways or navigable rivers. Few investors are big enough – or altruistic enough – to build hundreds of kilometres of roads. The large commercial farming schemes, therefore, seem to have things back to front. Rather than making the most of the local factors of production that are cheap – land and labour – they rely on capital-intensive machinery and inputs that will be costly to deliver. They try to impose a first-world farming system on a social and economic environment that could not be more alien. It is like trying to drive a Ferrari on a mountain track.

One project that is starting to exhibit these economic strains can be found a few miles away from Saudi Star's property in Ethiopia. It is under the control of a flamboyant Indian businessman named Sai Ramakrishna Karuturi. Six-foot tall and immaculately moustached, he was thrown out of six schools as a boy before gaining an engineering degree from Bangalore University and an MBA in the USA. By 2008 he had overseen an unlikely corporate metamorphosis, turning a family-run cable business in Bangalore, Karuturi Global, into the world's largest exporter of roses. Some of these roses came from greenhouses in highland Ethiopia.

In April 2008 Karuturi Global was offered a chance to lease a massive 300,000 hectares of land in Gambella to grow crops, for an annual rent of $1.15 per hectare. The company had no experience of arable farming. When Karuturi's father, who served as chairman, travelled to Gambella to negotiate with officials he concluded that it was too risky to take over a piece of land that was seventy-two kilometres from side to side. But he was over-ridden. 'Sign it right now,' his son shouted over the phone from Addis Ababa. 'I want it signed and sealed before they change their mind.' To him, it was too good an opportunity to miss. Karuturi boasted that he would soon be the biggest farmer in the world, producing cereals, rice and sugar and generating more than $500 million in profit every year. He brought in farmers from the Punjab, the USA, Uruguay and Australia to help him achieve this vision.

Since then, the project has endured a catalogue of mishaps. Karuturi imported Indian-made tractors to clear the land of trees and scrub, but they were not powerful enough, broke down frequently and had to be replaced by much more expensive American machines − 50 of them at a cost of $1 million each. After much delay, the company planted a maize crop in 2011, but the $15 million crop was washed away by floods. This came as no surprise to local villagers who showed Karuturi the water marks on trees from previous years. 'We were caught napping,' he admits. As a result, Dutch engineers were brought in to build a system of dykes and canals. The latest problem is the discovery that the property sits on the migration route of a million antelope, who naturally regard freshly planted crops as an 'all you can eat' buffet. The company is erecting a massive solar-powered electric fence to keep them out.

All told, by mid-2012 Karuturi had only prepared 12,000 hectares of land, without harvesting a substantial crop. The company had spent $128 million along the way. This works out at more than $10,000 per hectare, which is more than it would cost to buy an average piece of farmland in the USA. Karuturi is now approaching banks and trying to raise a loan of $250 million to complete the development, but the strains are starting to show. Karuturi Global's stock price has fallen 60 per cent since it started the Ethiopian farming venture. One visitor to the farm heard a frustrated Karuturi shout at a farm manager: 'I want crops. I want production. Come to the [Annual General Meeting] and see how investors roast me.'

At the time of writing Karuturi was still in the ring, fighting, but many other project developers have already slinked away in defeat. Most notably, practically every biofuels project launched with such fanfare a few years ago has now collapsed. Three examples from Tanzania tell the same dismal story. A UK venture, Sun Biofuels, folded in 2011 after investing $34 million over five years in a jatropha project. A Dutch firm, Bioshapes, spent almost $10 million on 34,000 hectares of land for jatropha, but only managed to plant 285 hectares before going bust in 2010. A large ethanol project set up by Swedish company SEKAB met a similar fate. The charity Action Aid has identified at least 30 abandoned biofuels projects in 15 African countries. It turned out that jatropha, the supposed wonder crop that would flourish on marginal land, only grew well on fertile soils, with plenty of water and fertiliser. Developers woefully underestimated the amount of work required to clear and plant thousands of hectares, especially where there was local opposition.

All across the world, land deals have stalled or collapsed. World Bank researchers found that farming had only started in 21 per cent of the schemes they investigated. 'This lag in implementation,' they found, 'was normally attributed to unanticipated technical difficulties, reduced profitability, changed market conditions, or tensions with local communities.' Unfortunately, failed deals still leave a trail of destruction in their wake. Communities have been cleared off their land and promised jobs on new plantations, only to see work stop and investors disappear. Large areas remain leased to foreign companies, which means locals cannot regain possession. If they do occupy the land illegally, this creates even more confusion between formal and customary rights. The land is in limbo. Sometimes, it seems, the only thing worse than a land grab is a *failed* land grab.

For those who understand the history of large-scale commercial farming ventures in Africa, these developments are not surprising. The last sixty years are replete with similar failures. After the Arab oil embargo of the 1970s, when the USA threatened to withhold food supplies, Saudi Arabia funded the establishment of mechanised farms for sorghum and sesame in central Sudan. Yields were poor, many farms were abandoned, and the forcible displacement of thousands of smallholders helped spark civil war in Sudan in 1983. In the same decade, the Canadian government funded the creation of state wheat farms in Tanzania – nomadic pastoralists now fight with local villagers over who should occupy the long-abandoned farms. The British government's development agency, the Commonwealth Development Corporation, recently conducted an assessment of its 179 investments in agribusiness over the past 50 years and found that two-thirds failed to produce adequate financial returns. Large-scale farming estates performed the worst.

It is striking how many of the recent land deals involve the acquisition of farms or infrastructure that were part of previous schemes – the Soviet-built dam in Gambella is just one example. Foreign investors are literally picking their way past rusted machinery and weathered signs, relics of past failures, when they arrive on their newly acquired land, full of grand visions. You would think it would give them cause for reflection.

In future, only three types of land deals are likely to survive. The first are smaller, humbler schemes that make a genuine effort to integrate with local farmers and produce real benefits for local communities. Rather than blindly trying to recreate Iowa or Mato Grosso in Africa, they will champion farming systems that make economic sense given local conditions. They will focus more on food staples for domestic markets, which are typically bigger than export markets in any case. And, as we shall see in the next chapter, land may be the least important part of these projects. They will focus just as much on infrastructure, processing and access to markets. There is a role for foreign investment in this, so long as investors are sufficiently patient and have realistic return expectations.

The second type of deal that may survive consists of commercial plantations for tropical commodities such as palm oil or sugar cane. These commodities require significant investment in processing facilities in order to unlock their value for world markets. Production is quite simple and does not suffer from diseconomies of scale like mainstream farming. Demand is growing quickly and at current prices production can be lucrative. These commodities can be grown most profitably in tropical developing countries. However, large-scale plantations that displace local communities, and do not produce real development benefits, will only be able to operate if local opposition is suppressed. Foreign investors can sometimes rely on compliant host governments and local elites to deploy force in this way. This may produce an economic return for investors but it will be ugly. It will not be for investors who genuinely care about corporate responsibility.

Finally, some of the uneconomic large-scale farming projects may survive. There are land grabbers who want to achieve security of supply at any price. They do not care whether the farming system makes economic sense. For example, when Saudi farmers were pumping aquifers dry to grow wheat at home, they received government subsidies worth five times the value of the crop. Therefore, Saudi Arabia may not mind funnelling hundreds of millions of dollars into expensive farming projects abroad. Operating these farms will require the suppression of local dissent. But, again, countries seeking food security for their own citizens may not be unduly sensitive about the rights of local communities in other parts of the world. Governments and parastatal companies with deep pockets and strategic motivations will continue to develop large farming estates in poor corners of the world so long as they are worried about the reliability of global food markets.

If this process continues, we may see the emergence of farming 'enclaves', where staff are flown in and out, locals are excluded and the majority of food is exported – with the connivance of local elites. Many oil and mining projects in Africa today are operated in this way, as 'states within states' completely separated from the local economy or society. For example, there is an ExxonMobil compound in Equatorial Guinea that has a Texan number as its local dialling code. Saudi investors appear to have a similar vision for their agricultural investments. In April 2012 the chairman of the Jeddah Chamber of Commerce, Saleh Kamel, announced that the Sudanese government had agreed to give up more than 800,000 hectares of farmland so that Saudi Arabia could develop a safe and steady food supply. Khartoum would make the land a free zone that is not subject to any form of taxation or duties and not covered by Sudanese laws. This sounds more like a Saudi colony than a commercial farming investment.

The Saudi Star farm in Gambella, where we began this chapter, is starting to look like a well-guarded enclave already. According to Anuak activists, the Ethiopian authorities responded to the attack on farm workers with a brutal crackdown, killing five local villagers. Ethiopian police and military now provide constant protection to the Saudi farm – one journalist likened it to an 'armed camp'. Saudi Star executives have taken the killings in their stride. 'Things are normalised. All our contractors are back to work,' the chief executive said from the safety of his office in Addis Adaba. There are no plans to change course. Indeed, in April 2012 it was announced that Al Almoudi had leased even more farmland in the northwestern region of Benishangul-Gumuz.

Committed land grabbers are seeing their plans through. The real test will come when the host country of one of these projects suffers an internal food crisis, due to a drought or crop failure. Will people stand by and watch trucks full of grain leave for the ports? Could any government or security apparatus prevent a popular revolt? Kofi Annan has said that it is 'a terrible business model' because 'to believe that if there is hunger at the doorstep the population will let you take [the food] away is itself naïve'. Yet, if there is a global shortage at the same time, what about the needs of the investor country that relies on these exports? Will it agree to forgo the food grown on its land when this is the reason it made the investment in the first place? What sort of pressure or inducements could it apply to local elites? This is a potentially explosive situation.

FEELING THE SQUEEZE
Amount of arable land available per person in 2050, hectares

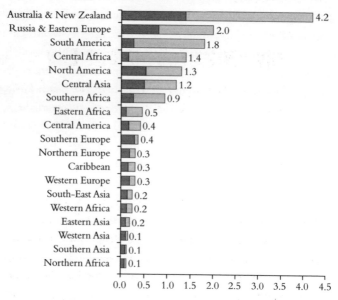

Australia & New Zealand 4.2
Russia & Eastern Europe 2.0
South America 1.8
Central Africa 1.4
North America 1.3
Central Asia 1.2
Southern Africa 0.9
Eastern Africa 0.5
Central America 0.4
Southern Europe 0.4
Northern Europe 0.3
Caribbean 0.3
Western Europe 0.3
South-East Asia 0.2
Western Africa 0.2
Eastern Asia 0.2
Western Asia 0.1
Southern Asia 0.1
Northern Africa 0.1

0.0 0.5 1.0 1.5 2.0 2.5 3.0 3.5 4.0 4.5

■ Currently cultivated land □ Available new land

1 hectare is about as big as 1½ football fields

Note: Total available land includes currently cultivated land plus all suitable forested and non-forested land outside protected areas

Source: Land data from IIASA, GAEZ 2009; population data from UN Population Division, World Population Prospects: the 2010 revision

10

HOW THIS STORY MIGHT END

*Dangerous trends, nightmare outcomes and the
geopolitics of food in the twenty-first century*

Earlier in this book we saw that there was no biophysical
reason why we could not feed a world of 9 billion people in
2050. Indeed, there is enough food to feed that many today.
But just because we can does not mean we will. It depends on
how food is distributed and priced, and whether people can
access and afford it. So far, as a species, we have spectacularly
failed to construct a just global food system – this is why one
in eight people go hungry while one in five are overweight.
Judging by the way the world responded to the recent crisis,
this will not change any time soon. When food inventories
ran low and prices spiked, nations and corporations tried to
manipulate markets to serve their own interests and scrambled
to establish control over food production resources.

How will these trends play out between now and 2050?
Predicting the future is a risky business but I suggest that three
things are likely to happen if we continue on the current path.
First, the imbalances within the global food system will widen,
which will put even more pressure on trade. Second, the way
this trade is conducted will be shaped by powerful states, as
food becomes a more important geopolitical issue. Third, we

are on the verge of an historic wave of agricultural expansion that will draw hitherto isolated parts of the world into the global food economy. This chapter will sketch out the implications of these developments. It will present some scenarios for how the global food system may evolve over the next forty years. Although not inevitable, it is possible to envisage scenarios that produce bleak outcomes for many people.

Widening imbalances

As we have seen, the biophysical potential of the planet for food production means there should be enough food to go around at a global level. But the picture looks very different from country to country. If we lay down all the trends that affect food security – population growth, ecosystem constraints, climate change, economic development and political systems – it emerges that some regions will be in a good position to feed their people, perhaps even to generate food surpluses. Others will face large food deficits. The gaps between the 'haves' and 'have nots' will widen. This will affect the composition of the five 'food blocs' outlined in Chapter Two. There will be winners and losers.

The USA and Canada will be among the big winners in the evolving food system. Populations are growing in North America, but there is still a large reserve of fertile land that can be brought into cultivation, and there may still be room to improve crop yields. Although parts of the American West are expected to suffer from reduced rainfall as the climate changes, the prime grain-growing areas will be less affected between now and 2050, and the zone of cultivation should shift northwards as temperatures increase. North America will continue to produce a massive food surplus, as it has for the past 150 years.

Nonetheless, North America's share of food trade will continue to fall, as the world comes to rely more on other regions as well. The industrialised exporting countries, Australia and New Zealand, are likely to grow their exports as more land is converted to agriculture (for example, in sub-tropical northern Australia), although this will be partly offset by a drying climate. Emerging Asian exporters such as Thailand, Vietnam and Myanmar may struggle to increase production, as there is little new land available for cultivation. The countries of the former Soviet Union, in particular Ukraine, Kazakhstan and Russia, have more potential. They could bring millions of hectares of fertile land into production and double their grain yields. A shrinking and ageing population should, in theory, create greater food surpluses – Russia is expected to have 16 million fewer people by 2050. Climate change could improve growing conditions in the north of the vast Russian land mass. Conversely, climate variability will probably lead to spectacular crop failures as well, so exports will gyrate from year to year.

The region with the greatest potential is undoubtedly South America. It has vast amounts of suitable land in reserve, even without touching the rainforests. Yields are still only half of what is physically attainable given the soils and the climate. The population of this region is expected to grow from 397 million now to 488 million in 2050, which is slow by historical standards. So, there should be plenty of surpluses for the rest of the world. Climate change may cause problems in some areas, for example northeast Brazil, but there are parts of this vast continent, for example Argentina and Uruguay, that may benefit. Most importantly, South America is already on the right trajectory, increasing food production and exports year on year. This shows that it has the social, political and economic capital necessary to realise its biophysical potential. South American countries, and especially Brazil, are best positioned to take advantage of the opportunities created by the new global food economy.

Asia will consume an ever larger share of exports from South America and other breadbaskets. Japan and South Korea will remain major buyers on world markets, although they will see a moderation in food demand as their populations age and decline. But it is the fast-growing Asian economies that will account for most new demand. They are unlikely to return to self-sufficiency any time soon.

The biggest economy is, of course, China. How dependent will it become on food imports? Some alarmists argue that China will eventually face a collapse in internal food production because of falling water tables, soil erosion, pollution and climate change, meaning that the country will have to fling itself on world markets for survival. This is overdone. China faces serious environmental problems but it is taking steps to address them. Climate science does not predict terrible changes for China; indeed, some models indicate that conditions for agriculture could improve. The country still achieves impressive increases in grain production year on year. Above all, demographics are on China's side: its population is expected to *fall* by 50 million between now and 2050 and then drop below 1 billion by 2100. China will import more food not because it is starving but because its wealthier population has more expensive tastes.

Instead, the region that we should be worried about is South Asia. This encompasses Pakistan, Bangladesh, Iran, Afghanistan and Nepal, as well as the largest country, India. The population of this region is set to explode from 1.7 billion today to 2.4 billion in 2050 – equal to all the people in the world in 1950. India alone will have an extra 450 million people, making it by far the most populous country in the world. There will be 400 million more Indians than Chinese in the world in 40 years' time.

Almost every environmental indicator for South Asia flashes red. About nine-tenths of all the suitable land is already being cultivated. By 2050 the region will have just 0.07 hectares of arable land per person, the lowest in the world. The crucial wheat-growing Punjab region is threatened by falling water tables and loss of soil fertility. Climate change is expected to scorch the heavily populated plains that stretch from Pakistan to Bangladesh, while disrupting the flow of the Ganges, the Indus and the Brahmaputra, which irrigate millions of hectares of cropland. Rising sea levels will encroach upon the crowded river deltas of Bangladesh. The one bright spot is that crop yields are less than half of what is technically possible, on a par with South America. But people will need to squeeze everything they can out of the land to have any chance of feeding themselves.

Far more likely is that South Asian countries will become major food importers. The consulting firm McKinsey & Company predicts that India will be importing 15 per cent of its grains by 2030 (compared to just 5 per cent for China). The sheer size of India means this will have an enormous impact on global food trade, especially if the failure of a monsoon causes a spike in imports in a particular year. The ripples sent out by China's recent dabbling in world markets may be as nothing compared to the waves caused by more than 2 billion hungry South Asian consumers.

Just as many populous Asian countries are likely to slide further away from self-sufficiency, other nations that already import food will have to import a lot more. Chief among these are the countries of North Africa and Western Asia, effectively the Arab world. The population of this region is expected to grow by 60 per cent between now and 2050, rising from 450 million to 720 million. There is only 0.10 hectares of arable land per person in this region, and there is little additional land that can be brought into cultivation. Moreover, this is the most water-stressed part of the world. Aquifers are being pumped at unsustainable rates, and there is growing competition for the waters of the Nile, the Tigris and the Euphrates. Climate change will dry out the region even more. The Arab nations make up only 5 per cent of the world's population, yet they consume more than 20 per cent of the world's grain exports today. Their massive food deficit is set to widen.

Where will the European Union fit into this evolving food system? The answer is not straightforward. Much of its good land is already being used, yields in core member states are already close to the maximum, and biofuels could swallow up more crops in the future. On the other hand, climate change impacts in the next forty years will be limited (outside the Mediterranean countries), new member states such as Poland and Romania have untapped agricultural potential, and a shrinking population should lead to more food surpluses. Higher food prices could encourage renewed investment in farming, while changes to subsidies – away from payments for holding land – could create stronger incentives for production. As a result, the European Union has some choice about its food future. Nevertheless, it is probably safest to assume that its position in the global food system will not change greatly – it will continue to export small amounts of wheat, meat, dairy and luxury foods, while sucking in large shipments of grains, oilseeds and other raw commodities.

And what of sub-Saharan Africa? Its fate is the hardest to predict because the trends shaping global food production will pull the region in different directions. On the one hand, sub-Saharan Africa will undergo extraordinary population growth. The number of people will more than double, from 878 million today to almost 2 billion in 2050. Most of this growth is locked in because of the huge number of young people already in these societies. Many African countries are beset by environmental challenges such as soil degradation, desertification, deforestation, water scarcity and recurring droughts. The region is expected to be one of the worst hit by climate change: for example, one study predicts that agricultural productivity in Southern Africa could fall by one-third between now and 2050. Alongside the environmental problems, many African countries have poor infrastructure, weak states and unproductive farming sectors. Sub-Saharan Africa is Ground Zero for many of the food production challenges discussed in this book.

On the other hand, sub-Saharan Africa has enormous potential to increase its food production. It vies with South America as the land bank for the world. In theory, it has more than 750 million hectares of suitable land that could be brought into cultivation, which is almost half all the arable land in use today globally. In Mozambique, Tanzania and Zambia, for instance, less than one-eighth of the potential farmland is actually cultivated. This means that the amount of arable land per person could be maintained even as the population doubles. Moreover, the 'yield gap' on cultivated land – the difference between what farmers actually grow and what they could grow using better techniques – is the highest in the world. African farmers could double or triple their yields and still be well below the theoretical maximum.

Sub-Saharan Africa is, therefore, a conundrum. If its agricultural sector does not improve, the region could suffer under the twin scourges of population growth and environmental change and become a massive net importer of food. Alternatively, if sub-Saharan Africa uses its natural resources to the full potential, it could not only satisfy its own needs but could become a breadbasket for the rest of the world. How this conundrum is resolved will be a major factor in determining the shape of the global food system in the twenty-first century.

The geopolitics of food

Irrespective of how Africa develops, one thing is clear. The imbalances in the global food system are set to grow. There will be an ever greater divergence between where food is grown and where it is needed. As a result, there will be greater pressure on trade to fill the gap. How will this trade be conducted? Through open markets and global cooperation? Unfortunately, the evidence provided by the response to the recent food crisis points in a different direction. Trapped in a Prisoner's Dilemma, food producers imposed taxes, quotas and bans on exports in an attempt to reduce domestic prices, while food importers hoarded food and panic purchased at almost any price. Private markets malfunctioned, as financial speculators magnified volatility and made it harder to manage risk. Canny commodity traders profited handsomely from the turmoil. The response of states and corporations was to try to establish captive supply chains, bypassing normal markets. They went all the way upstream in an effort to claim the ultimate means of production – land and water. The food crisis sparked a scramble for resources, the likes of which have not been seen for a hundred years.

One thing is clear from this response: food importing nations no longer trust open markets to provide. This is hardly surprising. Trade in food has never been free. Even the neo-liberal project of the 1980s only succeeded in reducing the food trade barriers of weaker developing countries. It barely dented the subsidies of Europe or North America, and never succeeded in convincing China or India to open their markets to a global free for all. The turmoil of recent years, and the shift from an era of abundance to one of relative scarcity, has only reaffirmed the belief of governments that food security is too important to be left to the market.

The Greek philosopher Socrates said that 'no man qualifies as a statesman who is entirely ignorant of the problem of wheat'. This will be truer than ever during the twenty-first century. We are at the beginning of a period when there will be intense competition over who has access to food and how the profits from it are shared. Food is set to become a much more important geopolitical issue. Those countries that produce agricultural surpluses will gain additional leverage. For countries that cannot produce enough to feed their people, food security will become a key driver for foreign policy. Some will have the wealth or power to secure what they need, while others could find themselves in a precarious position.

One country that stands to benefit is the USA, as it will continue to be the world's biggest food exporter for many years to come. In the past, control over food was an important diplomatic and military weapon for Washington. In both the First and Second World Wars, the USA denied supplies to its enemies and diverted food to its Allies on preferential terms. Commodity trading firms were forced to act under the instruction of the US government as the international grain trade became a 'public utility'. During the Cold War, Washington used subsidies to supply client states with cheap food, turning off the tap when unfriendly regimes came into power. When prices spiked during the early 1970s, American officials tried to extract political advantage by negotiating grain deals with the governments of the USSR, Poland and Japan. In 1980 President Carter withheld 15 million tonnes of American grain from the Soviet Union in retaliation for the invasion of Afghanistan.

More recently, this sort of food diplomacy has gone out of fashion. Washington made no attempt to control food exports when prices spiked in 2008 or 2012. The USA also shied away from using food as a weapon against its enemies. For example, the USA continues to sell food to Iran despite imposing wide-ranging sanctions on the country because of its nuclear programme. The value of total American exports to Iran actually rose by one-third from 2011 to 2012, chiefly because of grain sales. Lobbying by farmers and commodity traders (such as Cargill and Archer Daniels Midland) has helped keep every market open to American food.

Yet, in the event of war or serious crisis, control over a large proportion of the world's food exports will be a powerful weapon. It is bound to play a role in the country's complex relationship with China. In 2011, for the first time, China became the biggest single importer of American agricultural products. China spent $20 billion on imports from the USA that year. Soybeans are now the USA's second-biggest export to China, topping aircraft, cars and semiconductors. The American agricultural system, like its military strategy, is pivoting towards Asia.

A concrete manifestation can be seen at the Port of Longview in the Pacific Northwest, where huge silos have gone up as part of a $210 million grain export terminal, the first such facility to be built in the country for 25 years. Traditionally, US food surpluses were barged down the Mississippi River to ports on the Gulf of Mexico. Now, the growing volume of soybeans and maize destined for China is driving a reconfiguration of the transportation system. Billions of dollars are being invested in transcontinental railroads so that 100-car trains can take harvests directly from the Midwest to the Pacific coast.

Agriculture is one of the few bright spots in the USA's lopsided economic relationship with Beijing, helping to balance out a yawning trade deficit in manufactured goods. In the event of a political crisis, for example over Taiwan, American control of a large proportion of China's food imports could provide leverage. However, it will also create co-dependence, further enmeshing the two countries in each other's economies. Chinese consumers need American agricultural products, but American farmers also need the Chinese market and will be reluctant to give it up.

An era of relative scarcity should give emerging food exporters such as Brazil, Argentina, Russia and Ukraine a stronger hand in global affairs. The challenge for these countries will be reconciling competing domestic interests. Farmers and the rural economy will benefit from higher food prices and strong export demand. But consumers and the urban economy may suffer as domestic prices go up. Because households in many of these countries still spend a substantial share of their income on food, there will be calls for export restrictions, so that more of the agricultural surplus stays at home.

The outcome of this struggle will be determined by the relative influence of urban and rural lobbies. In Argentina, for example, the populist Kirchner government, which draws most of its support from the urban working class, is pursuing cheap food policies at the expense of farmers, imposing crippling export controls on beef and grains. Brazil, by contrast, where the agriculture sector has more political clout, has refrained from restricting exports. Availability on international markets, therefore, will sometimes depend on the *domestic* politics of food.

Food importing nations will seek to reduce these political risks by diversifying their sources of supply. The Chinese government is aware of the dangers of becoming too dependent on American food. It is therefore forging strategic relationships with a wide range of food exporters by signing trade agreements, providing low-cost loans, investing in local companies and agreeing currency swaps (so as to help position the Renminbi as a currency of international trade). This 'Going Out' strategy is part of a global Chinese effort to secure natural resources, not least in the energy and mining sectors.

One of the most interesting Chinese initiatives came to light at the end of 2012. Since 2008 China has offered a series of massive commodity-backed loans to countries in South America and Africa. They receive billions of dollars of infra-structure finance, while guaranteeing repayment in the form of raw materials, usually oil. In 2012 China extended this model to food. The Export-Import Bank of China agreed a $3 billion loan-for-crops deal with the government of Ukraine. Under this arrangement, Ukraine will receive much-needed finance to purchase agricultural technologies and inputs, and, in return, China will receive 3 million tonnes of Ukrainian maize each year. China is not trying to get food on the cheap – the value of the maize will be set according to prevailing market prices. Instead, China's goal is to secure a reliable line of supply outside of normal market channels.

Other wealthy food importers – such as Japan, South Korea, India and the oil-rich Arab states – will continue their efforts to secure supplies, whether by constructing integrated supply chains or going all the way upstream and acquiring land. Although this activity will be largely carried out by private companies, it will be encouraged and sometimes financed by governments as part of national food security policies. In this form of state capitalism, the lines between public and private will remain blurred.

We are likely to see more food alliances between importers and exporters. Just as oil dependency defined international relationships in the twentieth century, food trade will bind countries together in this century. The importance of these relationships will become clear in times of crisis. During the recent food crisis, countries that imposed export restrictions often made exceptions for allies or client states. For example, India exempted Bangladesh and Bhutan from its rice export ban, allowing stocks to flow at below the prevailing market price. Food importers will look to establish privileged relationships with suppliers so that they get first call during times of scarcity. Government to government deals will be common.

If food production is tied up in captive supply chains, long-term contracts and government to government deals, there will be less food available for open exchange. Global food markets may become thinner and more residual. When we add to this the other factors explored in this book – more extreme weather, less elastic demand, the coupling of food and energy prices, uncontrolled financial speculation – the result can only be extra volatility on international food markets. More frequent and more extreme price shocks will become the norm.

The losers in this scenario will be poor countries that lack the natural resources to feed their growing populations and do not have the wealth or political influence to secure supplies from abroad. They will have to make do with the crumbs that fall from the top table. According to FAO projections, under a business as usual scenario net imports of cereals by developing countries will more than double from 135 million tonnes in 2008/09 to 300 million tonnes by 2050. These countries will be highly exposed to international price shocks. A sudden rise in food prices will place a huge strain on their balance of payments, especially as it is likely to be accompanied by a simultaneous rise in energy prices. It will cripple the spending power of households that already allocate most of their income to food. Ultimately, price spikes will lead to more hunger, illness and premature death among the poorest sections of society unless safety nets are in place.

Higher food prices will also lead to conflict. In a recent report on 'Food Prices and Political Instability', two researchers from the International Monetary Fund provided empirical proof for something that most people intuitively knew. After studying the impact of variations in international food prices on 120 countries between 1970 and 2007, they found that increases in food prices in poor countries led to 'a significant deterioration of democratic institutions' and 'a significant increase in the incidence of anti-government demonstrations, riots, and civil conflict'. Or, as Bob Marley put it in one of his songs, 'A hungry mob is an angry mob.'

This instability is unlikely to stay within national borders. Hungry mobs tend to move to where food is available. This is already playing out in the West African Sahel, a belt of semi-arid land along the southern edge of the Sahara Desert. For decades the region has suffered from drought, soil degradation and rapid population growth. Many people have moved south, seeking land in better-watered areas. Since the late 1960s, 5 million people from Burkina Faso and Mali have migrated to neighbouring Côte d'Ivoire. The country fell into civil war in 2002, largely because of the uneasy relations between immigrants and local people and the growing shortage of land. This may be a sign of things to come. The Stern Report commissioned by the UK Treasury estimated that by the middle of the century 200 million people could be permanently displaced 'climate migrants'.

Military strategists and intelligence analysts take these threats seriously. A few years ago, the US National Intelligence Council, the body that provides long-range strategic analysis for the American intelligence community, issued a much-quoted report called 'Global Trends 2025'. It identifies food security as a major strategic issue in the coming decades. It describes how 21 countries, with a combined population of about 600 million, are already suffering from cropland or fresh-water scarcity, and how 36 countries, with about 1.4 billion people, are projected to fall into this category by 2025. Most of these countries can be found within an 'arc of instability' stretching from sub-Saharan Africa through North Africa, into the Middle East, the Balkans, the Caucasus, and South and Central Asia, and parts of Southeast Asia. These are countries with fast-growing populations, where most people are below the age of eighteen years. They are the countries most susceptible to conflict. A food price shock is the sort of spark that could set them alight. The blowback will be felt all around the world.

The final frontier

The 'arc of instability' drawn by the US National Intelligence Council includes countries that have abundant resources of land and water but are not using them to their full potential. Most are found in sub-Saharan Africa. In so far as they rely on food imports, they are vulnerable to the same price shocks as other countries that are not blessed with such natural endowments. Yet, they are also subject to another risk – exploitation, even colonialisation, by outsiders.

As we have seen, there is no biophysical reason why we cannot meet the growing demand for food between now and 2050. But it cannot be done only by relying on the advanced agricultural systems of North America, Europe or Asia alone. Instead, new land will have to be brought into production. Yield gaps will have to be closed. The regions with the greatest potential for increased production are South America and sub-Saharan Africa. They contain large areas of fertile lands that are sparsely populated and uncultivated, or cultivated with rudimentary techniques and oriented towards subsistence production for local communities. Now, the pressure is on to change how these lands are managed and to integrate them in the global food economy.

Throughout history, there have been periods of rapid change when territories have been brought under new agricultural systems and pulled into more powerful regional or global food economies. Change usually happened at the point of a sword and at the expense of indigenous peoples. The Roman Empire imposed its Mediterranean systems of grains, vineyards and animals on the tribes of Northwest Europe – Roman soldiers received land in return for their victories. The Chinese carried the legendary Five Grains from present-day Vietnam in the south to Korea in the north, building the world's most durable empire in between. In medieval Europe, Teutonic Knights from Germany conquered Slavic tribes to the east who still practised 'slash and burn' cultivation. They introduced a more productive farming system and created a vast cereal-growing region, served by rivers flowing into the Baltic Sea, which eventually became Prussia.

From the sixteenth century, Europeans brought wheat and livestock to the Americas, Africa, Australia and New Zealand, 'taming' the temperate grasslands. The opening up of the Argentinian Pampas only happened in the 1870s and 1880s and it entailed the killing or expulsion of large numbers of indigenous people. Settlers from Tsarist Russia brought new farming systems to Siberia, shuttling food back to St Petersburg on the Trans-Siberian Railway. In the late nineteenth century, French colonialists invested heavily in irrigation infrastructure in the thinly populated Mekong Delta in Vietnam, bringing farmers down from the north and laying the foundations for what is now one of the world's most important rice bowls. Soon after, when Japan found that domestic agriculture could no longer support an industrialising economy, it colonised Taiwan and Korea, turning them into rice and sugar producers for the home market.

All these agricultural expansions shared certain features. Societies with advanced farming systems that hit up against ecological limits at home conquered and colonised fertile lands that were seen as under-utilised. In almost all cases, these lands were already occupied. But the native farming systems were less productive, and their civilisations were weaker. Indigenous people were displaced, assimilated or exterminated. This process usually involved a transition from traditional communal property systems to individual private property rights – the enclosure of common lands. At the end of the process, much of this land was concentrated in the hands of the conquerors or of complicit native elites who had adapted to the new realities. And production was geared towards the export of commodities back to the imperial metropolis or into a globalised capitalist economy. Agricultural innovation spread around the world, but at massive human cost.

Thankfully, by the second half of the twentieth century, change usually happened in a different way. Innovations spread through cooperation rather than conquest. The 'Green Revolution' was promoted by charities such as the Rockefeller Foundation and by UN agencies, funded by rich-world governments. It was embraced by Asian countries that were experiencing rapid population growth – such as India and China – and rolled out without loss of sovereignty or foreign exploitation.

One reason for the peaceful spread of new farming systems was that the modern agricultural revolution relieved the pressure on land. For most of history, the main way to boost food supplies was to increase the amount of land under cultivation: when the global population multiplied five-fold between 1700 and 1961, the amount of cropland in the world also grew by five times. But in the next three decades, world population rose by 80 per cent but cropland only increased by 8 per cent. Instead, increased production came from higher yields. Rather than expanding the agricultural frontier, everyone focused on using the land within the frontier, and within their own borders, more productively.

Moreover, powerful countries such as the USA that possessed the new agricultural knowledge had large food surpluses. They did not need to force their more productive systems on less developed regions to feed people at home. If other countries chose to adopt these methods, so be it. But for those poorer countries that failed to do so, there was weak external pressure to change. People in these countries could just about survive on the cheap imports and food aid that was a by-product of global surpluses. The massive gap in productivity that had opened up between the most and least productive farmers could persist.

However, now that the world food system is characterised by scarcity, the gap in productivity has created a dangerous vacuum. Powerful countries with access to capital and agricultural technology are hitting the ecological limits of domestic food production. They look around the world and see land that is not being fully utilised by poorer, weaker states. All the science indicates that some of these less productive areas will have to close the yield gap and expand the area under cultivation, if there is to be enough food to go around. There are plenty of foreign states and investors willing to undertake this task if local governments are unable to take the necessary steps. Under-developed, resource-rich countries are being presented with an implicit ultimatum: 'use it or lose it'.

South America looks like it will be able to keep control of its agricultural development process. It is achieving impressive increases in food production year on year. It contains relatively strong states that can withstand outside pressures. Indeed, in the last two years Brazil and Argentina have introduced restrictions on foreign ownership of farmland, following a rush of reported land deals. They still welcome foreign investment but only if local partners keep control.

In contrast, most sub-Saharan African countries have much weaker state institutions. They are starting from a much less developed position in terms of infrastructure, education and wealth. Agricultural productivity has failed to keep up with population growth over the last three decades, even though many countries possess enviable amounts of fertile land and freshwater. For example, the World Bank talks about the African Guinea Savannah, a 1.5-million-square-mile band stretching across the middle of the continent, as containing 'the world's last large reserves of underused land'. Africa is where outside pressures to expand the agricultural frontier, and to integrate land into the global food economy, will be most intense. The recent 'land grabs' in Africa are the first manifestations.

There are some uncomfortable echoes from the colonial past in these land deals. Many involve the conversion of communal or public lands into private property. In his book *The Landgrabbers*, Fred Pearce warns that 'we could be witnessing the beginning of the final enclosure of the world's unfenced lands'. Large estates are being created and land ownership concentrated. Local people are being displaced to more marginal land or expected to work as wage labourers. The food grown on the land is destined for cash markets, rather than local subsistence. This fits the pattern of previous agricultural expansions that were marked by exploitation and loss of sovereignty.

The fact that private companies are in charge of most of these deals is not inconsistent with colonial precedence. From the sixteenth century onwards, chartered companies were used to spearhead European expansion into North America, the Caribbean, India and Africa. The British East India Company is the best example, practically carving out an empire in South Asia before handing it over to Queen Victoria. When the millionaire imperialist Cecil Rhodes seized East Africa in the late nineteenth century, he ruled through the British South Africa Company, which was given a Royal Charter by the British crown. The colourful cast of land speculators and dreamers that Rhodes attracted to Africa are not unlike some of the entrepreneurial individuals that we encountered in the previous chapter. It was imperialism on the cheap, 'informal if possible, formal if necessary'. Governments only intervened when the companies got themselves in trouble and required military protection, or when their exploitation of the natives became too offensive. The flag followed trade, rather than the other way around.

Finally, colonial powers have always acted through local elites. How else could a few hundred British administrators control a territory the size of India? All the recent land deals in Africa have been sanctioned by local officials or chiefs at some level. Many genuinely believe that foreign investment will benefit their people, but others may stand to gain personally. Once investments are made, there are subtle ways that foreign powers can maintain influence over local elites. Powerful individuals can be invited into corporate ventures as business partners, thus earning a financial reward from farming projects. Supportive governments can be propped up by cheap loans and arms sales. So long as the general populace do not have an effective check on their leaders (such as democracy), exploit-ative situations that benefit foreign countries or companies can continue for long periods – as the longevity of many African dictators amply demonstrates.

For all these reasons, there is a risk that land deals result in the exploitation of poor countries through a form of neo-colo-nialism. One advocacy group, Food First, warns that we may see the emergence of 'cereal republics', just like the 'banana republics' that developed in Central America a hundred years ago under the influence of US food corporations.

If we want to get an idea of where this could lead – a true nightmare scenario – then we could do worse than look at one of the most painful passages in the history of my homeland. In the sixteenth century, Ireland was a heavily forested island whose mostly Gaelic population subsisted on cattle husbandry and rudimentary arable farming. The full British conquest of Ireland, which started with Henry VIII and ended with the brutal Cromwell campaign, was accompanied by the confisca-tion of native lands and their transfer to thousands of English and Scottish settlers. These new settlers, backed by London finance, built roads, cleared forests and introduced more intensive farming systems. Ireland was dragged into the market economy of the British Empire. By the early nineteenth century Irish farming had split in two. There was an export sector, occupying the best land, which produced wheat, meat, butter and eggs for

Britain at a time of rapid industrialisation. Ireland was the source of three-quarters of its neighbour's food imports in the early 1800s. Meanwhile, the marginalised Catholic masses rented tiny plots on poor quality land and subsisted on a diet of potatoes.

When potato blight struck in 1845, the country's food staple rotted away. Starvation quickly followed. But there was no interruption to the export of food. Two-fifths of the Irish wheat crop was sent abroad on the eve of the famine. Half a million pigs were shipped across the Irish Sea in one year. Total Irish food exports in 1842 could have fed two million people. It was not that food was unavailable but that the majority of people were too poor to afford it. They could not compete with richer British consumers. And Irish commercial farmers, both Catholic and Protestant, were not prepared to forgo this market for the sake of charity. It is thought that 1 million Irish people died during the Great Famine and that a similar number were forced to emigrate. This is a graphic case study of how unequal land ownership, powerful economic incentives and complicit local elites can create a situation where foreign interests are served while local people starve.

The Irish experience in the mid-nineteenth century is a nightmare scenario, one that Africa must avoid at all costs. Yet, there is as much opportunity as threat in the current situation. The corollary of the pressure being exerted on African countries to grow more food is that these countries have the natural resources to be able to generate wealth for themselves. If they set themselves on the right development path, they can achieve food security, export agricultural surpluses, and get rich in the process. As Kofi Annan says, 'Africa has an opportunity not only to feed itself, but to feed the world.' How can this opportunity be grasped? How can we avoid the bleak outcomes sketched out in this chapter? It is time to stop speculating about what could go wrong and instead think about what should be done.

A WIDENING TRADE GAP UNLESS SOMETHING CHANGES
Net agricultural trade of developing countries – FAO projections, $ billion

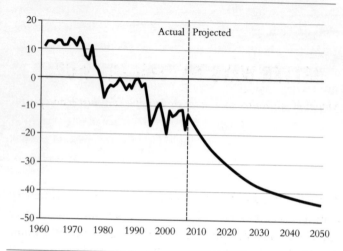

Source: N. Alexandratos & J. Bruinsma, World agriculture towards 2030/2050: the 2012 revision, FAO, 2012

11

BETTER WAYS TO FEED THE WORLD

Mapping out routes to a more sustainable and just food system

The world food crisis has unleashed some dangerous trends. If unchecked, they could lead to bleak outcomes for a large number of people. But there is nothing inevitable about this. Nothing is predetermined. The challenges are political and economic – man-made – not biophysically determined by some sort of remorseless Malthusian calculus. Therefore, through better political and economic choices it is within our power to shape a more just food system.

How can this be done? I believe there are four actions that governments, farmers, investors and citizens need to take to produce a fairer and safer world food system. They are: helping small farmers in poor countries to grow more food; putting ecology at the centre of food production; making financial markets work to address real challenges; and adapting to higher food prices and the shift to a bio-based economy. None of them depend on utopian schemes for world governance or altruistic behaviour by other nations. Many go against conventional wisdom or pierce through the fog of disagreement that obscures so many issues related to food and farming. Taken together they may be enough to set the world on a path towards food security for all.

The good news is that if we can get through the next few decades some of the pressures will ease. The Malthusian prediction that human population tends to increase exponentially, only to be held in check by famine or disease, has not been borne out. Instead, history shows that as societies get richer their populations grow more slowly and even start to contract. The number of people in the world is expected to grow by 2 billion between now and 2050, but it will probably only grow by another 1 billion thereafter. Total human population is expected to peak at just over 10 billion later in this century and then stabilise. The greatest squeeze on the world's food system, therefore, will be felt in the next forty or fifty years. If we can get over this hump, and establish food systems resilient to the oncoming challenge of climate change (no easy task), humanity should be able to sustain itself indefinitely.

Helping small farmers in poor countries to grow more food
You would think the idea that poor countries should grow more food would be uncontroversial. But for decades, many Western economists said it was not necessary. They argued that each country should pursue its comparative advantage. If modern farms in the USA, Brazil or Australia could produce grains and meat at lower cost, then it would be better for developing countries to import this food and focus their energies on other economic activities – making T-shirts, opening mines, or, if they insisted on practising agriculture, growing specialist cash crops for export. Better to earn the money needed to buy cheap food from abroad rather than slave away in unproductive, back-breaking peasant agriculture. 'Self-sufficiency' came to be derided as an old-fashioned concept, fit only for economic illiterates. This was best expressed by the US Secretary for Agriculture, John Block, during the Uruguay Round trade talks in 1986. '[The] idea that developing countries should feed

themselves is an anachronism from a bygone era,' he said. 'They could better ensure their food security by relying on U.S. agricultural products, which are available, in most cases, at much lower cost.'

This theory has been tested since the 1980s and found wanting. Many developing countries, especially in Africa, were forced to dismantle their agricultural subsidies and to open up to free trade. As a result, a majority are now net food importers. This has done little to improve their food security. Malnutrition has increased, economic growth has stagnated. It turned out that earning enough money to pay for imported food – no matter how cheap – was not so easy. Manufacturing growth remained sluggish even as refugees from a collapsing rural economy swelled the cities. Revenues from mining or oil exports tended to end up in the pockets of elites. As more and more farmers turned to growing cash crops, the prices of these commodities dropped on world markets, meaning that farmers had to work harder for less income. National food systems split in two, with an impoverished rural populace barely surviving on subsistence farming while city dwellers turned to imported food. Links between the rural and urban economy dissolved. This was not a recipe for inclusive, dynamic growth.

Looking forward, because of the structural changes taking place within the global food system, reliance on cheap imports will make even less sense than before. If food prices remain high, then the old calculations about comparative advantage – never very convincing in the first place – no longer hold. It is one thing to rely on imported food when it is cheap, but what if it costs twice as much? How will a poor country or a poor household afford it? On the other hand, higher world prices make it more likely that local farmers – so long as they have the right support – will be able to compete. Economists are supposed to believe in the power of prices. When the price of food on world markets changes as much, and for as long, as we have recently seen, this should change many of the old equations.

This is the situation in an average year. But one of the themes of this book is that we are likely to see more volatility in world food markets. The coupling of food and energy, more climatic extremes, less elastic worldwide demand for food, financial speculation in commodities, the locking up of supplies in vertically integrated supply chains – these are all reasons why prices are likely to rise and fall more viciously than over the last thirty years. This makes reliance on food imports an even riskier strategy than before.

However, growing more food at home is not just a good idea because of considerations of risk. Building a vibrant agricultural sector can kick-start a virtuous cycle of development that leads to prosperity all around. In most African countries more than three-quarters of the population are found in rural areas. Improving the productivity and profitability of agriculture will, therefore, benefit the largest part of the population. It is especially beneficial for the poor: the World Bank has found that agricultural growth is twice as effective at reducing poverty than growth in other sectors of the economy. If rural folk are more prosperous, they will act as a market for industrial goods and services, helping the development of cities. Indeed, agricultural development *requires* thriving industries, as farmers need inputs, machinery and infrastructure to improve their productivity. Rural and urban development go hand in hand. As the doyen of market capitalism, Adam Smith, observed over 200 years ago, 'the great commerce of every civilised society is that carried on between the inhabitants of the town and those of the country'.

We do not just have to rely on economic theory. There is a less impeachable source – history. Almost every single process of industrialisation and development (barring a few small city states) has begun with an agricultural revolution. Britain was renowned for its continuous rotation farming before factories and coalfields encroached on its green and pleasant land. The USA was a breadbasket for the world before Henry Ford started making cars. Japan achieved big yield increases in rice production in the 1880s, and again in the 1950s, which laid the foundation for bursts of industrial progress in each period. Most recently, China underwent a dramatic agricultural revolution in the 1980s – increasing food production by a third – before embarking on its breakneck dash to become the workshop of the world. Indeed, this suggests an axiom: it is extremely difficult for a large populous country to achieve industrial and economic development without first achieving a high level of agricultural productivity.

Of course, not every developing country can aim for food self-sufficiency. There will always be places without sufficient land or water to feed their populations. In these cases, trade must play a key role in food security. But there are many poor countries, especially in Africa, that could produce much more food, given their natural endowments. Increasing agricultural productivity should be a number one priority for these countries. Indeed, this may no longer be optional. As we have seen, there will be enormous pressures from powerful outsiders for countries with under-utilised natural resources to make a contribution to feeding the world. To ensure their independence, these countries will need to develop their farming sectors. They will need to use it, or risk losing it.

What is the best way to increase agricultural productivity in poor countries, especially in Africa, where there are millions of farmers cultivating small plots with rudimentary tools? There are two very different visions out there. In a famous 2008 article in *Foreign Affairs*, the Oxford economist Paul Collier argued that African countries could only produce enough food, at reasonable prices, if farms got bigger and more commercial. Bemoaning a Western 'romanticism' of the peasant farmer, he looked forward to the day when most people had got out of agriculture and had moved to the cities. He pointed to the large-scale, mechanised farming systems of Brazil and the USA as the model to which Africa should aspire.

There are certain problems with this argument. The first is that all the academic literature shows that small-scale farms of one or two hectares can be just as efficient as large-scale mech-anised farms. We explored the limitations of 'economy of scale' in agriculture in an earlier chapter. Millions of farmers across China, India and Southeast Asia produce just as much food per hectare as commercial operators in Iowa or Mato Grosso, with much less capital and machinery. Yields per worker are lower, but this is not necessarily a problem in societies where labour is plentiful and there are few other economic activities to absorb this labour. Indeed, a farming system that provides more employment will deliver wider social benefits than one that concentrates ownership and profits in a few hands.

The Collier argument also fails to recognise how and why developed economies ended up with large-scale mechanised farming systems in the first place. It did not happen overnight. The number of agricultural workers in the USA, UK, France and other advanced economies actually increased while they were industrialising during the nineteenth century. The departure of labour from farming only took place as the costs of labour rose, which was itself driven by the wages that farm workers could earn in the non-rural economy. In other words, it was the availability of good jobs in the cities that stimulated the mechanisation and consolidation of farming in advanced economies. Capital (and machinery) got cheaper, labour more expensive. The opposite conditions exist in most developing countries, where labour is cheap and capital expensive.

Over time, it may make sense for the number of farmers in Africa to shrink and for farms to grow in size. But this should happen because of the pull from other economic sectors, as part of a virtuous cycle of rural and urban development, not the push of a forced 'de-peasantisation'. Each country must proceed at its own pace.

It is argued that Brazil short-circuited this process by jumping straight to large-scale mechanised agriculture. Under the headline 'Big is Beautiful', *The Economist* trumpeted the achievements of 'productive giant operations' in Brazil over 'inefficient hobby farms'. However, studies by the World Bank show that this model evolved because credit was subsidised by the Brazilian government, making it artificially cheap for farmers to acquire machinery, fuel and fertilisers. Moreover, the results caused many social problems. The number of rural poor in Brazil actually increased during the 1990s (while falling by 400 million in China). Small farmers were forced off the land and into urban *favelas*, where there was little employment. The benefits of agricultural development flowed into the hands of the few: 3 per cent of the people own two-thirds of Brazil's arable land. And, although food production increased, it was not quite the 'miracle' that *The Economist* makes out. Between 1990 and 2006, sixteen other countries had higher rates of agricultural growth than Brazil, almost all based on smallholder agriculture.

One of these countries was Vietnam. It went through an equally impressive process of agricultural development but one that spread the economic benefits more widely. From the late 1980s the government abandoned a failed collectivisation policy, distributed land to small farmers and invested in rural infrastructure. The initial focus was on labour-intensive rice production but farmers later diversified into higher value exports such as rubber and coffee. In twenty years, Vietnam went from being a food deficit country to becoming the second largest rice exporter in the world. The poverty rate fell from 58 per cent in 1979 to just 15 per cent in 2007. At the same time, the country made more progress than any other in reducing hunger. Today, almost three-quarters of the population is still found in rural areas, mostly on small farms averaging half a hectare in size. Vietnam demonstrates that large farms are not necessary to achieve an agricultural revolution. The same lesson can be drawn from Thailand, which started on a similar development trajectory a decade earlier.

African countries are better off looking east than west. They can learn more by studying the experiences of Asian countries than trying to copy the USA or Brazil. They should put small-holder farmers at the centre of their agriculture strategies. If these farmers have the right support, there is no reason why they cannot spearhead an agricultural revolution that generates surpluses for local consumers and for world markets. Every major study on the future of food – whether by the UN FAO, the World Bank or the UK government's Foresight initiative – has come to this conclusion. Indeed, the World Bank recently dismissed the argument that 'modernised' agriculture requires a shift from smallholdings to large farms as 'a myth with little foundation in reality'.

How can a country kick-start an agricultural revolution based on smallholder farmers? The Asian experience shows that transformation does not happen on its own. These revolutions came about as a result of carefully executed national policies, not the invisible hand of the market. Governments provided farmers with secure land tenure (not necessarily privatised, but secure) so that they were willing to invest in improvements.

Governments put money into ensuring that farmers had the right knowledge, seeds, fertilisers, tools and access to credit. Governments invested in infrastructure such as roads, railways, storage facilities and markets, in order to link rural economies with urban centres.

None of these measures would have got very far, though, if the prices farmers received were not attractive enough to encourage production, or so volatile as to create daunting risks. All the Asian countries that achieved such advances in productivity managed international trade very carefully – and still do. They used subsidies, tariffs, price controls and reserve stocks to shield local markets from international pressures and to ensure that farmers operated in a low-risk environment. In taking these steps, they were simply following the lead of European and North American countries, which have long tried to manipulate trade to their advantage.

Any developing country serious about effecting an agricultural revolution must be prepared to use whatever policy tools are available to create the right environment for its farmers. The neo-liberal ideology that poor countries should open their borders to trade, and hope for the best, does not make sense. Ironically, under the existing WTO Agreement on Agriculture, developing countries have the right to impose quite heavy tariffs on food but often choose to waive them in pursuit of a cheap imports policy. It is time for governments to assert these rights and to seize new ones if necessary. All options should be on the table.

For African countries in particular, it may make sense to create regional trading blocs for food. It is one thing for continental-scale nations such as China or India to go it alone, but a country of just 5 or 10 million people will find it very difficult to achieve food security with such a policy. Rather than seeking national self-sufficiency, countries at a similar level of development may be better off pooling their food resources in a common agricultural trade area. This will provide market scale and production diversity. These blocs can then manage their interactions with world markets according to their needs.

Since the 1980s a neo-liberal adherence to free trade has been an article of faith in all the major multi-lateral institutions (such as the World Bank and the International Monetary Fund). They still tiptoe around the issue, even as evidence piles up that free trade in food can be disastrous for poor countries. Yet, cracks are starting to appear in the consensus. One man who has undergone a Damascene conversion is former US President Bill Clinton.

In the 1990s, the Clinton administration forced Haiti to open its economy to cheap American food imports. This helped to destroy the Haitian farming sector, driving people towards the slums of Port-au-Prince. It was one of the reasons Haiti was so exposed to the food price spikes in 2008 and the devastating 2010 earthquake. Clinton saw this first-hand when he was appointed as UN special envoy for Haiti after the natural disaster. It drove him to make a public *mea culpa*. Opening up Haiti to free trade 'may have been good for some of my farmers in Arkansas,' he told the US Senate Foreign Relations Committee, 'but it has not worked. It was a mistake.' He 'had to live everyday with the consequences'. Speaking more generally about the world food crisis, he told a UN audience that 'we all blew it, including me as president' by pressing developing country governments to get out of agriculture. 'Food is not a commodity like others,' he continued. 'We should go back to a policy of maximum food self-sufficiency. It is crazy for us to think we can develop countries around the world without increasing their ability to feed themselves.'

Some countries are already taking steps towards this goal. Senegal has switched its focus from cash crops for export to domestic production of rice, aiming to become self-sufficient by 2015. The Nigerian government is committed to introducing a total ban on rice imports by 2015, as an instrument for stimulating local production. When the new President of Malawi, Bingu wa Mutharika, came to power in 2004 he vowed to his cabinet that he would not beg for food aid from foreign capitals. Against the advice of international donors, he put in place a fertiliser and seed subsidy programme that helped more than a million farmers to triple maize production within two years. This gave the country resilience when world food prices spiked. Unlike many of its neighbours, Malawi did not suffer any increase in poverty or hunger in 2008. It was even able to export some of its maize surplus.

The economic sustainability of the Malawi subsidy programme has been questioned but it shows just how much can be achieved, and how quickly, through government support for smallholder agriculture. President wa Mutharika made the lesson clear at an African Union conference in 2010. 'For a long time,' he said, 'we were told poor African farmers in rural areas must compete through free market structures with highly advanced farmers in industrialised countries. Unfortunately, Africa accepted this falsehood. How wrong we have been and what a price we have paid.' He told the leaders present that the 'time has now come for Africa to stand up and take a decision to subsidise our poor farmers so that they can grow enough food beyond subsistence ... A nation that depends on other nations to feed it cannot claim sovereignty.'

Food is too important to be left to the market. Experience shows that governments must play a role in constructing secure, equitable food systems. But success requires *good* government. The intervention of inept or corrupt leaders in markets can make the situation worse. Governments must act in the interests of all the people, not just elites. Unfortunately,

many of the poorest countries do not possess such governments – it is one of the main reasons they are poor in the first
place. In these cases, citizens must organise, agitate and press
for change. For many of the most vulnerable people in the
world, the only protection against geopolitical threats will be
domestic political reform. Therefore, kick-starting an agricultural revolution may require a political revolution first.

Putting ecology at the centre of food production

The argument over whether African agriculture should be
built on smallholder farms or large-scale commercial operations mirrors a wider debate about how food should be
produced. This debate is just as relevant for Europe or North
America as it is for developing countries. As we have seen,
modern farming can be a dirty business. It can deplete finite
resources, degrade the environment and spew out greenhouse
gases. There is a general consensus that our food systems need
to be made more sustainable. But, again, there are two different
visions for how to achieve this.

On one side, there are those who see technology as the
answer. They believe that farmers everywhere should emulate
the high-input, industrialised systems that emerged in the
second half of the twentieth century. The goal should be to
produce the maximum amount of food as cheaply as possible,
using whatever fertilisers, chemicals and organisms that science
and agribusiness can provide. If there are negative environmental impacts, then the solution is more and better technology. Much hope is pinned on genetic modification. Even if
farming continues to pollute, it is better to intensify production on existing farmland so there is less need to expand into
the remaining areas of wilderness. 'If we are going to get
serious about solving global hunger,' the academic Robert
Paarlberg writes, it means 'learning to appreciate the modern,

science-intensive, and highly capitalized agricultural system we've developed in the West.'

Taken to its extreme, this position can lead to a simplification of agriculture, one that extracts it altogether from the natural world and tries to make it conform to principles of industrialization and mass production. Laurence Beltrão Gomes of the Brazilian farming company SLC Agrícola has boldly stated that 'we are not farmers'. Instead, they are 'a large company that uses state-of-the-art technology to produce high-quality soybean'. 'The same way you have shoemakers and computer manufacturers, we produce agricultural commodities.' Opponents who harp on about the environment are dismissed as elitists, 'agrarian romantics and populists', with little concern for the needs of the poor.

As anyone who has browsed a bookstore in Portland or Paris will know, a vigorous counter-movement has emerged with a completely different vision for how we should produce and consume food. Proponents of 'alternative agriculture' decry industrial farming as inherently unsustainable. Instead, they advocate farming systems that are rooted in biology, ecology and stewardship of the land. There is usually a strong social dimension to this movement, championing the small family farm against corporate behemoths. Organic farming is the most codified version of this approach, setting out standards that prohibit the use of synthetic fertilisers or agro-chemicals. The worldwide organic market was worth $52 billion in 2008, representing between 1 and 2 per cent of total food sales. Apart from 'organic', there are many other labels that describe branches of the alternative farming movement: 'biodynamic', 'community-based', 'extensive', 'free-range', 'permaculture', 'wise use', 'slow food'.

Taken to an extreme, this alternative approach can lead to an obscurantist, anti-science position that rejects modern forms of economic organisation. Synthetic fertilisers, agro-chemicals and genetically modified seeds are rejected on ideological grounds, no matter what science tell us about the actual risks. All companies over a certain size are condemned as exploitative. The small family farm is romanticised, even poeticised. For example, Professor Harriet Friedmann of the University of Toronto, when talking about her vision of agriculture, presents a 'buoyant image' of 'farming-gardening-playing coming together in the gardens of Gaia'. I am not sure this is how my uncle feels when he hauls himself on to his tractor on a drizzly Irish morning.

The debate about the future of farming has become highly polarised. But a truly sustainable agriculture will combine the best from both sides. It will place ecology at the centre while not forsaking modern technology.

Support for this view can be found in the archives of the Rothamsted Experimental Station in England, one of the oldest agricultural research institutions in the world. Its fields have been under continuous cultivation and monitoring since 1843. Some plots use traditional, organic practices, while others use modern seeds and chemicals. However, the records show that the best yields come from systems that rotate crops and incorporate farmyard manure, while applying moderate amounts of nitrogen fertiliser. Hybrid systems outperform all others.

This sort of approach has been called 'eco-agriculture' or 'agro-ecology'. It is not a set of prescriptive rules, rather a philosophical approach. It puts an emphasis on farmers understanding their local environment – the interaction of soils, water, climate, vegetation, birds and insects that comprises an agro-ecosystem. It seeks to alter, manage and mimic ecological processes, making the most of on-farm resources and minimising the use of off-farm inputs such as fertilisers and chemicals. It puts an emphasis on efficient use of water, not drawing out more than natural cycles replenish. A major focus is on improving the health of the soil by increasing organic matter and soil biotic activity. These systems tend to be highly diverse, incorporating crops, trees, animals (and sometimes fish) in symbiotic ways. The waste from one part of the system becomes the nutrient for another. The interaction between different species reduces the threat from pests. By better understanding and manipulating ecological processes, clever farmers can produce extraordinary results.

There are dozens of examples of successful agro-ecological farming systems from around the world. In Southeast Asia, integrated pest management, which employs crop diversity to control pests and only uses chemicals as a last resort, was introduced by millions of rice farmers from the 1980s. In Argentina, farmers stopped ploughing their land and instead used direct-seeding machines and herbicides to plant directly into the previous year's crop. This 'zero-tillage' system improved soil fertility and yields. Across Africa, farmers are discovering the wondrous properties of the *Faidherbia* tree: it fixes nitrogen from the atmosphere, then sheds its leaves early in the rainy seasons, fertilising the land at the perfect time for the crops growing below. Farmers have been able to double their maize yields while cutting the purchase of ammonia fertiliser.

In Iowa, some farmers have switched from the typical corn-soybean rotation to a multiple-crop rotation of corn, beans, oats and hay, while reincorporating livestock and making the most of crop residues. They have been able to cut costs as a result. In Madagascar, the French Jesuit Father Henri de Laulanié developed a system of rice intensification that flew against conventional wisdom – farmers were encouraged to plant rice more widely and to keep their fields moist rather than saturated. Yields doubled, resistance to pests increased, fertiliser use dropped. This system has since spread to forty countries in Asia, Africa and Latin America.

These farming systems may eschew expensive technologies but they are far from stupid. They are rooted in science, but with an emphasis on biology and ecology, not just chemistry and genetics. External inputs such as fertilisers, chemicals or machinery are not excluded, but they are used to complement biological processes, not replace them. It is a return to the original definition of 'technology', which comes from two Greek words: *technis*, which means art, skill, craft or the way something is gained, and *logos*, which means word or thought. 'Technology' does not just mean physical objects; it also refers to knowledge or mental objects. Knowledge-intensive agro-ecological systems, therefore, are advanced forms of human technology.

So far, agro-ecological innovations have mostly bubbled up from below, often developed by farmers or individual scientists who were prepared to kick against consensus views. Scientists have tended to focus on chemistry and genetics as these disciplines are better suited to the laboratory. Agribusinesses have concentrated on developing technology 'objects' that can be sold to farmers. Seeds and chemicals fit the bill; in contrast, it is impossible to patent a farming system. If more public funding is put into agro-ecological research, many more breakthroughs can be expected. Africa is especially in need of this sort of research as much existing technology is unsuited to its conditions.

What about genetic modification of crops and animals? Can it play a role in feeding the world? Genetic engineering is not the silver bullet that some proponents claim: so far, it may have helped to simplify farm management but it has done little to increase yields. At the same time, it is not the Frankenstein monster viewed by some critics with horror. Many applications of genetic science are not so different from traditional breeding methods – the new techniques just speed them up. Genetically modified crops have been grown for twenty years with little evidence of harm to humans. One justifiable concern is that genetic technology could lead to greater control by agribusiness over the food system but the solution to this is surely more public research so that improved seeds and animals are made available to farmers through other channels. In theory, there is no reason why genetic science cannot be compatible with ecological farming approaches. Why not 'Organic GMOs', seeds that have been engineered to flourish without external fertilisers or chemicals?

Nonetheless, when it comes to solving the food security problems of the world, genetic modification is still a technology of the future rather than today. And even if breakthroughs are made, it could be a long time before the world's poor farmers can afford high-tech seeds and animals. We must do more with the technology we have. The good thing is that we do not have to wait. There are plenty of examples of successful agro-ecological systems already in use. We just need to scale them up.

Agro-ecological approaches can help address the environmental challenges that we are likely to face during the rest of this century. Because of climate change, making our food systems more resilient to extreme weather events will be a stronger imperative than before. Specialised farms that only produce one or two crops are more vulnerable to climatic extremes than diverse agro-ecosystems producing many types of food. For example, following Hurricane Mitch in 1998, a study of 180 communities of smallholders in Nicaragua found that farming plots that used simple agro-ecological methods fared better than plots on conventional farms.

Agro-ecological farming systems also tend to create fewer environmental externalities. There is less waste, because all organic material is treated as a precious resource to be utilised on-farm. Nitrogen fertilisers and pesticides do not pollute waterways, because use of these inputs is minimised. Diverse, integrated farming systems have been shown to increase the amount of organic matter in the soil, which stores away more atmospheric carbon and improves the carbon balance of food production. And healthy soil full of organic matter holds water better, which reduces the need for wasteful irrigation. These are cleaner, greener systems.

But agriculture, if done the right way, can go beyond this. It can help *reverse* environmental damage. Millions of hectares of land around the world have been degraded by human activity. Soils have lost their fertility, hillsides have washed away, farms have been swallowed up by desert sands. This is a critical danger to people's food security right now. If we could restore some of this land it could pay a massive dividend. There are examples of agro-ecological systems that do just this, improving the health of soils, turning deserts green and making land productive again. Rather than just doing no environmental harm, they do the environment good.

One of the most forceful advocates for the positive power of land management is a stubborn octogenarian named Allan Savory. Born in what was then Rhodesia (now Zimbabwe), Savory spent his early career as a wildlife ranger, pondering why domesticated cattle degraded the land while larger herds of wild animals on the Serengeti thrived in healthy ecosystems. He noticed three things about the behaviour of the wild animals. First, they lived in huge groups – there might be half a million wildebeest in one herd. Second, they stayed bunched up because around the edge were lions, crocodiles or other predators trying to eat them. Third, they were constantly on the move as part of their seasonal migration – they would eat, dung and trample in an area for a day or two, then move on, not returning to the same patch for months. So, the animals would have a massive impact on the land for a short period of time, chewing up plant matter and recycling nutrients to the soil, but the ecosystem would then have time to recover.

When Savory looked at how farmers – both traditional pastoralists and rich white settlers – managed their livestock, he realised they did the exact opposite. They divided their animals into many little herds. They got rid of the predators so the animals behaved differently, spreading out to graze and hanging around water points. And they put a fence around their animals and kept them on the same land day after day, year after year. Instead of impact, then recovery, farmers produced a situation where small numbers of animals were constantly present, nipping in the bud any palatable plant that emerged. This had the effect of eating the good grasses out of the ecosystem, leading to a drop in productivity. In the worst cases, it caused the land to turn into desert.

Savory's insight was to see that farmers could restore the natural relationship between soils, grasses and grazing animals by mimicking nature. He began collecting cattle into a single herd. He divided the land into much smaller paddocks so that the animals stayed bunched up. He moved them from paddock to paddock according to a planned grazing system. The land got intense animal impact, followed by long periods of rest. The cattle did not come back to the same paddock for months. Savory brought this system with him when he moved to the USA in the 1970s. Under the banner 'holistic management', it eventually spread across the world and is now being used on more than 12 million hectares of land across the Americas, Africa and Australia.

Ranchers found that they could double the number of animals on the land while halving their costs of production. Because their soils and grasses were healthier, their farms were also more resilient to the droughts and floods that periodically affect dry grasslands. Here was an ecological farming system that was good for the environment while increasing productivity and profit, a way of producing large amounts of healthy, low-cost beef and lamb solely on pasture, without any need for feed grains. This has massive potential for global food security, as more than one-fifth of the world's land surface is made up of grazing land and demand for meat is growing. It also been recognised as one of the best ideas for fighting climate change because restoring grassland absorbs carbon from the atmosphere and puts it in the soil.

I have dwelt on this agro-ecological approach because I spent some years working on its application in Australia. I know it works. But there are many other examples of land regeneration at scale, from the Loess Plateau of northwest China, to the dusty Sahel region of Africa, to the forested hills of Central America. If we create the right sort of agro-ecological farming systems, we can pass on healthier, more productive landscapes to future generations. Rather than spending our natural capital, we can add to it.

Can these types of farming systems feed the world? The criticism most often made of organic farming is that it is a luxury of the middle classes, incapable of growing enough food. However, as the Savory example shows, there are plenty of opportunities to increase food production using agro-ecological approaches. This is particularly true in poorer developing countries. Three recent studies of projects in Africa showed that agro-ecological systems were able to increase crop yields by 80–100 per cent compared to traditional farming methods.

In the most highly developed farming regions of the world – including North America, Europe and Australia – the situation is more complex. Most studies show that switching from high-input, intensive systems to pure organic farming would probably cause crop yields to fall by one-fifth. But agro-ecology is not about giving up fertilisers or chemicals entirely, rather using them to maximum effect. The organic straitjacket does not apply. Rather than adopting dogmatic positions on the type of inputs farmers should use, the starting point should be the outputs we want the farming system to deliver. In countries of relative food abundance, where over-consumption is a problem, production may not be the only goal of agriculture. Other objectives include the income and health of the farmer, the quality of the food, the environmental impacts of its production and the sustainability of a farming system over time. When a broader set of goals is considered, agro-ecological approaches usually come out ahead.

Not too long ago these sorts of ideas would have been dismissed by many experts as, literally, for the birds. But over the past five years, most of the organisations to conduct serious studies on how to feed the world have arrived at the conclusion that ecology must be placed at the centre of agriculture. This includes the two Rome-based UN agencies (the Food and Agriculture Organization and the International Fund for Agricultural Development); the oldest scientific fellowship in the world (the Royal Society); an international study involving 900 experts from 110 countries (the International Assessment of Agricultural Knowledge, Science and Technology for Development, or IAASTD); and the French Agricultural Research Centre for International Development (CIRAD). 'Sustainable intensification' and 'ecological intensification' are the new buzzwords in these circles.

National governments are starting to reflect this shift in their policies. China's eleventh Five-Year Plan emphasised the need to reduce the food system's environmental footprint and included measures for the promotion of organic and ecological agriculture. In 2009 the Philippines stopped its fertilizer subsidies and introduced a strategy aimed at promoting the use of balanced combinations of inorganic and organic fertilisers. Even Brazil, the poster boy for industrial farming, is starting to change. An act on agrarian reform passed in 2010 prioritises rural extension activities that help family farms implement ecological agriculture. What was alternative is now becoming mainstream. The new consensus is that ecology must be at the centre of the next agricultural revolution if we are to create sustainable food systems that deliver for all.

Making financial markets work for food security

Increasing food production through sustainable agriculture will require investment, not only in the farming systems themselves but in the roads, railways, irrigation, schools and markets needed to support agricultural development. The FAO estimates that net investments of $83 billion a year must be made in agriculture in developing countries if there is to be enough food for 9 billion people by 2050.

Much of the investment will come from farmers, ploughing some of their profits back into the land. Governments should provide a substantial amount, as part of national agriculture development strategies. Poorer countries can be assisted by rich donors and multi-lateral agencies such as the World Bank. But financial investors such as banks, pension funds and fund managers can also play a role. So long as capitalism is the dominant form of economic organisation in the world, financial capital needs to be recycled back into productive sectors of the economy so it can be used to fund new infrastructure, enterprises and activity. If done right, this can generate a return for investors, thus helping to fund all our pensions. 'For more than two decades', David Hallam of the FAO explains, 'we have been trying to persuade governments and investors around the world to invest in agriculture to halt the downturn in food production. So it is difficult for us to turn around and argue against it now.'

Where is this financial capital needed? When I attended an agricultural investment conference recently, I heard a moderator ask the manager of a large European pension fund if he invested in agriculture. 'Yes,' he replied, 'we invest in commodity futures via index funds'. He was confusing two things. This is not investment in agriculture. It is speculation on commodity prices, a very different animal.

Defenders of investor participation in futures markets argue that it deepens liquidity and improves the operation of these markets. Yet, as we have seen, the flood of speculative capital in recent years has increased volatility, raised the cost of hedging and made futures markets work less well for those who really need to manage risk. Betting on commodity futures does nothing to improve the productivity or sustainability of the world's food systems. Not one extra bushel of wheat is grown as a result; not one farmer is helped to create a profitable enterprise. Lord Turner, chairman of the UK Financial Services Authority, has declared that much financial activity is 'socially useless'. This is a perfect example. Commodity futures markets should be tightly regulated to ensure that they serve the interests of farmers, traders and consumers, rather than becoming a casino for financial speculators. Responsible investors should consider whether it is ethical or wise to deploy their capital in this way – especially as they are just as likely to be losers in what is a zero sum game.

Where investment *is* required is in addressing the challenges identified in this book – increasing agricultural productivity in developing countries, ensuring that farmers can earn a decent livelihood, getting safe and nutritious food from farm to fork, improving the sustainability of food systems everywhere. This is not a zero sum game. Investment can help create a food system that delivers better outcomes for everyone.

In developed countries, investment can help the transition to more sustainable production systems. The average age of farmers in North America and Australia is close to sixty. Young people have been leaving rural areas for the cities as quick as they can, often encouraged by parents who do not see agriculture as a rewarding career. Investment can facilitate the transition from farmers ready to retire to a new generation willing to try out new ideas. It can also help build the transport, storage and on-farm infrastructure that will be needed to sustain food production in coming decades.

In poor countries, where most people rely on the land for a livelihood, there are right and wrong ways to go about investment. The grabbing of land with the goal of creating farming enclaves is likely to harm local communities. It is probably also politically and economically unsustainable, unless investors have deep pockets and are backed by force. If foreign investment in developing countries is to play a constructive role, other models are needed, ones that help small-scale farmers rather than displacing them.

The former UN Secretary-General Kofi Annan made this plain in a speech in Cape Town in 2009. 'One-off land deals will solve neither Africa's food crisis nor the long-term threats to global food security,' he said. 'Africa's breadbaskets must be developed in ways that benefit the continent's major food producers – smallholder farmers. That is the surest route to feeding the continent and producing for export.'

There are a number of tried and tested investment models that can benefit local farmers. Companies can use 'contract farming' or 'out-grower' schemes, providing the materials, finance and training that farmers need to improve productivity, and then buying the produce from them at a pre-agreed price. Pepsi Foods successfully use this approach in the Indian state of Punjab to source tomatoes, chillies, potatoes and Basmati rice. An investor can develop a nucleus farm and use this as a base to establish relationships with local farmers. For example, in Morocco the government designed a programme whereby commercial farmers could lease fifty hectare parcels so long as they committed to work with nearby smallholders. More than thirty partnerships have been launched in the last three years. Other investments may avoid farming altogether and instead focus on upstream activities – seeds or machinery, perhaps – or downstream enterprises – such as processing, logistics or marketing. To give one example, Indian investment in the Tilda rice processing plant in rural Uganda is providing a market and livelihood for more than a thousand local farmers who sell their crops to the mill. All these schemes have one thing in common – they are investing in farmers, not just farmland.

One of the most innovative projects in recent years is the Chiansi irrigation project in Zambia. InfraCo, a private company funded by European donor governments, has designed a scheme under which it will develop irrigation infrastructure on the Kafue River. This is an area that suffers from unreliable rainfall and chronic food insecurity. Six hundred and fifty small-scale farmers have pooled their unused land and formed a cooperative, which leases land to a commercial farming company in which the cooperative holds an equity stake. The commercial farm will grow wheat and soybeans in large quantities, while local farmers receive year-round free irrigation on their garden plots. Villages will also benefit from better drinking water, new electricity supplies and access to credit. When the costs of development have been recouped, the farmers' cooperative will take full control of the irrigation infrastructure and the farming company. This is a systemic, inclusive approach to agricultural development that fills real gaps – water availability, energy supply and access to markets. It is based on a pilot scheme, covering 150 hectares, that has been operating successfully in this part of Zambia since 2008.

Can financial capital play a role in supporting agro-ecological farming systems? The two concepts – the two worlds – rarely go together, and with good reason. Another thing you will notice if you attend an agricultural investment conference in London or New York is that almost every speaker begins his or her presentation with the same sort of photographs: a brand new John Deere tractor: a centre-pivot irrigation system linked to fancy electronic controls; bags of Monsanto seeds or barrels of Bayer pesticides. The investment story presented is usually about buying under-utilised land, investing capital in new seeds, fertilisers, machines or irrigation, and implementing a 'modern' high-input, mechanised farming system. This is the sort of narrative financial investors expect to hear, perhaps because it makes farming sound like the industrial sectors they are used to investing in.

However, there is a strong economic rationale for placing ecology at the heart of agriculture. Profitability in farming is driven not by high yields but by good margins – the difference between the price a farmer gets and the costs of production. High-input, mechanised farming systems emerged during a time of cheap energy, which kept costs down. But if oil and natural gas prices stay high, so will the cost of fertilisers, chemicals and diesel fuel. This will alter the cost structure of agriculture. It will make more sense for farmers to replace fertilisers with nitrogen-fixing legumes; to cultivate the natural enemies of pests rather than to spray pesticides; to save on fuel by ploughing less. Animal producers who rely on purchased feed, rather than using pastures, will feel the squeeze more than most, as grains and oilseeds are likely to be more expensive. Because of the changes sweeping through the global food system, the economic calculus is tilting in favour of systems that minimise external inputs and make the most of on-farm natural cycles.

Smart investors will see that farming systems caught between rising input prices and volatile commodity prices are a risky business proposition. Instead, low-input, agro-ecological farming systems offer a more profitable and lower risk option. 'What has become increasingly clear,' according to Professor Jules Pretty of Essex University, a leading researcher on agro-ecology, 'is that many modern specialized farming systems are wasteful.' Farmers with more complex, integrated systems have found they 'can cut down many purchased inputs without losing out on profitability or even yields'. The best returns from agriculture will belong to those who can control their costs of production and maintain or enhance the productivity of their main asset, the land.

Investors can play a special role in helping to restore degraded land. The seventeenth-century English philosopher Francis Bacon once said that 'the improvement of the ground is the most natural way of obtaining riches'. In many parts of the world today there are lands that have been mined for their timber or nutrients and left degraded. Investment is needed in farming systems that can nurture these ecosystems back to health. This is building natural capital that can be passed on to future generations. But it can also generate financial returns for farmers and their investors.

There are signs that financial capital is starting to flow towards agro-ecological approaches. European pension funds are investing in the scale-up of Allan Savory's holistic grazing system on cattle farms in Australia. Agrica, a farming company backed by international investors, has introduced the system for rice intensification first developed in Madagascar to 250 small farms in Tanzania. In Kenya, the Unilever Tea Company is managing a programme that will help smallholders improve soil and water conservation on 8,000 hectares of land. It is just a start, but an encouraging one.

We are at the beginning of a wave of financial invest-ment in agriculture and the global food system. Persistently high food prices guarantee this. Proponents of sustainable agriculture complain about how hard it is to scale up agro-ecological systems. The academic and governmental estab-lishment has traditionally been geared towards high-input industrial production models; farmers are conservative and resistant to change; capital is scarce. The coming flow of investment into agriculture, if harnessed, could help change this. Investors can finance existing agro-ecological farmers or acquire land in partnership with these farmers, so that these systems can be implemented more widely. They can invest in differentiated supply chains and certification programmes so that consumers can choose food that is more sustainably produced. The economic logic is compelling. It may be an unlikely alliance, but there is no reason why financial investors cannot help accelerate the agro-ecological revolution that the world needs.

Learning to love high prices – and bioenergy

In this book I have talked a lot about high food prices. It is the most visible symptom of the strain on the global food system. Dozens of reports describe how high prices have swelled the ranks of the hungry and caused misery for the poor. The impli-cation is that we need to get food prices back down as quickly as possible and stop doing things that keep prices high, such as promoting biofuels. Yet, during the previous twenty years there were as many reports complaining that food prices were too *low*. According to these reports, the downward slide in prices was crippling farmers in rich and poor countries alike, forcing some out of the sector and driving others to suicide. The very same NGOs that are now most vocal in their criticism of high food prices were calling for measures to raise prices just a few years ago. This should indicate that the issue of price is more complicated. It is not simply the case that high prices are 'bad' and low prices are 'good'.

People go hungry not because of high food prices but because they cannot afford to pay these prices. And inability to pay has as much to do with income levels and purchasing power as the price of food. This is why malnutrition is found among the poorest sections of developing countries. Rich countries are largely immune – wealth is the best guarantee of food security.

Three-quarters of the world's hungry can be found in rural areas. They are either farmers, or landless labourers who rely on farms for employment. Their income levels, their ability to pay for food, are driven by the health of the rural economy. For decades, the rural economy in many developing countries stagnated. Farmers were faced with low and volatile prices, because of weak linkages with urban markets and downward pressure from subsidised imports. Even if they produced a bumper crop this only served to crash prices in the local market, which meant there was little incentive to invest in productivity. These farmers lacked the high and stable prices that were needed to raise incomes and to encourage invest-ment in production.

If the right enabling environment is in place, higher prices can boost the rural economy and help set off the virtuous cycle of development that is so desperately needed. This is what happened in China. Between 1976 and 1980 the relative price of agricultural products rose by 40 per cent. Rather than impoverishing the country, it encouraged Chinese farmers to invest more in their land, and as they became richer the economy grew. The recent structural rise in global food prices has benefited some countries too. Unsurprisingly, rural households in Vietnam gained. In India, the number of malnourished people actually went down in 2007 and 2008 because higher prices helped farmers and the rural economy, where most hunger is concentrated.

Of course, not everyone benefits from higher food prices. Poor urban consumers in developing countries, who make up one quarter of all malnourished people, suffer the most because they have to pay more for food. Rural landless people can be hit if they do not see any rise in wages, as can small-scale farmers who are net purchasers of food. There are ways to mitigate the shock of higher prices on these groups. Governments can create safety nets to help the most vulnerable. One of the efficient methods is to provide food vouchers or cash payments to women, as this tends to spread the benefits throughout households. In the long run, if countries can kick off a virtuous cycle of rural and urban development, and incomes rise across the city and countryside, there should be less need for these safety nets.

Higher prices, the chief symptom of the 'food crisis', could be exactly what the global food system needs. They will attract investment into a sector that has been neglected for so long. They will provide a stimulus to rural development in some of the poorest countries in the world. They will cause governments to think twice about relying on cheap food imports as these imports will be more expensive. Higher prices will encourage everyone to reduce waste, as food becomes more precious. Maybe it is time we started paying what food is really worth.

Prices are a reflection of global demand. The same people who lament high food prices usually criticise the rich consumers of the world for accounting for an unfair share of this demand. 'Do not eat meat,' we are told, because animals consume grain that could otherwise be fed to the poor. 'Reduce food waste' so that more is available for the rest of the world. The strongest criticisms are reserved for biofuels and the government policies that support them. NGOs complain that biofuels take food out of the mouths of the hungry and divert it to the cars of the rich. Land grabs in Africa, the clearing of rainforests for palm oil, and the doubtful carbon benefits of converting maize to ethanol all add to the bad press. In a recent campaign, Oxfam stated that if the land used to produce biofuels for the EU in one year had been used to grow wheat and maize, it could have fed 127 million people. Science writer Matt Ridley made the lurid claim that biofuels, by raising food prices, were responsible for 'killing an estimated 192,000 people' in 2010.

The implication is that if only rich countries consumed less, food prices would come down and fewer people would starve. Although there is some truth in this, it mistakes symptom for cause. The real problem is not how rich countries choose to dispose of their agricultural surpluses but the fact that poor countries do not produce more themselves. It is underproduction, not over-consumption. Even when rich countries subsidised food exports and suppressed world food prices – producing the very opposite effect to recent biofuels policy – global hunger was not any lower than now. The world's poorest cannot access the rich world surpluses at almost any price. Rather than promoting dependence on cheap imports, the ultimate solution is for developing countries to improve the productivity of their agriculture, so that more food is produced where it is needed and more people earn the money to buy it. Once again, we come back to the critical importance of kick-starting rural development through an agricultural revolution.

Within this context, there is no reason why the provision of bioenergy, even though it may keep food prices higher, cannot be an output of sustainable and equitable farming systems, alongside food. In the advanced economies it is one solution to the problem of over-production that has bedevilled farming for the past fifty years. It can encourage investment and bring wealth back to struggling farming communities. Across the Corn Belt of the USA there is plenty of evidence that this is already happening. 'The ethanol industry has reju-venated rural America,' according to Todd Becker, the chief executive officer of Omaha-based Green Plains Renewable Energy. 'The brain drain out of rural America has been incred-ible. We're able to bring it back with good, high-paying jobs.' Cleaner forms of second generation bioenergy could generate the same economic impacts without some of the environ-mental flaws.

In the poorest countries, bioenergy is already the norm. For example, in Tanzania, Ethiopia and the Democratic Republic of Congo, nine-tenths of all energy comes from biomass, in the form of charcoal, fuel wood, crop residues and even cow dung. The introduction of new feedstocks, technologies and distribution networks could create a market for more efficient and cleaner bioenergy products. This could boost the incomes of farmers, while reducing dependence on imported oil and improving a country's balance of payments. Just as developing countries have skipped landline communication for mobile telephony, some experts believe that they could leapfrog fossil fuel dependence and instead build vibrant indigenous bio-based economies.

Smallholder-based bioenergy projects will have the greatest poverty impacts. One good example can be found in the West African country of Mali. Award-winning Mali Biocarburant is a company that is part-owned by small-scale farmers. They grow stands of jatropha trees on their land. The company purchases the jatropha seed, turns some of it into animal feed and converts the rest into biodiesel, which is sold in local towns. This business provides new sources of revenue for farmers – jatropha seeds plus company dividends – while helping Mali improve its energy self-sufficiency.

The interface between food and bioenergy markets will require careful regulation. Farmers and traders will choose to what extent they divert land and crops from food to bioenergy based on relative prices. This creates a risk that they will chase more lucrative energy markets instead of feeding people. Poor food consumers may not be able to compete with richer people who want to fuel their cars. The first priority, therefore, should be satisfying food needs. Only surpluses should be converted to energy.

However, if handled carefully, bioenergy demand can actually help to strengthen food security. It can keep more people in agriculture, and encourage farmers to grow more. This extra production can act as a buffer for the world. In theory, if a major crisis crippled supply, crops could be diverted back from energy markets to food markets.

Is this unrealistic? In the summer of 2012, as drought ravaged the American maize harvest, there were calls for the US Department of Agriculture to suspend the ethanol mandate so that more of the country's crop could be used for food. (To be precise, almost all the extra maize would have been converted into animal feed, and those calling most loudly for a suspension of the mandate were livestock producers.) In the end, the department resisted the pressure and let markets ration demand. But this event shows how bioenergy demand can act as a buffer for our food supply. The amount of US maize converted to ethanol in 2012 – about 40 per cent of the crop – was more than the total shortfall caused by the drought. If there had been no ethanol market, most of this maize would not have been grown in the first place. There would have been an absolute shortage, and the option to divert surplus grain into the food supply chain would not have existed. Bioenergy demand ensured that the output of American farmers was well above the amount needed for the food sector, which put extra options on the table when drought hit.

A call to action

We began this book by tracing the history of agriculture. By the turn of the century, a global food system had emerged that was characterised by low prices and seeming abundance, even if imbalances, injustices and perversities lurked below the surface. Over the past five years, the tectonic plates of the food system have shifted. Changing diets, the diversion of food towards bioenergy, extreme weather events and ecological constraints have come together to produce a situation of relative scarcity, driving food prices higher. The shock waves have rattled governments and left people hungry. Although Malthusian predictions of future collapse are overdone, there are reasons to believe that food will stay more expensive, that prices will be volatile and that global imbalances will widen over the next fifty years, as the number of people in the world exceeds 9 billion.

Ideally, we would deal with these pressures through cooperation and exchange. However, the recent 'World Food Crisis' sparked unbridled competition and profit-seeking by governments and corporations alike. Countries manipulated trade to reduce food prices at home, even if this meant beggaring or starving their neighbours. Private markets malfunctioned as the influx of speculative capital made prices more volatile. Commodity firms tried to strengthen their grip on the world's food system by buying up rivals and creating vertically integrated supply chains. The most striking phenomenon is the flurry of land acquisitions in poor countries by powerful outsiders. These are dangerous trends which, if unchecked, could result in bleak outcomes for large parts of humanity.

There is nothing inevitable about this. Our food economy is determined by political choices. This chapter has sketched out an alternative way forward that could result in a more benign scenario. Two major themes stand out. The first is the need to help small farmers in poor countries to produce more food. This can kick-start a virtuous cycle of rural and urban development in these countries, while reducing their dependence on rich-country surpluses. The second theme is the importance of switching to agro-ecological farming systems that use fewer non-renewable resources, pollute less and enhance the fertility of the land, while still producing sufficient quantities of food. Financial investors can support both these goals by investing in real assets and enterprises, rather than betting on food prices. We may have to get used to permanently higher food prices, but this is not necessarily a problem if the most vulnerable are protected by safety nets and if higher prices help drive the long-term changes that are needed.

What role can we play as individuals in bringing about these changes? At this point in a book on food, it is customary to talk about what we can all do as consumers to effect change. The implication is that if we only ate differently many problems would be solved. There are certainly ways for individuals to help. We can eat more fresh foods rather than processed junk, buy directly from food producers where possible, use food certification schemes to make choices when shopping. Seeking out food that is grown in a sustainable way sends a signal all the way back through the supply chain. If there is one type of food worth thinking about most carefully, it is food that comes from animals (including fish). This is where the greatest variation in production methods exists. Choices made here cascade through the food system because of the multiplier effect of animal feed. Sustainable animal products may cost more right now, but it is a price worth paying.

Nonetheless, it is important not to over-estimate the power of the consumer. Most people do not have the time or inclination to buy directly from farmers or to interrogate the source of their food. Supermarkets, wholesalers and food processors have a huge influence on determining what we eat. Moreover, simple prescriptions such as 'go vegan' or 'buy organic' are seductive but do not work. Meat, fish and dairy can be the most sustainable foods, depending on how they are produced. Similarly, there are brilliant agro-ecological farming systems that do not have organic certification, either because farmers decide it is not worth the hassle or want the option to use non-organic interventions if necessary. There are no straightforward answers, no strict rules. All we can do is find out as much as possible about where our food comes from and make the choices that our circumstances allow.

Instead, we may be able to have a bigger impact as food citizens. If there is one theme that runs throughout this book, it is that government policy has a huge effect on food systems. The natural world is only one factor in whether people eat or go hungry, and whether they get rich or stay poor from agriculture. Similarly, there is no such thing as a free market in food – and never has been. Instead, winners and losers in the global food system are determined by choices about the political economy. If we are going to make the transition to a sustainable and just food system this means altering the political and economic framework in which we all operate. The global food system is largely man-made, so it is within our power to change it.

Effecting political change is difficult, especially when so many issues cut across economic sectors and national boundaries. This is why some of us may be able to make our biggest and most direct contribution not as citizens or consumers but as *doers*. Building a just and sustainable food system will require more farmers, researchers, investors and food entrepreneurs with the spark of innovation and the passion to drive structural change. We need people to roll up their sleeves and develop the technologies, systems and business models that will address the challenges outlined in this book. Instead of wringing our hands about the unsustainability of the modern food system, let us get out there and do something about it.

Nowhere is this needed more than in agriculture. Over the past hundred years, farming came to be seen as a backward economic sector, something you might be born into but wouldn't choose to join. Fewer and fewer young people decided to study agriculture or pursue a career on the land, which is one reason why the average age of farmers in Europe, North America and Australia is close to sixty. Even if a person remained on the family farm, this did not always have positive connotations: the saying was that if a farmer had two sons he would send the smart one to university, while the dumb one stayed at home to run the farm.

This may be changing. Because of high food prices, there is money to be made in agriculture. Investment is flowing into the sector. As other economic sectors struggle to recover from a global financial crisis, the business of growing food, energy and other biological materials on the land looks more enticing. More than a few bankers have swapped their pinstripe suits for wellington boots.

The new emphasis on agro-ecological systems should make a career in agriculture even more attractive. These systems place a premium on farmer knowledge. Instead of low-skilled machinery operators, they require thoughtful land managers. Instead of farming by numbers, they demand constant experimentation, observation and adaptation. The need for innovative ways to make more of natural resources will be particularly appealing to young farmers. Not only can they earn a decent income, they can gain the tremendous satisfaction of knowing they left the land in better condition than before. The rest of society will cheer them on. People's insatiable appetite for TV programmes and magazines about food shows no sign of abating. If chefs are the new rock stars, farmers may not be far behind.

Thousands of years ago, the Chinese were rescued from their misery by Emperor Shennong who, according to legend, had the head of an ox, the body of a man and a stomach that doubled as a plant laboratory. Today, we cannot rely on the appearance of a superhuman figure like the Emperor of the Five Grains. Instead, we need the best and the brightest to turn their attention to food, not only as farmers but as scientists unlocking new innovations, as entrepreneurs linking different parts of the supply chain, as investors backing new ways of doing things. There is no time to waste. Our food system is already failing hundreds of millions of people around the world. Over the next forty years the pressures will intensify. The challenge is a big one: how to produce more food with fewer non-renewable resources, without wrecking the environment, and in a way that creates prosperity for all. It can be done but it will require a massive effort. One thing is sure: we can no longer take food for granted.

ACKNOWLEDGEMENTS

This book is the product of five years of research, thinking and work on issues related to food, agriculture and the sustainable management of land. I would like to thank Justin Mundy for first introducing me to this subject and for acting as a mentor and an intellectual sparring partner throughout. Andreanne Grimard, David Barley, Lucy Holmes, Tony Juniper, David Edwards, Charlotte Cawthorne and the rest of the merry band at The Prince's Rainforests Project and The Prince's International Sustainability Unit provided plenty of input and encouragement during the book's long gestation. I have also benefited from conversations with Gerald Nelson, Tom Slayton, Javier Blas, Alex Bakir, Ann Berg and Leslie Lipper.

My practical understanding of the business of farming has been greatly helped by spending many hours in a car with my Australian colleagues at SLM Partners, Tony Lovell and Bruce Ward. Sadly, Bruce passed away in September 2012 – his deep wisdom and humility have left a lasting impression. Tony continues to combine ecology, finance and 'manly can-do' to achieve extraordinary results. My other colleagues at SLM Partners – Jack Gibbs, Hylton Murray-Philipson and David Ward – have all contributed to the ideas in this book and have helped to demonstrate how they can be put into practice. Words are just the prelude, action is far more important.

Chris Lane, a salty son of Walsall, did heroic work in reading through the manuscript and suggesting improvements. I thank Mark Ellingham and the rest of the staff at Profile Books for taking on this project and enthusiastically supporting it. My agent Maggie Hanbury has been a wise counsellor during the publishing process, and I am grateful to Maurice Walsh for making this introduction. Finally, I would like to thank Naomi for tolerating the many travels and long hours of seclusion that were needed to write this book. Hopefully, it was worth it.

SOURCES

I have benefited from countless books, papers, reports and conversations related to this topic over the last five years. Rather than attempting a comprehensive bibliography, this section provides sources for specific information and arguments presented in the text.

Introduction

Further details on the Saudi project in Ethiopia are in Ch. 9 of this book. Population predictions are from UN Population Division, *World population prospects, the 2010 revision*, 2010.

Ch. 1 A brief history of food

For Shennong see Lihui Yang & Deming An, *Handbook of Chinese mythology*, Oxford University Press, 2008. Figures for the number of edible plants, calories from crops and protein sources are from ICARDA, *Caravan*, No.128, Dec 2008 and the UN Food and Agriculture Organization (FAO).

For the section on the early origins of agriculture, the most insightful book is Marcel Mazoyer & Laurence Roudart, *A history of world agriculture: from the Neolithic age to the current crisis*, Earthscan, 2006. This section also draws on Mark Tauger, *Agriculture in world history*, Routledge, 2011; Thomas Sinclair and Carol Janas Sinclair, *Bread, beer and the seeds of change: agriculture's imprint on world history*, CABI Publishing, 2010; Francesca Bray, *The rice economies: technology and development in Asian societies*, University of California Press, 1986;

and Christian Anton Smedshaug, *Feeding the world in the 21st century: a historical analysis of agriculture and society*, The Anthem Press, 2010.

These same sources inform the rest of this chapter. In addition, the role of farming in eighteenth-century Britain is described in Tim Blanning, *The pursuit of glory: Europe 1648–1815*, Penguin, 2008; information on the amount of arable land in the 'New World', the falling costs of transport and the expansion of irrigated land is from Giovanni Federico, *Feeding the world: an economic history of agriculture, 1800–2000*, Princeton University Press, 2005; the history of fertilisers is from G. J. Leigh, *The world's greatest fix: a history of nitrogen and agriculture*, Oxford University Press, 2004; the value of crop protection in 2008 is given by Phillips McDougal, *AgriFutura*, April 2010; the impact of the Green Revolution is cited in Robert Paarlberg, 'Attention Whole Foods Shoppers', *Foreign Policy*, May/June 2010 and the International Fund for Rural Development (IFAD), *Rural poverty report 2011*, Rome, 2011.

Ch. 2 On the brink

Professor Haddad was speaking at the launch of Foresight's report on *The future of food and farming*, published by the UK Government Office for Science in 2011. Unless otherwise stated, all data on food trade in this chapter is from FAOSTAT or the FAO Statistics Division. Data on national GDP is from UNStats or the CIA Factbook.

Anthony Weis, *The global food economy: the battle for the future of farming*, Zed Books, 2007, cites the number of farmers in the USA and the importance of livestock. The story of high fructose maize syrup is described in Raj Patel, *Stuffed and starved: markets, power and the hidden battle for the world food system*, Portobello Books, 2008. US foreign food policy is covered in these two books, as well as in Dan Morgan, *Merchants of Grain*, Penguin, 1980.

The Economist article on the Cerrado is from 26 August 2010, which also describes the growth in Brazilian output. Details on the Chinese famine can be found in *South China Morning Post*, 6 July 2008 and Frank Dikötter, *Mao's great famine: the history of China's most devastating catastrophe, 1958–62*, Bloomsbury, 2011. The agricultural transformation since then is described in David Spielman and Rajul

Pandya-Lorch (ed.), *Millions fed: proven success in agricultural development*, IFPRI, 2009, and Robert Paarlberg, *Starved for science: how biotechnology is being kept out of Africa*, Harvard University Press, 2008. Data on crop yields and arable land in China is from FAOSTAT. India's agricultural revolution is showcased in Robert Paarlberg, 'Attention Whole Foods Shoppers', *Foreign Policy*, May/June 2010. Data on subsidies is from *AFP*, 21 Sep 2011.

GCC reliance on food exports is explored in *Emirates Business 24/7*, 17 Jan 2010 and *Financial Times*, 24 Feb 2011, while Japan's food dependence is highlighted in *The Japan Times*, 11 Feb 2000 and Christian Anton Smedshaug, *Feeding the world in the 21st century: a historical analysis of agriculture and society*, The Anthem Press, 2010. Eighteenth-century Britain is explored in Thomas Sinclair and Carol Janas Sinclair, *Bread, beer and the seeds of change: agriculture's imprint on world history*, CABI Publishing, 2010; the country's nineteenth-century dependence on imports in James Belich, *Replenishing the earth: the settler revolution and the rise of the Angloworld*, Oxford University Press, 2011; and the current situation in DEFRA, *UK food security assessment*, 2009. The ups and downs of EU food self-sufficiency are explained in H. von Witzke & S. Noleppa, *EU agricultural production and trade: can more efficiency prevent increasing 'land-grabbing' outside of Europe?*, Agripol, and in Smedshaug, *Feeding the world*.

The performance of African agriculture is described in FAO, '2050 – Africa's food challenge', 28 Sep 2009; UNCTAD, *Technology and Innovation Report 2010* ; Michael Fleshman, 'A harvest of hope for African farmers', *Africa Renewal Online*, 21 Sep 2011; and Weis, *The global food economy*. Data on the numbers working in farming and the prevalence of malnutrition is from IFAD, *Rural poverty report 2011* and FAO, *The state of food security in the world 2012*. Information on Egypt is from UNDP, on Mexico from Weis, *The global food economy*, and on the Philippines from Bruce Tolentino, *The globalization of food security: rice policy reforms in the Philippine*, Philippine Institute for Development Studies, 2002. Global food trade policy is outlined in Derek Headey & Shenggen Fan, *Reflections on the global food crisis*, IFPRI, 2010. Akin Adesina is quoted in Fleshman, 'A harvest of hope'.

Giovanni Federico gives his upbeat assessment of modern agriculture in *Feeding the world: an economic history of agriculture, 1800–2000*, Princeton University Press, 2005. The decline in investment is described in FAO, *Foreign direct investment: win-win or land grab*, 2009. Stagnating yields are identified in Alex Evans, *The feeding of the nine billion*, Chatham House, 2009. The impacts of obesity and micronutrient deficiency are examined in Foresight, *The future of food and farming*. The latest data on hunger is from FAO, *The state of food security*. The numbers dying from hunger are from Smedshaug, *Feeding the world* and David John Shaw, *World food security: a history since 1945*, Palgrave Macmillan, 2007. Mazoyer and Roudart were writing in *A history of world agriculture: from the Neolithic age to the current crisis*, Earthscan, 2006. Useful context for the state of the world's food system can also be found in Patrick Westhoff, *The economics of food: how feeding and fueling the planet affects food prices*, Pearson Education, 2010.

Ch. 3 The world food crisis

Unless otherwise stated, all data on food trade, production and consumption in this chapter is from the USDA Production, Supply and Distribution online database, which has the most up-to-date estimates. A good source for historical commodity prices is www.indexmundi.com.

Details on the Haitian food riots can be found in BBC, 'Haitian Senators vote to fire PM', 12 Apr 2008 and http://www.counterpunch.org/2008/04/21/the-u-s-role-in-haiti-s-food-riots/. Data on the prevalence of hunger is from FAO, *The state of food security in the world 2012*. Riots in Mozambique are described in IRIN, 'Mozambique: price increases "irreversible"', 2 Sep 2010, while events in North Africa are covered in Annia Ciezadlo, 'Let them eat bread', *Foreign Affairs*, 23 Mar 2011. The two quotes on the causes of the food crisis are from Alex Evans, *The feeding of the nine billion*, Chatham House, 2009, and the High Level Task Force on Food Security, *Comprehensive framework for action*, UN, 2008. Data on global consumption vs production of major food staples is from USDA.

The best source of population data is the UN Population Division, although the US Census Bureau also tracks global trends. '219,000 more mouths to feed' is from Lester Brown, *World on the edge: how to prevent environmental and economic collapse*, Routledge, 2011. Faster growth of meat consumption in developing countries is explored in Credit Suisse, *Higher agricultural prices*, 2007.

The volume of ethanol production in the USA is presented in Renewable Fuels Association, *Industry Statistics: Monthly U.S. Fuel Ethanol Production/Demand*, retrieved 30 Apr 2011. Ziegler and Monbiot are quoted in *The Guardian* on 6 Nov 2007. The High Level Panel of Experts on Food Security and Nutrition released an otherwise excellent report on *Price volatility and food security* in July 2011. For the political dimension of US food policy see Robert Paarlberg, *Food politics: what everyone needs to know*, Oxford University Press, 2010. Data on Brazilian ethanol is in Renewable Fuels Association, *Industry Statistics: 2010 World Fuel Ethanol Production*, retrieved 30 Apr 2011, whereas details on EU policies are found in Christian Anton Smedshaug, *Feeding the world in the 21st century: a historical analysis of agriculture and society*, The Anthem Press, 2010. For the break-even point of biofuels see *The Guardian*, 5 Jun 2011.

The Russian heatwave is described in *Time* magazine, 2 Aug 2010. Data on Australian wheat exports is from FAOSTAT and the impact on sugar exports from The Prince's International Sustainability Unit, *What price resilience? Towards sustainable and secure food systems*, Jul 2011. Losses from the Texan drought are estimated in *Financial Times*, 6 Sep 2011, while the impacts of the 2012 US drought are described in Bloomberg, 21 Aug 2012 and *Financial Times*, 10 & 30 Aug 2012. One recent report on climate extremes is IPCC, *Managing the risks of extreme events and disasters to advance climate change adaptation*, 2012. Others are referenced in *Financial Times*, 13 Jul 2012. Höppe is quoted in John Carey, 'Storm warnings: extreme weather is a product of climate change', *Scientific American*, 28 Jun 2011.

Estimated US yield growth is from Smedshaug, *Feeding the world*. Plateauing rice yields are described in B. McIntyre, H. Herren, et al, *Agriculture at the crossroads: International Assessment of Agricultural*

Knowledge, Science and Technology for Development, Island Press, 2009. Pesticide resistance is discussed in Gordon Conway, *The doubly green revolution: food for all in the twenty-first century*, Cornell University Press, 1999, while recent superweeds are assessed in *New York Times*, 3 May 2010. Information on Jealot's Hill is from a personal visit. The proportion of crops lost to pests is from Smedshaug, *Feeding the world*, as is the loss of arable land in China. The global figure for annual loss of usable land is from David Montgomery, *Dirt: the erosion of civilizations*, University of California Press, 2008. The section on water scarcity draws on Lester Brown, *World on the edge*, as well as Andrew Rice in the *New York Times*, 16 Nov 2009 and *Arabian Business*, 3 Mar 2010.

The dependence of fertilisers on natural gas is from C. J. Dawson and J. Hilton, 'Fertiliser availability in a resource-limited world: production and recycling of nitrogen and phosphorus', *Food policy*, vol. 36, 2011. Gray is quoted in *Financial Times*, 12 Jan 2011. Figures on rising input costs for American farmers are from USDA, *Amber waves*, Mar 2011. Over-exploitation of fisheries is discussed in FAO, *The state of world fisheries and aquaculture 2010*. Data on aquaculture and the 1 billion who rely on fish for protein is from FAO, 'Fish consumption reaches all time high', 2011. The Chile collapse is in UPI, 'Disease decimates salmon farms in Chile', 2010 (http://www.upi.com/Science_News/2010/08/17). The quote on sustainability is from Foresight, *The future of food and farming*, UK Government Office for Science, 2011.

Ch. 4 Was Malthus right?

The Mathus quote is from *An essay on the principle of population*, 1798, Ch. VII. For neo-Malthusians, warnings see William Paddock and Paul Paddock, *Famine 1975! America's decision: who will survive?*, Little Brown, 1967; Paul R. Ehrlich, *The population bomb*, Ballantine Books, 1968; and H. Donnella et al, *The limits to growth*, Earth Island, 1972. The latter's sales figures are from Wikipedia: http://en.wikipedia.org/wiki/The_Limits_to_Growth. 'Die-off' predictions are discussed in Cormac Ó'Gráda, *Famine: a short history*, Princeton University Press,

SOURCES

2010. For the alternative view, see Ester Boserup, *The conditions of agricultural growth: the economics of agrarian change under population pressure*, Allen & Unwin, 1965 and John Maddox, *Doomsday syndrome: an assault on pessimism*, Macmillan, 1972. One example of the return of Malthusian thought, this time fuelled by climate change, is Julian Cribb, *The coming famine: the global food crisis and what we can do to avoid it*, University of California Press, 2010. The Ehrlich and Brown quotes can be found in *The Guardian*, 23 Oct 2011 and Lester Brown, *World on the edge: how to prevent environmental and economic collapse*, Routledge, 2011.

IIASA's GAEZ v3.0 model is online at http://webarchive.iiasa.ac.at/Research/LUC/GAEZv3.0/. A more user-friendly analysis of this data is presented in G. Fischer et al, *Scarcity and abundance of land resources*, SOLAW Background Thematic Report – TR02, FAO, 2011. All data on land use and availability is from these sources unless otherwise stated. The shrinking of US cropland is explored in E. Wesley Peterson, *A billion dollars a day: the economics and politics of agricultural subsidies*, Wiley-Blackwell, 2009. The ideal growing conditions in Europe are identified by Klaus Hahlbrock, *Feeding the planet: environmental protection through sustainable agriculture*, Haus Publishing, 2009. Adesina is quoted in UNCTAD, *Technology and innovation report 2010*. For FAO prediction of 10 per cent land expansion see Jelle Bruinsma, *The resource outlook to 2050*, Expert Meeting on How to Feed the World in 2050, FAO, 2009. Climate change impacts are discussed in FAO, *The state of the world's land and water resources for food and agriculture: summary report*, 2011; Foresight, *The future of food and farming*, UK Government Office for Science, 2011; and IPCC, *The AR4 synthesis report*, 2007. For a recent paper that warns of more near-term impacts see World Bank & Potsdam Institute, *Turn the heat down: why a 4°C warmer world must be avoided*, 2012.

Energy use in food systems is from High Level Panel of Experts on Food Security and Nutrition, *Price volatility and food security*, July 2011. Early forms of biofuels are cited in Christian Anton Smedshaug, *Feeding the world in the 21st century: a historical analysis of agriculture and society*, The Anthem Press, 2010. '3 per cent of global energy consumption' is from Charles Godfray et al, 'The future of the global food system', *Philosophical Transactions of the Royal Society – Biological Sciences*, 2010, No. 365. The importance of nitrogen fertiliser is outlined in J.W. Erisman et al, 'How a century of ammonia synthesis has changed the world', *Nature Geoscience*, 1, 2008. US gas reserves are given in http://www.naturalgas.org/business/supply.asp and the figure for gas consumption in fertilisers is from Paul Fixen, 'World fertilizer nutrient reserves – a view to the future', *Better crops*, Vol. 93, No.3, 2009. Electrolysis is cited in The Royal Society, *Reaping the benefits: science and the sustainable intensification of global agriculture*, Oct 2009. G. J. Leigh, *The world's greatest fix: a history of nitrogen and agriculture*, Oxford University Press, 2004, contains the story of Kristian Birkeland. Phosphate reserve data is from C. J. Dawson & J. Hilton, 'Fertiliser availability in a resource-limited world: production and recycling of nitrogen and phosphorous', *Food Policy*, 36, Supplement 1, Jan 2011.

Simplistic statistics on water 'used' in food are presented in http://www.waterfootprint.org/Reports/Hoekstra-2008-Waterfootprint-Food.pdf and George Monbiot writing in *The Guardian*, 23 Dec 2002. Water use in transpiration is from Thomas Sinclair and Carol Janas Sinclair, *Bread, beer and the seeds of change: agriculture's imprint on world history*, CABI Publishing, 2010. Over-extraction of water for irrigation is covered in Fischer et al, *Scarcity and abundance of land resources*; FAO, *The state of the world's land and water resources*; AQUASTAT, FAO's online global information system on water and agriculture; and Water Resources Group, *Charting our water future*, 2009. For a positive assessment of water availability see CGIAR Challenge Program on Water & Food, *Water, food and poverty in river basins: defining the limits*, 2011. For a comprehensive review of the environmental externalities of agriculture, see Foresight, *The future of food and farming*.

Population predictions are from UN Population Division, *World population prospects, the 2010 revision*, 2010. The global middle class is analysed in McKinsey & Company, *Resource revolution: meeting the world's energy, materials, food and water needs*, 2011. Meat consumption data is from Smedshaug, *Feeding the world*. FAO, *The state of the world's land and water resources* provides the standard estimates of required increases in food production. Food waste in Britain is cited in Danish Academy of Technical Sciences (ATV), *Food for all forever*, 2010 and ways to reduce waste are presented in Foresight, *The future of food and farming*. Data on use of cereals to feed animals is in FAO, *Food outlook*, Nov 2011. The cost of obesity and the potential to divert more grains for human consumption are discussed in two UNEP reports, *Towards a green economy: pathways to sustainable development and poverty eradication*, 2011, and *The environmental food crisis*, 2008. The role of political economy in causing famines is explored by Amartya Sen in *Development as freedom*, Oxford Paperback, 2001.

Ch. 5 This time is different

The idea that price rises would only be temporary can be found in E. Wesley Peterson, *A billion dollars a day: the economics and politics of agricultural subsidies*, Wiley-Blackwell, 2009 and Robert Paarlberg, *Food politics: what everyone needs to know*, Oxford University Press, 2010. Further examples are given in High Level Panel of Experts on Food Security and Nutrition, *Price volatility and food security*, July 2011, as is the quote from Prof. Timmer. For the perils of 'new paradigms' see Carmen Reinhart & Kenneth Rogoff, *This time is different: eight centuries of financial folly*, Princeton University Press, 2009.

Energy price projections are given in International Energy Agency, *World energy outlook 2011*. Case studies assessing the 'true cost' of food are presented in The Prince's International Sustainability Unit, *What price resilience? Towards sustainable and secure food systems*, Jul 2011, which this author helped to write. The cost of bringing new, marginal land into cultivation is highlighted in FAO, *Save and grow: A policymaker's guide to sustainable intensification of smallholder crop production*, 2011 and Gordon Conway, *The doubly green revolution: food for all in the twenty-first century*, Cornell University Press, 1999. Constraints are presented in G. Fischer et al, *Scarcity and abundance of land resources*, SOLAW Background Thematic Report – TR02, FAO, 2011. Costs in Mato Grosso are based on analysis of information provided by the Chicago Board of Trade, Wells Fargo and USDA, *Soybean transportation guide*, 2008. Biofuels as a per cent of future transport fuels is covered in Günther Fischer & Sylvia Prieler, *Impacts of biofuel expansion on world food systems and the environment*, ELOBIO, 2010, and R. Murphy et al, 'Global developments in the competition for land from biofuels', *Food Policy*, 2011, doi:10.1016/j.foodpol.2010.11.014. Projections for diversion of food to biofuels are in OECD/FAO, *Agricultural outlook 2012*. The impact on food prices is estimated in Fischer & Prieler, *Impacts of biofuel expansion*. Josef Schmidhuber discusses how biofuels will place a floor under food prices and Brazil sugar markets in *Biofuels: an emerging threat to Europe's food security*, Notre Europe, 2007, while the US maize example is in *Financial Times*, 2 Feb 2011. For the long-term potential of bioenergy see Hans Langeveld & J. Dixon, 'Development perspectives of the bio-based economy: the need for a systems approach', 9th European IFSA Symposium, 4–7 July 2010. The historic use of land in USA for biofuels is from Christian Anton Smedshaug, *Feeding the world in the 21st century: a historical analysis of agriculture and society*, The Anthem Press, 2010. Losses in the US pork industry are given in *Financial Times*, 10 Sep 2012.

Predictions of high prices in the future can be found in Thomas Helbling & Shaun Roche (IMF), 'Rising prices on the menu', *Finance & Development*, Mar 2011; Gerard Nelson et al, *Food security, farming and climate change to 2050*, IFPRI, 2010; Chatham House, *The feeding of the nine billion*, 2009; D. Willenbockel, *Exploring food price scenarios towards 2030 with a global multi-region model*, Oxfam Research Report, 2011; Goldman Sachs research quoted in *Bloomberg*, 31 Mar 2010; Deutsche Bank Climate Change Advisors, *Investing in agriculture: far-reaching challenge, significant opportunity*, 2009; Nomura, *The coming surge in food prices*, Sep 2010; Foresight, *The future of food and farming*; and OECD-FAO, *Agricultural outlook 2011–2020*.

Commodity price volatility is analysed in Stefan Tangerman, *Policy solutions to agricultural market volatility: a synthesis*, International Centre for Trade and Sustainable Development, 2011. Income and inelasticity are discussed in High Level Panel of Experts, *Price volatility and food security*. Extreme weather events are the focus of Oxfam, *Extreme weather, extreme prices*, Sep 2012 and Nelson et al, *Food security, farming and climate change.* For Russian agriculture, see Dan Morgan, *Merchants of Grain*, Penguin, 1980; Mark Tauger, *Agriculture in world history*, Routledge, 2011; and *Financial Times*, 28 Aug 2012 & 8 Nov 2012. Hafez Ghanem, the FAO's assistant-general for economic and social development, makes the point that increased reliance on the Black Sea region will lead to more market volatility in FAO, 'No food crisis seen, but greater market stability needed', 7 Sep 2010. The IFPRI quote on trade is from Nelson et al, *Food security, farming and climate change.*

Ch. 6 Starve thy neighbour

There is a vast literature on the Prisoner's Dilemma available online. Its application to American and European subsidies is referenced in Kyle Bagwell & Robert Staiger, 'Strategic trade, competitive industries and agricultural trade disputes', 2000.

Unless otherwise stated, the information on rice markets is drawn from an interview with Tom Slayton and from his paper 'Rice crisis forensics: how Asian governments carelessly set the world rice market on fire', Centre for Global Development, Working Paper No. 163, March 2009, with some additional material from Derek Headey, *Rethinking the global food crisis: the role of trade shocks*, IFPRI, Mar 2010. Saudi subsidies are mentioned in Thomas Lippman (Council on Foreign Relations), 'Saudi Arabia's quest for "food security"', *Middle East Policy*, Vol. 17, No. 11, Spring 2010. The section on wheat markets is based on Headey, *Rethinking the global food crisis* and Oxfam, *The impact of Russia's 2010 grain export ban*, 2011. Information on African events is from *Agritrade*, 6 Oct 2011 and Heidi Fritschel, 'Overcoming traders' block', *IFPRI Insights*, Vol. 1, Issue 1, 17 Oct 2011. The FAO survey is described in Ramesh Sharma, *Food export restrictions*, FAO, May 2011. The impact on prices is estimated by W. Martin and K. Anderson in 'Export restrictions and price insulation during commodity price booms', World Bank Policy Research Working Paper, 2011. Franck Galtier makes the case that trade restrictions are one of the few tools available to countries in 'What can the international community do to help developing countries manage food price instability?', CIRAD, May 2011. Many of the arguments made in this chapter are supported by a recent report edited by Simon J.Evenett and Frédéric Jenny, *Trade, competition and the pricing of commodities*, Centre for Economic Policy Research, 2011.

The story of Sir John Boyd Orr is found in Amy Staples, 'To win the peace: the Food and Agriculture Organization, Sir John Boyd Orr, and the World Food Board proposals', *Peace & Change*, Vol. 28, No. 4, October 2003, and David John Shaw, *World food security: a history since 1945*, Palgrave Macmillan, 2007. Boyd Orr presents his own ideas in John Boyd Orr, *The white man's dilemma*, Barnes & Noble, 1965. The 'one of the boldest' quote is from R. P. Sinha, 'World food security', *Journal of Agricultural Economics*, XXVII, 1, 1976. Shaw provides much detail on food governance initiatives in subsequent decades, as well as the quote from Aziz. *Time*, 11 Nov 1974, has an excellent feature on the World Food Summit of 1974. Wry reflections on the 2009 summit can be found in Reuters, 18 Nov 2009. WTO and G20 efforts are reviewed in Fritschel, 'Overcoming traders' block'. Shaw, a former FAO official, makes the comment on 'the graveyard of aspirations'. Pinstrup-Anderson was speaking at IFPRI on 21 Nov 2011 – his talk is available online.

Philippines policy is described in Slayton, 'Rice crisis forensics'; Chinese subsidies in AFP, 21 Sep 2011; Chinese imports in Reuters, 'China imports corn, soy to rebuild state reserves', 13 Oct 2011; and the growth of Chinese stocks in High Level Panel of Experts on Food Security and Nutrition, *Price volatility and food security*, July 2011. Measures taken by other countries are described in http://makanaka.wordpress.com/2011/03/05/food-reserves-strategic-foodgrain-stocks-and-port-protests/. Recent action by Russia and Ukraine is probed in *Financial Times*, 19 & 22 Oct, 6 & 8 Nov 2012. For the Thai proposals, see Slayton, 'Rice crisis forensics' and USDA, 'Thailand grain and feed OREC 2008,' 7 May 2008; while Russia's flirtation with a grain cartel is described at http://www.stratfor.com/weekly/20100809_drought_fire_and_grain_russia and http://www.russianintelligencer.com/articles/grain-cartel.html. The Korean report is Samsung Economic Research Institute, *New food strategies in the age of global food crises*, 2011. Neo-liberal angst at government policy is expressed in *The Economist*, 19 Nov 2009 and *Wall Street Journal*, 18 Jul 2012.

Ch. 7 Trading in the wind

Anthony Ward's career is described in *Financial Times*, 23 Jul 2010. The *Financial Times* produces the best coverage of day-to-day developments in these markets. The value of Amarjaro cocoa contracts is cited in Ann Berg, 'The rise of commodity speculation: from villainous to venerable', in Adam Prakash, *Safeguarding food security in volatile global markets*, FAO, 2011. Criticism of hedge funds is quoted in Reuters and *The Guardian*, 6 Jul 2010, and in *Financial Times*, 29 Jul 2010. Berg summarises the history of food speculation in 'The rise of commodity speculation'. Sarkozy is quoted in *New York Times*, 6 Feb 2011, while speculators are blamed for many things in *The Independent*, 23 Aug 2012 and *The Guardian*, 2 Aug 2012.

The lack of understanding of commodity markets among economists is critically evaluated in Institute for Agriculture and Trade Policy (IATD), *Excessive speculation in agriculture commodities: selected writings from 2008–2011*, 2011. UNCTAD, *Price formation in financialized commodity markets*, 2011, provides a good overview of how these markets work, as well as details on exchanges worldwide. Emily Lambert, *The futures: the rise of the speculator and the origins of the world's biggest markets*, Basic Books, 2011 charts the colourful history of American markets, although it is light on critical analysis. The Rabobank trader is quoted in *Euromoney*, Sep 2011. Position limits and soft red wheat futures are discussed in Berg, 'The rise of commodity speculation'; the amount of money flowing into commodities is quantified in High Level Panel of Experts on Food Security and Nutrition, *Price volatility and food security*, July 2011 and *Financial Times*, 19 Jul & 4 Dec 2011; and UNCTAD, *Price formation*, tracks the number of outstanding contracts. The dominance of high frequency traders is assessed in *Financial Times*, 17 Jun 2012.

Van Praag is quoted in *Daily Mail*, 29 Jun 2011. C. L. Gilbert presents his research in 'Speculative influences on commodity futures prices 2006–2008', UNCTAD Discussion Paper, No. 197, March 2011. IATD, *Excessive speculation in agriculture commodities* contains similar arguments. Details on Ann Berg are from her website (http://www.annberg.com/biography.html) and *Daily Mail*, 29 Jun 2011. She presents her views in 'The rise of commodity speculation'. Herd behaviour in financial markets is discussed in UNCTAD, *Price formation*, as are traders talking about the 'Wall Street mentality' and 'lemmings'. The 2008 trader hoping for 'one more fool' was quoted by Per Pinstrup-Anderson in a talk at IFPRI on 21 Nov 2011. The candid Goldman Sachs analyst – an oil analyst although the same principal applies to food markets – is quoted in Andrew Awad & Woody Canaday et al, 'The Global Commodities Boom', Greenwich Associates, May 2008. For coffee market 'squeezes' see *Financial Times*, 14 Feb 2012. The US Senate Sub-Committee report is in IATD, *Excessive speculation in agriculture commodities*, as are details on reductions in hedging in Kansas in 2008. The 'casino' quote is from UNCTAD, *Price formation*, while the comments on sugar are contained in *Financial Times*, 30 May 2012. For recent efforts to curtail speculation see *Financial Times*, 25 Jan, 16 Feb & 19 Aug 2012. Increased correlation is explored in *Financial Times*, 26 May 2011 & 26 Mar 2012.

Ch. 8 Stirring the alphabet soup

The best source of information on commodity trading firms is the *Financial Times*. Its commodities team, led by Xavier Blas, has tracked key developments since 2008. The history of the ABCD firms and Glencore is covered in Dan Morgan, *Merchants of Grain*, Penguin, 1980; the Berne Declaration, *Commodities: Switzerland's most dangerous business*, 2011; and on the company websites. Further details on Louis Dreyfus are presented in *Bloomberg Markets Magazine*, 31 Jan 2012 and *Financial Times*, 6 Sep 2012, while the latter compared Cargill to ExxonMobil on 19 May 2010. Glencore's history is also discussed in Al Jazeera, 9 May 2011. Tax avoidance is one of the main themes of Berne Declaration, *Commodities*. The latter quotes a Boston Consulting Group report on the total share of grain trade controlled by the ABCDs (73 per cent in 2003), while data on Glencore's market share (9 per cent in 2010) is revealed in its public offering documents. These five companies probably control around 80 per cent of the grain trade, although no one is really sure. Samsung Economic Research Institute, *New food strategies in the age of global food crises*, 2011, warns of market dominance, as do Simon J. Evenett & Frédéric Jenny, *Trade, competition and the pricing of commodities*, Centre for Economic Policy Research, 2011 and Per Pinstrup-Anderson in a talk at IFPRI, 21 Nov 2011. Company revenues and profits are estimated from company reports, press interviews by Louis Dreyfus executives and data in the Glencore offering documents. The Deutsche Bank report on Glencore is dated 6 Jun 2011. 'Short' positions are discussed in UNCTAD, *Price formation in financialized commodity markets*, 2011, while the profitability of futures speculation can be deduced from the Glencore public offering documents (which reveal that 'directional price betting' accounted for 14 per cent of company profits in 2010), ABCD company annual reports and information on Louis Dreyfus in *Financial Times*, 24 Apr 2011. Glencore's bet on wheat prices is revealed in *Financial Times*, 24 Apr 2011. Oxfam is quoted in *The Independent*, 23 Aug 2012, and similar views can be found in Raj Patel, *Stuffed and starved: markets, power and the hidden battle for the world food system*, Portobello Books, 2008. Data on the Cargill transport network is from 'Cargill Fast Facts', Mar 2012, available on the company website. ADM losses are from private information.

Noble is profiled in *Forbes*, 4 Dec 2009 and in Berne Declaration, *Commodities*. Information on Olam is from *Financial Times*, 24 Sep 2010 & 19 Aug 2012 and confidential interviews. Marubeni's actions are discussed in *Financial Times*, 28 Nov 2010 & 29 May 2012 and Reuters, 31 May 2012. Mitsui is profiled in *Nikkei Weekly*, 17 Jan 2011. South Korea's attempts to create a grain trading infrastructure are covered in *Financial Times*, 10 Jan 2011; *The Korea Herald*, 24 Mar 2011; *Bloomberg Business Week*, 25 Apr 2011; and US Grains Council press release, 1 Mar 2012. China's activities in South America are explored in *Washington Times*, 1 Feb 2012. Olam's land deals are described in *Daily Trust*, 23 Feb 2011; Bloomberg, 19 Jan 2012; Agrimoney.com, 29 May 2012; and *Financial Times*, 19 Aug 2012. Mitsui's desire for land is explored in Fred Pearce, *The landgrabbers: the new fight over who owns the earth*, Eden Project Books, 2012, while the Chongqing Grain Group is covered in *Want China Times*, 15 Mar 2012. Sunny Verghese is quoted in *Financial Times*, 19 Aug 2012. The Viterra deal is analysed in *Financial Times*, 15 Mar 2012 and *The Globe and Mail*, 28 May 2012. The GrainCorp battle can be found in *Financial Times*, 22 & 25 Oct 2012. The Goldberg quote is in Reuters, 31 May 2012. The Verghese interview can be found at http://video.ft.com/v/1583879207001/ Olam-sees-more-agriculture-M-A. Figures on mis-pricing in Africa are from Global Financial Integrity, *Illicit financial flows from Africa: hidden resource for development*, 2010.

Ch. 9 Land grabs

The rice ceremony is described in *Middle East Online*, 3 Feb 2009 and *Addis Fortune*, 14 Sep 2009. Details on Al Amoudi can be found in *Ethiomedia*, 3 Dec 2009 and *New York Times*, 22 Nov 2009. Ethiopian policy towards land deals is presented in the same *New York Times* article, and in *Washington Post*, 23 Nov 2009 and Bloomberg, 9 May 2012. Al Amoudi's business plans and machinery purchases are detailed in *Irish Times*, 30 Jan 2010, *The Observer*, 7 Mar 2010 and *Addis Fortune*, 21 Feb 2010. The tribal situation and the link between 'villagization' and foreign land deals are analysed in Human Rights Watch, *Waiting here for death: forced displacement and "villagization" in Ethiopia's Gambella Region*, 2012. Omot Ochan's story is contained in Fred Pearce, *The landgrabbers: the new fight over who owns the earth*, Eden Project Books, 2012. The attack on Saudi Star workers is reported by Bloomberg, 30 May 2012. The Solidarity Movement statement appears in *African Agriculture*, 6 Jun 2012.

The World Bank report is *Rising global interest in farmland*, 2011 and the Oxfam figures are quoted in Bloomberg, 22 Sep 2011. Unless otherwise stated, figures on the extent and location of land deals in this chapter are taken from the Land Matrix database, available online at http://landportal.info/landmatrix and accessed on 27 July 2012. (This database contains 924 deals. All deals identified as domestic in origin (274) have been removed to focus on foreign deals (the remaining 650). However, the origin of investor is not given for 224 of the remaining deals. These deals have been included with foreign deals for the purposes of the analysis, although in reality a number are likely to be domestic in origin.) The World Bank quote is from *Rising global interest in farmland*. For the role of local deal-makers see France 24, 25 Dec 2009 and *This is Africa*, 2 Jul 2012. Consistent with the Land Matrix data, two-thirds of the land deals tracked by World Bank, *Rising global interest in farmland*, were in Africa.

Saudi activities are described in *Financial Times*, 24 May 2009 and GRAIN, *Against the grain*, 29 Nov 2010. Qatari land deals are described in AFP, 9 Jul 2009, *Time*, 13 Mar 2009, *The National*, 12 Dec 2009 and *Gulf Times*, 1 Jun 2010. The UAE official is quoted in *Gulf News*, 12 Jul 2012. South Korean deals are detailed in *The Korea Herald*, 23 Mar 2011 and *Asahi Simbun*, 20 Feb 2012. Financial investors, including Susan Payne, are profiled in *Wall Street Journal*, 29 Oct 2010, *New York Times*, 16 Nov 2009 and *The Observer*, 7 Mar 2010. The Sime Darby project is assessed in Ecological Internet, 'Malaysia's hollow democracy: government censors internet criticism of global rainforest for oil palm land grab', 16 May 2009. A good review of biofuels projects can be found in *The Guardian*, 5 Jun 2011. Agricola's plans are cited in *Zawya*, 6 Apr 2010, while *The Telegraph*, 28 Jun 2009 covers Indian activities. The figure for total deals in South Sudan is from *The Times*, 2 Jul 2011. Heilberg's activities are covered widely, especially in *Financial Times*, 9 Jan 2009, Reuters, 27 Jan 2009, BBC, 28 Jan 2009, *Fortune*, 10 Jun 2009 and *Rolling Stone*, 27 May 2010. Germany's policy coordinator for Africa, Guenter Nooke, blamed Chinese land acquisitions in Ethiopia for contributing to famine in the Horn of Africa in *Der Spiegel*, 28 Jul 2011. The reality of Chinese activity is presented in SIANI, 'Chinese "land grabs" in Africa – the reality behind the news', 27 Apr 2012. A wealth of additional detail on land deals can be found at www.farmlandgrab.org, although because this is mostly a collection of media reports not all of it can be relied on.

The figure for customary tenure in Africa is from FAO, 'Information Sheet on Climate Change and Biofuels for the High-Level Conference on World Food Security', 2008. The limited economic benefits of land deals at a local level are mentioned in FAO, 'Foreign Direct Investment – win-win or land grab?', 2009. The environmental impacts of land deals are described in Pearce, *The landgrabbers*. The World Bank points out the risks in *Rising global interest in farmland*. For an eloquent description of emotional attachment to the land in Africa see Chido Makunike writing in Woodrow Wilson International Center for Scholars, *Land grab? The race for the world's farmland*, 2009. *The Globe and Mail*, 16 Nov 2009 notes the 'hot button issue' at the World Food Summit. The attack on the farm manager is covered in *How We Made it in Africa*, 9 Jun 2012. The Daewoo project is referenced in *This is Africa,* 2 Jul 2012. Diseconomies of scale in agriculture are dealt with in Giovanni Federico, *Feeding the world: an economic history of agriculture, 1800–2000*, Princeton University Press, 2005; World Bank, *Rising global interest in farmland*; and Lorenzo Cotula et al, *Land grab or development opportunity: agricultural investment and international land deals in Africa*, IIED, 2009. The Karuturi Global farm is profiled in *Times of India*, 26 Sep 2009, *Business World*, 2 Jun 2012 and *How We Made it in Africa*, 12 Jun 2012. Failed biofuel projects are described in *The Observer*, 29 Oct 2011, *Mail & Guardian* online, 10 Mar 2012 and on the ActionAid website at http://www.actionaid.org.uk/102838/biofuels_research.html. The World Bank findings on stalled deals are in *Rising global interest in farmland*. This report also refers to the history of unsuccessful deals, as do CNN, 5 Jul 2012 (for Sudan) and *Arusha Times*, 5 May 2006 and *The Citizen*, 18 Jun 2012 (for Tanzania). CDC's track record is explored by Graham Dixie in 'What does the past teach us about agribusiness investments?', World Bank, Nov 2011. Saudi wheat subsidies are cited in *The Globe and Mail*, 30 Jan 2009. Padraig Carmody, *The new scramble for Africa*, Polity Press, 2011 assesses the emergence of enclave capitalism in Africa. The latest Saudi plans in Sudan are revealed in *Sudan Tribune*, 9 Apr 2012. Reprisals in Gambella were reported by the Anywaa Survival Organisation on 3 May 2012, although they have not been independently verified. The 'armed camp' reference is from *African agriculture*, 6 Jun 2012, and the latest announcements by Saudi Star are in Bloomberg, 5 Apr & 30 May 2012. Kofi Annan was quoted in *This is Africa*, 2 July 2012.

Ch. 10 How this story might end

Unless otherwise stated, the analysis of land availability and population in this chapter is based on IIASA's GAEZ v3.0 model and the projections in UN Population Division, *World population prospects, the 2010 revision*, 2010. Climate change impacts are drawn from IPCC, *The AR4 synthesis report*, 2007, and Gerard Nelson et al, *Food security, farming and climate change to 2050*, IFPRI, 2010.

For warnings about Chinese agriculture see Lester Brown, *Who will feed China? Wake-up call for a small planet*, Norton & Company, 1995, and *World on the Edge: How to Prevent Environmental and Economic Collapse*, Routledge, 2011. Water scarcity in India is presented in CGIAR, *Climate, agriculture and food security*, Dec 2009; UNEP, *The environmental food crisis*, 2008; and Water Resources Group, *Charting our water future*, 2009. Projections for Indian and Chinese grain imports are given in McKinsey & Company, *Resource revolution: meeting the world's energy, materials, food and water needs*, 2011. Food importing by the Arab world is examined by Earth Policy Institute, 2 May 2012, *Emirates Business 24/7*, 17 Jan 2010 and Reuters, 7 Apr 2010. African agriculture's susceptibility to climate change is made clear in Günther Fischer, 'World food and agriculture to 2030/50', Expert Meeting on How to Feed the World in 2050, FAO, 2009. The figures for uncultivated land in E. Africa are given in Vera Songwe & Klaus Deininger, 'Foreign investment in agricultural production', World Bank, ARD, Issue 45, 2009.

The geopolitics of food are explored by Lester Brown in 'The new geopolitics of food', *Foreign Policy*, May/June 2011. US food diplomacy in the twentieth century is explored in Dan Morgan, *Merchants of Grain*, Penguin, 1980, while data on exports to Iran are found in Reuters, 15 Oct 2012. The importance of US food exports to China is cited in *Financial Times*, 20 Mar 2012 and *DTN*, 27 Apr

2012. The westward reconfiguration of American logistics is described in *Financial Times*, 12 Jul 2010. The broader context of China's search for resources is examined in Padraig Carmody, *The new scramble for Africa*, Polity Press, 2011. China's loans-for-oil deals are analysed in Associated Press, 6 Jun 2011, while the recent deal with Ukraine is reported in *Financial Times*, 19 Sep 2012. India's special treatment of neighbours is described in Derek Headey, *Rethinking the global food crisis: the role of trade shocks*, IFPRI, Mar 2010. Projected cereal imports by developing countries are in FAO, 'How to feed the world in 2050', 2009. The IMF findings are in Rabah Arezki & Markus Brückner, 'Food prices and political instability', IMF Working Paper, Mar 2011. The Bob Marley song is 'Them Belly Full (But We Hungry)'. The conflict in Côte d'Ivoire is explored in Camilla Toulmin & Saleemul Huq, 'Adapting to climate change: insights from the West African Sahel', in ICARDA, *Caravan*, Dec 2008, while climate migration is covered in Nicholas Stern, *Stern review on the economics of climate change*, HM Treasury, 2006. The US scenario planning is found in National Intelligence Council, *Global Trends 2025*, 2008.

The agricultural expansion of the Roman Empire is described in Mark Tauger, *Agriculture in world history*, Routledge, 2011; the role of Teutonic Knights in Marcel Mazoyer & Laurence Roudart, *A history of world agriculture: from the Neolithic age to the current crisis*, London, Earthscan, 2006; the taming of the grasslands and Japanese colonialism in James Belich, *Replenishing the earth: the settle revolution and the rise of the Angloworld*, Oxford University Press, 2011; and French policy in Indochina in Francesca Bray, *The rice economies: technology and development in Asian societies*, University of California Press, 1986. The World Bank report on the African Guinea Savannah is quoted in Fred Pearce, *The landgrabbers: the new fight over who owns the earth*, Eden Project Books, 2012, which talks about the 'final enclosure' of land. The parallels with Cecil Rhodes are drawn by Robin Palmer in 'Would Cecil Rhodes have signed a Code of Conduct? Reflections on Global Land Grabbing and Land Rights in Africa, Past and Present', presented at the International Conference on Global Land Grabbing, IDS Sussex, 6–8 Apr 2011. Formal vs informal empire is the topic of a well-known article by John Gallagher & Ronald Robinson, 'The imperialism of free trade', *The Economic History Review*, Vol. VI, no. 1, 1953. The complicity of African elites is identified in Carmody, *The new scramble for Africa*. Food First warned of 'cereal republics' in a press statement on 4 Feb 2010. Food exports during the Irish Famine are detailed in Belich, *Replenishing the earth*. See also Cormac Ó'Gráda, *Famine: a short history*.

Ch. 11 Better ways to feed the world

10 billion is the median projection in UN Population Division, *World population prospects, the 2010 revision*, 2010. Block is quoted in Eric Holt-Gimenez & Raj Patel, *Food rebellions! Crisis and the hunger for justice*, Food First Books, 2009. The fall in value of tropical commodities is explored in Peter Robbins, *Stolen fruit: the tropical commodities disaster*, Zed Books, 2003. The effectiveness of agricultural growth in reducing poverty is a major theme of the *World Development Report 2008* by the World Bank. For the symbiosis between rural and urban growth see Christian Anton Smedshaug, *Feeding the world in the 21st century: a historical analysis of agriculture and society*, The Anthem Press, 2010 and, much earlier, Adam Smith, *The wealth of nations*, 1776. Sources for the role of agriculture in industrial revolutions are the same as for Ch. 1, with additional material from Gordon Conway, *The doubly green revolution: food for all in the twenty-first century*, Cornell University Press, 1999. The Collier article is 'The politics of hunger: how illusion and greed fan the food crisis', *Foreign Affairs*, Nov/Dec 2008. Details on the shrinking of the agricultural labour force in advanced countries can be found in Giovanni Federico, *Feeding the world: an economic history of agriculture, 1800–2000*, Princeton University Press, 2005. *The Economist* article on Brazil appeared on 26 Aug 2010, whereas a deeper analysis of the patterns of Brazilian farm development can be found in World Bank, *Rising global interest in farmland*, 2011. *The Guardian*, 14 Mar 2008 refers to unequal land ownership in Brazil. Country comparisons of growth rates are based on FAOSTAT data. Vietnam is profiled in IFAD, *Rural poverty report 2011*, Rome, 2011; World Bank,

Rising global interest in farmland; and Joachim Von Braun, 'Food security risks must be comprehensively addressed'. IFPRI, 2009. For strong endorsements of the importance of smallholders see Foresight, *The future of food and farming*, UK Government Office for Science, 2011; FAO, *Save and grow: A policymaker's guide to sustainable intensification of smallholder crop production*, 2011; and B. McIntyre, H. Herren, et al, *Agriculture at the crossroads: International Assessment of Agricultural Knowledge, Science and Technology for Development*, Island Press, 2009. The World Bank quote is from *Rising global interest in farmland*.

Government policy in Asia is described in IFAD, *Rural poverty report 2011* and by the FAO at http://www.fao.org/docrep/W7442E/w7442e07.htm#TopOfPage. Clinton's comments on Haiti were reported by The Huffington Post, 20 Mar 2010, while his comments on food self-sufficiency were relayed by the Associated Press on 11 Feb 2009. Senegal's new policy is described in UNCTAD, *Technology and Innovation Report 2010*; Nigeria's is in CTA, *Agritrade*, 12 Aug 2012. The Malawi case study is presented in Andrew Dorward & E. Chirwa, 'The Malawi agricultural input subsidy programme: 2005–6 to 2008–9', *International Journal of Agricultural Sustainability*, 9, 1, 2011 and in *Africa Renewal*, Vol.22, No. 3, Oct 2008. The president is quoted in Reuters, 29 Mar 2010.

Robert Paarlberg's views are in 'Attention Whole Foods Shoppers', *Foreign Policy*, May/June 2010. One cheerleader for industrial agriculture is Gary Blumenthal, who writes in Woodrow Wilson International Center for Scholars, *Land grab? The race for the world's farmland*, 2009. Beltrão Gomes is quoted in *The Guardian*, 13 Mar 2008. 'Agrarian romantics' is from Robert Paarlberg, *Starved for science: how biotechnology is being kept out of Africa*, Harvard University Press, 2008. The size of the organic market is given in IFAD, *Rural poverty report*. Friedmann is quoted in Anthony Weis, *The global food economy: the battle for the future of farming*, Zed Books, 2007. For scientists that advocate a synthesis between ecology and technology see Conway, *The doubly green revolution* and David Montgomery, *Dirt: the erosion of civilizations*, University of California Press, 2008. Professor Conway of Imperial College London, a former president of the Rockefeller

Foundation, calls the emergence of ecology as a sophisticated discipline 'the second great revolution in modern biology' alongside genetics. Rothamstead's archives are explored in G. J. Leigh, *The world's greatest fix: a history of nitrogen and agriculture*, Oxford University Press, 2004. Similar findings from farm plots in the USA were recently published by Iowa State University – see *New York Times*, 19 Oct 2012. Agro-ecology or eco-agriculture is defined by Olivier de Schutter in a report for the UN Human Rights Council, 20 Dec 2010; by Louise Buck & Sara Scherr in The Worldwatch Institute, *State of the world 2011: innovations that nourish the planet*, 2011; and by Jules Pretty in *Monthly Review*, Vol. 61, Issue 6, Nov 2009. Integrated pest management is profiled in The Royal Society, *Reaping the benefits: science and the sustainable intensification of global agriculture*, Oct 2009; zero-till in Argentina in David Spielman and Rajul Pandya-Lorch (ed.), *Millions fed: proven success in agricultural development*, IFPRI, 2009; agro-forestry in World Agroforestry Centre, 'Agro-forestry using the Faidherbia tree in sub-saharan Africa'; complex crop rotations in Iowa in *The New American Farmer*, 2005 and *New York Times*, 19 Oct 2012; and rice intensification in IFAD, *Rural poverty report 2011*. The idea of 'organic GMOs' is floated by the Royal Society in *Reaping the benefits*, but IFAD explains how GMOs will remain out of reach for poor farmers in *Rural poverty report 2011*. Hurricane Mitch is discussed in the de Schutter report for the UN. Details on Allan Savory and the holistic grazing system can be found in Allan Savory, *Holistic management: a new framework for decision making*, Island Press, 1998; Mark Stevenson, *An optimist's tour of the future*, Profile, 2011; and the website of the Savory Institute http://www.savoryinstitute.com/. Other sources are in the author's possession. The amount of grazing land is in FAO, *The state of the world's land and water resources for food and agriculture: summary report*, 2011. The grazing system was selected by the Virgin Earth Challenge for its contribution to climate change mitigation. See http://www.virgin.com/people-and-planet/blog/virgin-earth-challenge-announces-leading-organisations. Large-scale land restoration is also taking place in China, as described in World Bank, 'Restoring China's Loess Plateau', 2007.

Studies showing the potential in developing countries are Jules Pretty et al, 'Resource-conserving agriculture increases yields in developing countries', *Environmental Science and Technology*, Vol. 40, No. 4, 2006; Jules Pretty et al., 'Sustainable intensification in African agriculture', *International Journal of Agricultural Sustainability*, Vol. 9, No. 1, 2011; and Catherine Badgleya & Ivette Perfecto, 'Can organic agriculture feed the world?', *Renewable Agriculture and Food Systems*, 22, 2007. Yield reduction in organic systems in advanced countries is described in Verena Seufert et al, 'Comparing the yields of organic and conventional agriculture', *Nature* http://dx.doi.org/10.1038/nature11069, 2012. The studies advocating agro-ecology have already been mentioned except for the work of CIRAD which can be found at http://www.cirad.fr/en/innovation-expertise/skills-and-expertise/inventing-an-ecologically-intensive-form-of-agriculture-to-feed-the-planet. China's new policy is referenced in IFAD, *Rural poverty report* and Brazil's in the de Schutter report for the UN.

Investment needs are estimated in FAO, 'How to Feed the World in 2050', 2009; Hallam is quoted in *The Independent*, 3 May 2009; and Turner's remarks are reported in *The Guardian*, 27 Aug 2009. The Kofi Annan speech at Cape Town is contained in an AGRA press release, 11 Jun 2009. The Pepsi example can be found in Chandra Shekara (ed.), *Private Extension: Indian experiences*, National Institute of Agricultural Extension Management, 2001; the Moroccan programme is outlined in the *McKinsey Quarterly*, Apr 2011; and the Tilda plant is covered in Reuters, 14 Aug 2009. Information on the Chiansi project can be found in Private Infrastructure Development Group, *InfraCo Africa: Progress Review 2010* and at http://www.infracoafrica.com/images/library/files/Chiansi.pdf. The Jules Pretty quote is from the *Monthly Review*, and Bacon is quoted in David Montgomery, *Dirt: the erosion of civilizations*, University of California Press, 2008. For Agrica's activities see http://www.agrica.com/html/project2.html and for Unilever see Buck & Scherr in *State of the world 2011*.

Price rises in China are described in Federico, *Feeding the world*, benefits in Vietnam are covered in IFAD, *Rural poverty report*, and improvements in nutrition in India are listed in FAO, *The state of food security in the world 2012.* The Oxfam claim on biofuels is aired in *The Guardian*, 17 Sep 2012, while Ridley was writing in *Raconteur on Sustainable Agriculture and Food Security*, 7 May 2011. For a more positive assessment of the role of biofuels see Dr Jeremy Wood quoted in R. Murphy et al, 'Global developments in the competition for land from biofuels', *Food Policy*, doi:10.1016/j.foodpol.2010.11.014, 2011. Becker is quoted in Reuters, 20 Nov 2011. Josef Schmid-huber discusses the reliance of poor countries on biofuels in *Biofuels: an emerging threat to Europe's food security*, Notre Europe, 2007. The potential is outlined in Hans Langeveld & J. Dixon, 'Development perspectives of the bio-based economy: the need for a systems approach', 9th European IFSA Symposium, 4–7 July 2010. The Mali case study is presented in IFAD, 'The growing demand for land: risks and opportunities for smallholder farmers', Discussion Paper, 2010. The idea of adjusting biofuel mandates when food markets come under pressure has been endorsed by a group including the FAO, IFAD, the IMF, OECD, UNCTAD, WFP, the World Bank and the WTO, in a joint statement on international food prices for the G20, 4 Sep 2012.

The appeal of ecological farming approaches to young farmers is noted by IFAD in its *Rural poverty report 2011*.

INDEX

global food crisis and 52–5
Russia/Ukraine/Kazakhstan
exports 32
surpluses 28–9
trading 139, 140, 143, 148, 152,
153, 162–75
US exports 29–30
to China 220
see also specific grains
Cerrado farmland (Brazil) 31,
103–4
change (to better global food
systems) 225–7, 233–70
cheap food *see* prices
Chiansi irrigation project 257–8
Chicago Board of Trade 139, 142,
146, 149, 154, 155
China 33–4, 52–3, 132–3
agro-ecological farming 254
ancient 7–8, 13, 270
aquifers 66
barely self-sufficient 33–4,
54, 69
commodity trading by 172–3
food reserves 133, 171
future predictions 214, 220,
221
futures markets in 142
global food crisis and 52–3
high prices in 262
land deals, limited extent
195–6
rice 119
USA and, food alliances
219–20, 221
Chongqing Grain Group 173,
174
climate, as factor determining
suitability of land for
agriculture 77–84

climate change (incl. global
warming) 45, 60–3, 75, 82–4,
91, 111, 212, 213, 214–15, 216,
234, 252
agro-ecological farming and
249, 252
see also weather extremes
Club of Rome 74
cocoa 40, 48, 137–8, 139, 140,
141, 152, 154, 169, 170
Collier, Paul 238–9
colonialism 4, 226, 228–30
commodities
markets *see* trading
tropical, land deals involving
207
competition between trading
firms 168
lack 177
from new firms 168–76
computers
futures trading strategies
146–7, 151
modelling 74
climate change and extreme
weather events and their
effects 83
International Institute for
Applied Systems Analysis
77–9
supply and demand 109
conflict and war 4, 219–20, 223,
224
consumer power 264–5
contango 143
cooperation 123, 125, 126, 127,
266
in Prisoner's dilemma 116, 125
corn syrup (high fructose maize
syrup) 29, 40, 48

301

rule-based trade system and
its failure 125–32
taxonomy/typology of
23–42
glyphosate 64
Goldberg, Ray 176
Goldman Sachs 108, 148, 152,
191
Gomes, Laurence Beltrão 245
governance (food), failure 125–32
governments 268
agro-ecological farming and
253–4
foreign, land grabs by 181–91
local, opposition to land grabs
and 201–2
manipulation of food trade
by 50
see also politics
grains see cereals/grains
Granger causality test 157–8
Gray, John 67
grazing system for cattle, Savory's
(holistic) 250
Greece, ancient 11–12
Green Revolution 21, 33, 34, 41,
82, 120, 226–7
greenhouse gases 22, 58, 76, 82,
83, 85, 91, 92, 102, 244
guano 18–19
Guinea Savannah 228

Haber–Bosch process 19, 67, 86,
87, 88
Haddad, Professor Lawrence 25
Hail Agricultural Development
Company (HADCO) 189
Haiti 49, 242
earthquake 47–8
Hallam, David 255

Hassad Food 189–90
health problems 44
heatwaves, Russia 60, 62, 122
hedge funds 138, 143, 144, 145,
150, 153, 154, 165
cocoa 137–8
Heilberg, Phillipe 194–5
herbicides 20
resistance 64
high frequency trading 146, 151,
155, 156
high fructose maize syrup 29,
40, 48
history of food 7–23, 126–8,
225–6
colonialism 4, 226, 228–30
financial aspects 138–9
Ireland 230–1
prices 99–100
Hoppe, Professor Peter 62
Hurricane Mitch, Nicaragua 249
hybridisation (plants) 19–20, 21,
27, 30
hydraulic civilisations 10
hydraulic fracturing 87
hydrogen in Haber–Bosch
process 19, 87

import(s)
surges 122, 124, 125
tariffs 27, 32, 34, 36, 37, 38, 41,
59, 116, 117, 120, 123, 125,
129, 130, 132, 192, 241
see also demand
importing countries
food alliances between
exporting and 219–22
future predictions 214–15
poor 39–42
rich 35–9